MEE Essay Questions

Released Multistate Essay Examination Questions

AmeriBar
Phone (800) 529-2651 • Fax (800) 529-2652

MEE Essay Questions

Copyright 2017 AmeriBar

ISBN 1-44049-239-5

TABLE OF CONTENTS

* Limited actual prior MEE questions are available. Additional practice questions not from prior MEEs have been provided. This subject is a subject traditionally tested on the MBE. It has only been testable on the MEE since July, 2007.

Introduction

This book contains actual past Multistate Essay Examination questions and corresponding analyses. Each examiner analysis contains an exhaustive discussion of all pointable issues. Therefore, the examiner analyses are much more detailed than a typical passing examinee answer.

This book also contains a limited number of additional practice questions (non-MEE) and sample answers for select subjects tested on the Multistate Bar Exam ("MBE"). Because the sample answers to the practice questions are actual applicant answers, they may contain spelling, grammatical, or even legal errors. However, they have been classified as representative good answers.

Preface

The Multistate Essay Examination (MEE) is developed by the National Conference of Bar Examiners (NCBE). This publication includes the questions and analyses from prior MEE tests. Each test includes six 30-minute questions. In the actual test, the questions are simply numbered rather than being identified by area of law. For more information, see the *MEE Information Booklet,* available on the NCBE website at www.ncbex.org.

The model analyses for the MEE are illustrative of the discussions that might appear in excellent answers to the questions. They are provided to the user jurisdictions to assist graders in grading the examination. They address all the legal and factual issues the drafters intended to raise in the questions.

Description of the MEE

The MEE consists of six 30-minute questions and is a component of the Uniform Bar Examination (UBE). It is administered by user jurisdictions as part of the bar examination on the Tuesday before the last Wednesday in February and July of each year. Areas of law that may be covered on the MEE include the following: Business Associations (Agency and Partnership; Corporations and Limited Liability Companies), Civil Procedure, Conflict of Laws, Constitutional Law, Contracts, Criminal Law and Procedure, Evidence, Family Law, Real Property, Secured Transactions (UCC Article 9), Torts, and Trusts and Estates (Decedents' Estates; Trusts and Future Interests). Some questions may include issues in more than one area of law. The particular areas covered vary from exam to exam.

The purpose of the MEE is to test the examinee's ability to (1) identify legal issues raised by a hypothetical factual situation; (2) separate material which is relevant from that which is not; (3) present a reasoned analysis of the relevant issues in a clear, concise, and well-organized composition; and (4) demonstrate an understanding of the fundamental legal principles relevant to the probable solution of the issues raised by the factual situation. The primary distinction between the MEE and the Multistate Bar Examination (MBE) is that the MEE requires the examinee to demonstrate an ability to communicate effectively in writing.

Instructions

The back cover of each test booklet contains the following instructions:

You will be instructed when to begin and when to stop this test. Do not break the seal on this booklet until you are told to begin.

You may answer the questions in any order you wish. Do not answer more than one question in each answer booklet. If you make a mistake or wish to revise your answer, simply draw a line through the material you wish to delete.

If you are using a laptop computer to answer the questions, your jurisdiction will provide you with specific instructions.

Read each fact situation very carefully and do not assume facts that are not given in the question. Do not assume that each question covers only a single area of the law; some of the questions may cover more than one of the areas you are responsible for knowing.

Demonstrate your ability to reason and analyze. Each of your answers should show an understanding of the facts, a recognition of the issues included, a knowledge of the applicable principles of law, and the reasoning by which you arrive at your conclusion. The value of your answer depends not as much upon your conclusions as upon the presence and quality of the elements mentioned above.

Clarity and conciseness are important, but make your answer complete. Do not volunteer irrelevant or immaterial information.

Answer all questions according to generally accepted fundamental legal principles unless your jurisdiction has instructed you to answer according to local case or statutory law. (UBE instructions: Answer all questions according to generally accepted fundamental legal principles rather than local case or statutory law.)

MEE RELEASED ESSAY QUESTIONS

AGENCY & PARTNERSHIP
July 2002

Sunrise Lodge is a corporation that develops and operates luxury resort hotels. Sunrise recently began constructing a hotel in East Beach, a beach town on the Atlantic coast of the United States. Sunrise hoped to give the East Beach hotel a local flavor by using local sources for materials.

Sunrise hired Adam to be its interior design agent on the East Beach project. The contract between them, which was for a one-year term, included the following language:

Adam has the discretion to make selections for interior floor and wall coverings, works of art, furniture, plumbing fixtures, and lighting fixtures for East Beach hotel, provided that (a) the cost of such purchases does not exceed the budgeted amounts listed in Exhibit A, (b) all purchases will be made from local vendors, and (c) the items selected are within the quantity and style guidelines described in Exhibit B. Adam shall inform vendors that purchases are for Sunrise East Beach and should arrange for Sunrise to be billed on a 30-day net basis.

The style guidelines in Exhibit B include a comprehensive list of themes and styles typical of an Atlantic fishing village like East Beach, including lighthouses, whitewashed wood, lobster traps, wicker furniture, and sailboats.

After hiring Adam, Sunrise sent a letter to prospective local suppliers on Sunrise stationery signed by the Sunrise president, announcing Adam's appointment as follows:

Sunrise Lodge is delighted to announce the appointment of Adam, a well-known local interior designer, to act on its behalf in the selection of interior floor and wall coverings, works of art, furniture, and plumbing and lighting fixtures for the Sunrise East Beach hotel. We are confident that-working only with local suppliers-Adam will exercise a wonderful creative flair in coming up with just the right look for this exciting project. Know that you deal with Sunrise when you deal with Adam on this project.

During the first months of Adam's one-year term, Adam entered into the following transactions with suppliers who had received Sunrise's letter.

First, Adam contracted with Tahini for the main lobby area of the hotel to be decorated entirely in a Tahitian theme. The items for the Tahitian decor are within the budget and are from a local supplier. However, they are not within the Exhibit B style guidelines.

Second, Adam contracted with Moby for the guest rooms to be decorated using authentic themes from the Atlantic seaboard region as required by Exhibit B. The decor selections are within budget and are from local suppliers, but the Sunrise officials do not like the design.

Sunrise has refused to pay either vendor and has terminated Adam's contract.

1.   On what agency principles, if any, is Sunrise liable to Tahini and Moby on their respective contracts? Explain.

2.   Is Adam liable to Sunrise as a result of the contracts with Tahini and Moby? Explain.

3.   May Sunrise terminate Adam's agency before the end of their one-year contract term without incurring liability to Adam? Explain.

MEE RELEASED ESSAY QUESTIONS

AGENCY & PARTNERSHIP
February 2003

Lessor owns and manages apartment buildings in the town of Utopia.

Handy is the sole proprietor and only employee of a small business called "Rapid Repairs." Most of the income from this business is generated by making small household repairs for homeowners and apartment dwellers in Utopia. Handy has a good reputation for performing quality work and charging reasonable rates.

One year ago, Lessor contracted for an indefinite period with Handy to perform repair work at several apartment units that Lessor owns in Utopia. The tenants of these units are told to make requests for repairs by calling a telephone number listed as "Lessor's Repair Line."

Under the Lessor/Handy contract, any call to "Lessor's Repair Line" actually rings directly through to Rapid Repairs. Handy is obligated to investigate any tenant's request for repair within 24 hours. Before actually making any repair, however, Handy is required to contact Lessor, describe the nature of the repair, and seek authorization to proceed. Once authorized to make the repair, Handy must make it within 24 hours. Lessor is obligated to pay Handy $50 per hour for any work done pursuant to the contract (including investigating repair requests) and, in addition, to reimburse Handy's out-of-pocket expenses.

The Lessor/Handy contract further provides that Handy:

- may perform similar work on other apartment buildings, but may not perform work "on the side" for Lessor's tenants in Lessor's buildings;
- must provide his own tools;
- may not perform any electrical work, but must subcontract it to a licensed electrician, approved by Lessor, who will work under Handy's supervision.

Last month, Tenant called "Lessor's Repair Line." Handy answered. Tenant said he had a cracked sink drainpipe. Handy immediately investigated. After obtaining permission from Lessor to repair the sink, Handy returned to make the repair. While Handy was making the repair, Tenant asked Handy to install an electrical outlet in the apartment for Tenant's computer. Despite his contract with Lessor, Handy agreed to do so, but told Tenant there would be a charge of $200 as it was an improvement to the apartment, not a repair covered under the lease. Tenant agreed to pay $200 for a new outlet. Tenant assumed that the money would go to Lessor, but Handy intended to keep it for himself.

Handy was negligent in installing the electrical outlet. The outlet caused a fire, which destroyed Tenant's personal property. Tenant never paid for the installation work.

On what alternative theories should Tenant argue that Lessor is liable for Handy's negligence, and what is the likely outcome on each theory? Explain.

MEE RELEASED ESSAY QUESTIONS

AGENCY & PARTNERSHIP
July 2003

Adam, Barbara, and Carl are partners in a beverage distribution business. They have no written partnership agreement. The partnership distributes alcoholic and nonalcoholic beverages to bars and restaurants throughout State A. Jane owns one of these bars. She also owns a number of pinball and video game machines, which are located in many of the same bars and restaurants served by the partnership. In past dealings with the partnership, Jane has dealt exclusively with Carl.

A number of beverage distribution businesses have expanded into the pinball and video game machine business. To capitalize on this trend, Jane decided to sell her pinball and video game machines. At about the same time, Adam, Barbara, and Carl decided that their partnership should consider expanding into the pinball and video game machine business. The partners agreed that Carl would approach Jane to obtain information about the number of machines she had for sale, their locations and condition, and the associated revenues and expenses. However, because the opportunity represented a new line of business, Adam and Barbara instructed Carl not to finalize a deal with Jane without first discussing the terms with them.

When Carl met with Jane, she said that she owned 127 machines located in 72 bars and restaurants. After they visited 50 bars and saw 98 machines, Carl decided he had seen enough. Carl told Jane he would go back to the office to "run some numbers" and would call her soon.

Based on Jane's representations and his observations of 98 machines, Carl decided to offer $225,000 for all of Jane's 127 machines. Jane accepted the offer and signed the contract Carl had drafted. Carl signed the contract on behalf of the partnership. At no time, however, did Carl consult with Adam or Barbara before finalizing the deal. Adam and Barbara later discovered that the revenue generated by the machines was insufficient to justify the contract price.

1.   **Is the partnership bound by the contract that Carl signed? Explain.**

2.   **Can the partnership recover from Carl any loss on the contract with Jane? Explain.**

MEE RELEASED ESSAY QUESTIONS

AGENCY & PARTNERSHIP
February 2004

One year ago, Randy and Sandy formed a partnership to manufacture widgets. They did not enter into a written partnership agreement. Randy contributed $10,000, and Sandy contributed $5,000 to the partnership. They participated equally in the management of the partnership and shared the profits equally.

The widget market has since declined, and business has been slow. Last Monday, Randy told Sandy, "I don't want to do this anymore. I am quitting this partnership." Randy then left town on an extended vacation. At that time, the partnership still had some short-term widget contracts to fulfill and owed trade creditors $30,000.

The next day, Barney, a widget broker, met with Sandy at the widget factory. Barney knew about Randy and Sandy's partnership but had not previously done business with the partnership. For over a month, Sandy had been soliciting a long-term contract to produce widgets for Barney. Without telling Barney about Randy's statement the previous day, Sandy, on behalf of the partnership, entered into a contract with Barney to produce 500,000 widgets a year for three years.

After Randy's departure, Sandy, using her own funds, paid the $30,000 owed to trade creditors.

1. **What is the effect of Randy's statement, "I don't want to do this anymore. I am quitting this partnership"? Explain.**

2. **Is the partnership bound by the contract with Barney? Explain.**

3. **What contribution, if any, can Sandy claim from Randy for Sandy's $30,000 payment to trade creditors? Explain.**

MEE RELEASED ESSAY QUESTIONS

AGENCY & PARTNERSHIP
July 2004

Best Care Hospital, one of five hospitals in City, operates the largest emergency room in City. Best Care advertises extensively about the quality of care provided in its emergency room. It has billboards strategically placed throughout City urging local citizens to come to Best Care "because Best Care's emergency room doctors are the absolute *best* and will really *care* for you." In fact, Best Care employs no doctors; instead it contracts with seven doctors in City to staff the emergency room on a 7-day, 24-hour basis. These contracts provide:

1. Each doctor is an "independent contractor," not an "agent/employee," and may conduct a private practice but may not work in any other emergency room;
2. Each doctor is responsible for the manner in which he or she provides medical care and for the purchase of malpractice insurance;
3. Each doctor is authorized to purchase supplies and equipment for Best Care's emergency room from a list of approved vendors located in City and within Best Care's price guidelines;
4. Each doctor is periodically reviewed by Best Care's governing board to assure that each doctor provides quality care;
5. Each doctor independently bills patients for services provided; and
6. All emergency services are performed in the Best Care emergency room using supplies and equipment provided by Best Care.

Three months ago, Owen, a local orthopedist and one of the doctors with whom Best Care contracts, ordered a portable X-ray machine costing $25,000 from Vision, a company located in a town 450 miles from City. Vision is not on Best Care's approved vendor list and Owen did not consult with anyone at Best Care before he placed the order. When Owen ordered the machine, which was to be custom-designed for Best Care, he truthfully told Vision that he was one of the seven emergency room doctors at Best Care and needed the machine for the emergency room.

Owen also stated that he was acting on behalf of Best Care. Vision had had no previous dealings with Owen or Best Care and agreed to make the machine according to the custom specifications provided by Owen. When Vision shipped the X-ray machine, Best Care refused to accept delivery, even though the price for the machine was within its price guidelines. Best Care claimed that Owen had no authority to purchase the machine on its behalf. Vision filed an action for breach of contract against Best Care.

Last month, Anita was hit by a bus. When the ambulance arrived, Anita asked the ambulance driver to take her to Best Care, quoting the billboard claim that "Best Care's emergency room doctors are the absolute *best*." When Anita arrived at the emergency room, she was treated by Owen. Owen correctly told Anita that she needed immediate surgery. During the operation, Owen negligently severed one of Anita's arteries, and she bled to death. Anita's estate has filed a wrongful death action against Owen and Best Care for damages resulting from Owen's negligence.

1.   Is Owen an independent contractor or servant (employee) of Best Care? Explain.

2.   Is Best Care liable to Vision for breach of contract? Explain.

3.   Assuming Owen is an independent contractor, is Best Care liable to Anita's estate for Owen's negligence? Explain.

MEE RELEASED ESSAY QUESTIONS

AGENCY & PARTNERSHIP
February 2005

For many years, Ruth owned and operated a restaurant as a sole proprietorship doing business as (d/b/a) Ruth's Family Restaurant. In 2001, Ruth sold the assets of the restaurant to Scott. Ruth and Scott agreed that: (1) the restaurant would operate under the name "Ruth's Family Restaurant"; (2) Ruth would manage the restaurant for Scott but would have no ownership interest in the restaurant; (3) all necessary licenses would remain in Ruth's name; and (4) Ruth would hire all employees, but only on an at-will basis (as is customary in the restaurant business). No one other than Ruth and Scott was aware that Scott had bought the restaurant.

Prior to Scott's purchase of the restaurant, Ruth had purchased supplies from Wholesale Restaurant Supply Co. (Wholesale), always signing the contracts as "Ruth, d/b/a Ruth's Family Restaurant." Following Scott's purchase of the restaurant, Scott instructed Ruth in very clear terms not to make any purchases of restaurant supplies from Wholesale in the future. Ruth complied with this instruction for the next several months.

In 2003, Ruth hired Nora, her niece, as assistant manager of the restaurant under a written employment contract for a 20-year term. Ruth signed the contract as "Ruth, d/b/a Ruth's Family Restaurant."

Soon after Nora was hired, she pointed out to Ruth that Wholesale's prices were generally less than those of the other local supply company. Despite Scott's clear prohibition, Ruth resumed buying supplies from Wholesale, again signing all contracts as "Ruth, d/b/a Ruth's Family Restaurant."

When Scott discovered what Ruth had done, Scott took over management of the restaurant, discharged Nora and Ruth, and refused to pay thousands of dollars of invoices from Wholesale for restaurant supplies delivered to the restaurant.

Wholesale has sued Scott to recover on the outstanding invoices. Nora has sued Scott for breach of the employment contract.

Under agency law:

1.   **Is Scott liable to Wholesale? Explain.**

2.   **Is Scott liable to Nora? Explain.**

MEE RELEASED ESSAY QUESTIONS

AGENCY & PARTNERSHIP
February 2006

Rich, who lives in Smalltown, recently bought a sports utility vehicle (SUV) from Dealer in Capital City, which is located approximately 60 miles from Smalltown. Rich asked if Dealer would have the SUV delivered to him in Smalltown. Rich offered to pay the driver $75. Dealer does not ordinarily deliver SUVs to its customers. Nonetheless, Dealer agreed to have Sales, a full-time salesperson employed by Dealer, deliver the SUV to Rich's house because Dealer was eager to please Rich. At the end of the normal workday, Dealer gave Sales directions to Rich's house in Smalltown. As Sales prepared to drive off in the SUV, Dealer told him, "Drive straight to Rich's house, no detours. Drive carefully and no speeding. I don't want any dents in that SUV."

On his way to Rich's house, Sales stopped to visit Friend, who was in the process of moving. Friend was distraught because the movers had not shown up. Friend asked Sales if he would like to earn $200 by transporting "a few loads" in the SUV. Sales agreed and transported many of Friend's belongings in the SUV. Friend paid Sales $200.

Helping Friend took several hours, so Sales was running late. In his rush to Rich's house, Sales negligently ran over Ped, who was trying to cross the street. Ped was seriously injured.

Dealer learned that Sales had used the SUV to help Friend move and demanded the $200 Friend had paid Sales.

1.   **Can Ped recover from Dealer for Sales's negligence? Explain.**

2.   **Must Sales give Dealer the $200 he earned helping Friend move? Explain.**

MEE RELEASED ESSAY QUESTIONS

AGENCY & PARTNERSHIP
July 2006

Two years ago Nephew asked Uncle for a loan to purchase a tire dealership. Uncle agreed. Nephew decided to name the new business "Monster Tires" and to focus on selling oversized tires made by Big Rubber, Inc. Uncle agreed to accept 50% of the profits generated by Monster Tires, instead of a fixed payment, until the loan was fully repaid.

One year after Monster Tires was established, Nephew approached Friend, who had a knack for sales and marketing and was well-connected in the trucking business. Friend agreed to join Monster Tires in exchange for a one-third share of all of its profits. Friend and Nephew approached Uncle to renegotiate the repayment of the loan. Uncle was excited by Friend's ideas to expand the business and agreed to forgive the loan and instead accept a one-third share of all of the profits of Monster Tires. Uncle also offered to let Monster Tires use one of his properties rent-free so that Monster Tires could open a second location.

Nephew and Friend both worked full time at Monster Tires. Friend began an aggressive sales campaign and spent a significant amount of time entertaining potential customers. Uncle was not involved in the day-to-day operations of Monster Tires.

Nephew, Uncle, and Friend were all present when Monster Tires opened its second store. The store was packed with potential customers, but Uncle was dismayed by the sparse inventory. When a representative of TireCo asked Uncle about placing its line of tires in the stores, Uncle agreed and signed a large purchase order for TireCo tires without consulting either Nephew or Friend.

After the store opening, Uncle, Nephew, and Friend went out to celebrate. Friend suggested that Monster Tires should buy a yacht for entertaining. Nephew agreed because he wanted to expand to a third location near the beach. Uncle vehemently protested and said: "We can't afford a yacht. I forbid you to purchase one." Two weeks later, Friend signed a contract with Custom Yachts to purchase a yacht for Monster Tires.

Monster Tires is now refusing to pay both TireCo and Custom Yachts.

1.   **Is Monster Tires liable to TireCo for the tires Uncle ordered? Explain.**

2.   **Is Monster Tires liable to Custom Yachts for the yacht Friend ordered? Explain.**

3.   **Are Uncle, Nephew, and Friend personally liable on either of the contracts? Explain.**

MEE RELEASED ESSAY QUESTIONS

AGENCY & PARTNERSHIP
February 2007

Astoria Limited Partnership (Astoria) is a properly formed limited partnership. The general partner of Astoria is Baker, an individual. The limited partners are Tim, Uma, and Vivian, who are also individuals. Under the limited partnership agreement, distributions and voting rights in the limited partnership are allocated to Baker (10%), Tim (30%), Uma (30%), and Vivian (30%).

The limited partnership agreement of Astoria gives the limited partners the right to remove Baker as the general partner—with or without cause—if the holders of 60% of the voting rights concur.

Three weeks ago, articles appeared in the business press raising questions about Baker's management of Caldonia Limited Partnership (Caldonia). While the articles did not specifically mention Astoria, the misconduct documented in the articles—contracts between Caldonia and a janitorial company owned by Baker that charged greatly inflated fees for its services—raised concerns on the part of Astoria's limited partners. Tim wrote Baker requesting that Baker, in his capacity as the general partner of Astoria, provide: (1) copies of any contracts between Astoria and any entities related to or controlled by Baker, (2) copies of any contracts for janitorial services between Astoria and any entity, (3) copies of Astoria's federal and state tax returns for the past three years, and (4) copies of all correspondence between Astoria and any other parties for the past five years. Alternatively, Tim requested access to Astoria's records in order to secure copies of the documents himself.

Baker responded by refusing all four of Tim's requests. Thereupon, Tim contacted Uma and Vivian to request their votes that Baker be removed as the general partner. Tim also proposed that the three limited partners, Tim, Uma, and Vivian, agree in writing to jointly run Astoria until a suitable replacement for Baker could be found.

1.   **Did Baker act wrongfully in refusing to provide Tim the information and documents he requested? Explain.**

2.   **If the limited partners do no more than remove Baker as general partner of Astoria, will they be liable to persons who transact business with Astoria? Explain.**

3.   **If the limited partners remove Baker and run Astoria until a replacement general partner can be found, under what circumstances will they be liable to persons who transact business with Astoria? Explain.**

MEE RELEASED ESSAY QUESTIONS

AGENCY & PARTNERSHIP
July 2007

Talker is a persuasive salesperson, Fixer is a talented carpenter, and Manager is an experienced small business manager. The three are friends and often discussed going into business together. Two months ago they orally agreed to form a cabinet restoration business and to share profits equally.

The three friends began doing business under the name TFM Restored Cabinets (TFM). Manager collected accounts receivable, paid all bills, and distributed the profits equally among the three. Fixer restored the cabinets, and Talker marketed them. The three friends operated independently in performing their respective duties, but they met periodically to discuss and decide other business matters.

Everything went smoothly until Fixer announced that he intended to hire Crafty to help with the restoration work because there was more work than one carpenter could handle. Talker and Manager opposed hiring Crafty. They believed that most of TFM's customers were attracted by Fixer's reputation and that the business would be harmed if Crafty performed restoration work. Despite their objections, Fixer hired Crafty.

One month later, Crafty quit after Manager refused to pay for the work that Crafty had performed.

1.   **What is the legal relationship of Talker, Fixer, and Manager? Explain.**

2.   **Did Fixer have authority to hire Crafty on behalf of TFM? Explain.**

3.   **Under what circumstances, if any, could Crafty collect from Talker the wages TFM owes Crafty? Explain.**

MEE RELEASED ESSAY QUESTIONS

AGENCY & PARTNERSHIP
July 2008

Fifteen years ago, Amy, Beck, and Curt formed a partnership, "Amy, Beck, and Curt Co.," to engage in a retail shoe store business. The partnership is for a 25-year term. All real estate owned by the partnership is titled to "Amy, Beck, and Curt Co., a partnership."

While the partnership has done well, the three partners have not managed their respective personal finances successfully. In order to deal with personal financial problems, Amy borrowed $25,000 from Green, Beck borrowed $50,000 from Red, and Curt borrowed $75,000 from White. The three partners each have defaulted on their respective loans.

Green, Red, and White are pursuing various avenues to recover what is owed to each of them.

Green has obtained a judgment against Amy, who is judgment-proof, and is considering attaching the partnership real estate.

Red has taken no legal action against Beck but wants to collect the amount of his loan to Beck from Beck's interest in the partnership.

Curt has assigned all of his interest in the partnership to White. After the assignment, White asked to inspect the partnership books and records and demanded the right to participate in the management and affairs of the partnership. White is also considering the possibility of collecting Curt's debt by forcing a dissolution and winding up of the partnership.

1.   **Can Green, as a judgment creditor of Amy, attach and execute upon the partnership real estate? Explain.**

2.   **What steps should Red take to collect the amount of his loan to Beck from Beck's interest in the partnership? Explain.**

3.   **Does White have a right to inspect partnership books and records and to participate in the management of the partnership? Explain.**

4.   **Can White force a dissolution and winding up of the partnership? Explain.**

MEE RELEASED ESSAY QUESTIONS

AGENCY & PARTNERSHIP
February 2009

Hanson's Fruitcakes (Hanson's) is the largest producer of fruitcakes in the world. The company was founded 150 years ago and uses an original secret recipe closely guarded by the company.

Because of a significant drop in the demand for fruitcakes, Hanson's decided to expand its product line to include other baked goods that will not compete with its fruitcakes.

Because Hanson's has limited experience producing baked goods other than fruitcakes, it decided to hire Taster as a consultant. The contract between Hanson's and Taster provided as follows:

(1)   Taster would travel for six months tasting baked goods at "high-end" bakeries. Taster was expressly authorized, on behalf of Hanson's, to buy the recipes of any baked goods he thought Hanson's could produce successfully. Taster was expressly prohibited from committing Hanson's to pay more than $5,000 cash for any one recipe, because market research confirmed that baked-goods recipes typically sold for prices between $3,000 and $6,000.

(2)   Hanson's would disclose to Taster the secret recipe for Hanson's fruitcake so that Taster would not inadvertently agree to buy any baked-goods recipes that were substantially similar to the fruitcake. Taster is required to keep Hanson's recipe secret from everyone.

Hanson's president announced the company's plans to expand its product line at the annual baking industry trade show attended by everyone in the baking industry. At the trade show, Hanson's president stated: "Hanson's is breaking new ground in the baking industry by hiring a consultant, Taster. Taster will be entering into contracts to buy recipes from other bakers on Hanson's behalf." Hanson's president did not disclose the precise terms of the Hanson's-Taster contract.

Purporting to act on behalf of Hanson's, over the next four months Taster entered into contracts to buy the following recipes:

(1)   Boysenberry-granola muffins for $4,000 from Monumental Muffins,
(2)   Almond-pecan tarts for $6,000 from Bakers Bonanza, and
(3)   Chocolate truffle cake from Parisian Delights in exchange for a copy of Hanson's secret fruitcake recipe.

Purporting to act on behalf of Hanson's, Taster also entered into a contract with Ironcast Enterprises to buy a sophisticated baking oven for $5,000.

Is Hanson's legally bound to any of the four contracts made by Taster? Explain.

MEE RELEASED ESSAY QUESTIONS

AGENCY & PARTNERSHIP
July 2009

Six months ago, Andy, Ben, and Carol executed a document entitled "Metropolitan Limited Partnership Agreement" (the Agreement). Under the terms of the Agreement, Andy, Ben, and Carol were to be "limited partners" in the "Metropolitan Limited Partnership" (MLP). The Agreement provided that each would contribute $500,000 to the venture, which they each did.

The Agreement also provided that Warren would be the "general partner" of MLP, but Warren never signed the Agreement.

The Agreement further provided that the venture would buy undeveloped land and hold it for development. The land was purchased, and a deed for the land naming "Metropolitan Limited Partnership" as grantee was executed, delivered, and recorded. In the MLP name, Andy, Ben, and Carol also hired a marketing company, Marketing, to develop a campaign to resell the land as "Metropolitan Estates."

Two months after the Agreement was executed by Andy, Ben, and Carol, Marketing sued MLP, and Andy, Ben, and Carol individually, for nonpayment of amounts due to Marketing for services it had provided to MLP. MLP is unable to pay Marketing because the land, its only asset, has substantially depreciated due to an economic downturn.

Immediately after Marketing filed suit, Andy, Ben, and Carol filed a Certificate of Limited Partnership in the name of Metropolitan Limited Partnership in the appropriate state office.

Two weeks after the Certificate of Limited Partnership was filed, Zack went onto the land owned in the name of Metropolitan Limited Partnership and fell down an uncovered well. Zack died as a result of injuries suffered in the fall. Zack's estate has filed a wrongful death action against Andy, Ben, and Carol individually.

1. **What type of entity is the Metropolitan Limited Partnership? Explain.**

2. **Can Marketing recover from Andy, Ben, and Carol personally for the amounts it is owed by Metropolitan Limited Partnership? What steps must it follow if it tries to do so? Explain.**

3. **If Zack's estate is entitled to damages, can it recover from Andy, Ben, and Carol personally for the wrongful death claim? What steps must it follow if it tries to do so? Explain.**

MEE RELEASED ESSAY QUESTIONS

AGENCY & PARTNERSHIP
July 2010

On January 2, Fran opened Petals, a floral shop, and operated it as a sole proprietorship. Petals soon ran into financial difficulties, and Fran could not pay its bills.

On March 1, Fran asked her friends Gina and Hank for financial help.

On April 1, in response to Fran's request, Gina delivered a check payable to "Petals" to Fran. In exchange for this contribution, Fran agreed to pay Gina 25% of the monthly net profits of Petals for as long as Petals remained in business. Gina also agreed that, if Petals suffered losses, she would share those losses with Fran.

Gina began working at the shop with Fran and helped Fran with business planning for Petals.

On April 2, also in response to Fran's request, Hank delivered a check payable to "Petals" to Fran and noted on the memo line of the check "loan to Petals." Hank agreed to accept 25% of the monthly net profits of Petals until his loan (plus interest) was repaid in full.

Fran used the proceeds of the checks from Gina and Hank to purchase equipment, supplies, and a delivery truck in the name of Petals.

Beginning in April, on the last day of each month, Fran distributed to both Gina and Hank 25% of Petals' monthly net profits.

On September 1, Gina wrote a letter to her son Ivan stating that she was assigning to Ivan, as a gift, all of her interest in Petals effective immediately. Gina gave a copy of that letter to Fran. Fran told Gina, "I don't want anything to do with Ivan." Gina continued to be active in the business operations of Petals.

On September 30, Fran distributed the monthly net profits of Petals to Gina and Hank, but distributed nothing to Ivan.

On October 10, Ivan demanded that Fran distribute Gina's share of Petals' net profits to him and that she also allow him to inspect the books and records of Petals.

On October 15, Gina learned that Fran was using Petals' delivery truck on Sundays to transport her children to their soccer games. Gina demanded that Fran stop doing so, but Fran refused, noting that the truck was not being used for Petals' business on Sundays.

1.   **What is the legal relationship among Fran, Gina, and Hank? Explain.**

2.   **Is Ivan entitled to Gina's share of the monthly net profits of Petals? Explain.**

3.   Is Ivan entitled to inspect the books and records of Petals? Explain.

4.   Is Fran entitled to use the delivery truck on Sundays to take her children to their soccer games? Explain.

MEE RELEASED ESSAY QUESTIONS

AGENCY & PARTNERSHIP
July 2011

Portable Shredder Services (PSS) is a partnership that operates a mobile shredding business. When a client needs paper shredded, PSS sends a truck and a crew to perform the operation.

Adam, Beth, and Chris are partners in PSS. Each of them contributed $50,000 in start-up capital, and each actively works in the business.

The PSS partnership agreement provides in relevant part that (1) each partner is required to devote substantially all of the partner's working efforts to the business and (2) any partner can withdraw from the partnership upon giving six months' written notice. The partnership agreement contains no other relevant provisions modifying any of the statutory default rules.

PSS has not been profitable. Adam is convinced that the assets of PSS are worth more than the value of the business as a going concern. He believes that the only way he can receive a fair price for his share of partnership assets is if those assets are sold. Beth and Chris, on the other hand, wish to continue operating the business, if they can.

Adam would like to withdraw immediately from the partnership in order to force Beth and Chris to cease the operations of PSS immediately and sell the partnership's assets.

Adam has asked your law firm to answer the following three questions:

1.   **If Adam immediately withdraws from the partnership, what will be the consequences (a) to him and (b) to the partnership? Explain.**

2.   **If Adam gives six months' written notice before withdrawing from the partnership, what will be the consequences (a) to him and (b) to the partnership? Explain.**

3.   **If the partnership's business is wound up after Adam's withdrawal, will he be liable for partnership debts incurred during the winding-up process after his withdrawal? Explain.**

MEE RELEASED ESSAY QUESTIONS

AGENCY & PARTNERSHIP
February 2012

A man and a woman validly formed a partnership ("Garden Partnership") to fix commercial gardening equipment. Several months after Garden Partnership began operations, it hired an employee who was a skilled mechanic.

The employee negligently repaired a piece of equipment for a customer. As a result, the customer was severely injured. The customer successfully sued Garden Partnership and recovered a judgment for $500,000, which has not been paid.

Shortly after entry of this judgment, the man and woman took the necessary steps to qualify Garden Partnership as a limited liability partnership, and they renamed it "Garden LLP."

Shortly thereafter, the man and woman decided to expand the business. Because they needed more capital, they agreed to admit an investor as a partner. The investor contributed $50,000 and became a partner in Garden LLP.

1.   Is Garden LLP liable for the $500,000 judgment against Garden Partnership? Explain.

2.   Are the man and woman personally liable to the customer for the $500,000 judgment against Garden Partnership? Explain.

3.   Is the investor personally liable to the customer for the $500,000 judgment against Garden Partnership? Explain.

MEE RELEASED ESSAY QUESTIONS

AGENCY & PARTNERSHIP
February 2013

Over 5,000 individuals in the United States operate hot-air balloon businesses. A hot-air balloon has four key components: the balloon that holds the heated air, the basket that houses the riders, the propane burner that heats the air in the balloon, and the propane storage tanks.

The owner of a hot-air balloon business recently notified several basket and burner manufacturers that she or her agent might be contacting them to purchase baskets or burners. The owner did not specifically name any person as her agent. Basket and burner manufacturers regularly receive such notices from hot-air balloon operators. Such notices typically include no restrictions on the types of baskets or burners agents might purchase for their principals.

The owner then retained an agent to acquire baskets, burners, and fuel tanks from various manufacturers. The owner authorized the agent to buy only (a) baskets made of woven wicker (not aluminum), (b) burners that use a unique "whisper technology" (so as not to scare livestock when the balloon sails over farmland), and (c) propane fuel tanks.

The agent then entered into three transactions with manufacturers, all of whom had no prior dealings with either the owner or the agent.

(1) The agent and a large manufacturer of both wicker and aluminum baskets signed a contract for the purchase of four aluminum baskets for a total cost of $60,000. The agent never told the manufacturer that he represented the owner or any other principal. The contract listed the agent as the buyer and listed the owner's address as the delivery address but did not indicate that the address was that of the owner rather than the agent. When the baskets were delivered to the owner, she learned for the first time that the agent had contracted to buy aluminum, not wicker, baskets. The owner immediately rejected the baskets and returned them to the manufacturer. Neither the owner nor the agent has paid the basket manufacturer for them.

(2) The agent contacted a burner manufacturer and told him that the agent represented a well-known hot-air balloon operator who wanted to purchase burners. The agent did not disclose the owner's name. The agent and the burner manufacturer signed a contract for the purchase of four burners that did not have "whisper technology" for a total price of $70,000. The burner contract, like the basket contract, listed the owner's address for delivery but did not disclose whose address it was. The burners were delivered to the owner's business, and the owner discovered that the agent had ordered the wrong kind of burners. The owner rejected the burners and returned them to the manufacturer. Neither the owner nor the agent has paid the burner manufacturer for the burners.

(3) The agent contracted with a solar cell manufacturer to make three cells advertised as "strong enough to power all your ballooning needs." The agent did not tell the manufacturer that he was acting on behalf of any other person. One week after the cells were delivered to the agent, he took them to the owner, who installed them and discovered that she could save a lot of money

using solar cells instead of propane to power her balloons. The owner decided to keep the solar cells, but she has not paid the manufacturer for them.

Assume that the rejection of the baskets and the burners and the failure to pay for the solar cells constitute breach of the relevant contracts.

1.   **Is the owner liable to the basket manufacturer for breach of the contract for the aluminum baskets? Is the agent liable? Explain.**

2.   **Is the owner liable to the burner manufacturer for breach of the contract for the burners? Is the agent liable? Explain.**

3.   **Is the owner liable to the solar cell manufacturer for breach of the contract for the solar cells? Is the agent liable? Explain. (Do not address liability based upon restitution or unjust enrichment.)**

MEE RELEASED ESSAY QUESTIONS

AGENCY & PARTNERSHIP
July 2013

After a dump truck unloaded gravel at a road construction job site, the trucker negligently drove away with the truck bed still in a raised position. The raised truck bed hit an overhead cable, causing it to fall across the highway.

The telephone company that owned the fallen cable sent one of its employees to the scene in a company vehicle. The employee's responsibilities were expressly limited to responding to cable-damage calls, assessing damage, and reporting back to the telephone company so that a repair unit could be dispatched.

The foreman of the road construction job site asked the telephone company employee if the foreman's crew could lift the cable off the highway. Fearful that the cable might be damaged by traffic, the telephone company employee said, "Go ahead, pick it up. Just don't damage the cable." The foreman then directed his crew to stretch the cable over the highway so that traffic could pass underneath.

Shortly thereafter, a bus passing under the telephone cable hit the cable and dislodged it, causing the cable to strike an oncoming car. The driver lost control of the car and hit a truck carrying asphalt to the road construction site. As a result of the collision, hot asphalt spilled and severely burned the foreman.

The foreman is now threatening to sue the telephone company on the ground that it is responsible for its employee's negligence in authorizing the road construction crew to stretch the cable across the highway. The telephone company argues that, even assuming that its employee was negligent, the telephone company is not liable because:

1.   the telephone company employee's acts were outside the scope of his employment and thus cannot be attributed to the telephone company; *No - w/in scope*

2.   there is no other agency theory under which the foreman could hold the telephone company liable for its employee's acts; and *apparent authority*

3.   the telephone company employee's acts were not the proximate cause of the foreman's injuries. *yes - foreseeable*

Assess each of the telephone company's responses.

apparently within foreseeable

MEE RELEASED ESSAY QUESTIONS

AGENCY & PARTNERSHIP
February 2014

Five years ago, Adam and Ben formed a general partnership, Empire Partnership (Empire), to buy and sell antique automobiles at a showroom in State A. Adam contributed $800,000 to Empire, and Ben contributed $200,000. Their written partnership agreement allocated 80% of profits, losses, and control to Adam and 20% to Ben. No filings of any type were made in connection with the formation of Empire.

Three years ago, a collector purchased one of Empire's antique cars for $3,400,000. The collector was willing to pay this price because of Ben's false representation (repeated in the sales contract) that a famous movie star had once owned the car. Without the movie-star connection, the car was worth only $100,000. One month later, when the collector discovered the truth, he sued Adam, Ben, and Empire for $3,300,000 in damages. The lawsuit is still pending.

Two years ago, Adam and Ben admitted a new partner, Diane, to Empire in return for her contribution of $250,000. The three agreed to allocate profits, losses, and control 75% to Adam, 10% to Ben, and 15% to Diane. Before joining the partnership, Diane learned of the collector's claim and stated her concern to Adam and Ben that she might become liable if the claim were reduced to a judgment.

Following Diane's admission to Empire, the three partners sought to convert Empire into a limited liability partnership (LLP). Adam's lawyer proposed to file with State A a "statement of qualification" making an LLP election and declaring the name of the partnership to be "Empire LLP." Ben's lawyer stated that this would not work and that a new LLP had to be formed, with the assets of the old partnership transferred to the new one. In the end, the conversion was done the way Adam's lawyer suggested with the approval of all three partners.

One year ago, a driver purchased a vintage car from Empire LLP, based on the representation that the car was "fully roadworthy and capable of touring at 70 mph all day." The driver took the car on the highway at 50 mph, whereupon the front suspension collapsed, resulting in a crash in which the car was destroyed and the driver killed. The driver's estate sued Adam, Ben, Diane, and Empire LLP for $10,000,000. The lawsuit is still pending.

Although profitable, Empire LLP does not have resources sufficient to pay the collector's claim or the claim of the driver's estate.

Assume that the Uniform Partnership Act (1997) applies.

1. **Before the filing of the statement of qualification,**

   (a)   **was Adam personally liable on the collector's claim? Explain.**

   (b)   **was Diane personally liable on the collector's claim? Explain.**

2.   After the filing of the statement of qualification, was Adam, Ben, or Diane personally liable as a partner on (a) the collector's claim or (b) the driver's estate's claim? Explain.

MEE RELEASED ESSAY QUESTIONS

AGENCY & PARTNERSHIP
February 2016

Four years ago, a man and a woman properly formed a partnership to own and manage a multi- million-dollar apartment complex. They qualified the partnership as a limited liability partnership (LLP). The complex required a good deal of maintenance, and they anticipated regular borrowings of up to $25,000 to cover maintenance expenses as is customary in this industry.

While the partnership agreement contained no limitations on the authority of the partners to act for LLP, two months after LLP was formed the man and the woman agreed that neither partner would have authority to incur indebtedness on behalf of LLP in excess of $10,000 without the consent of the other partner. They then signed a statement of partnership authority describing this limitation, but this statement was never filed.

Over the next two years, the man regularly borrowed amounts from LLP's bank to cover the complex's ordinary maintenance expenses. The amounts borrowed ranged from $5,000 to

$9,000, and the man did not ask for the woman's consent when he entered into these loans on behalf of LLP.

Earlier this year, the man, without the woman's knowledge, asked the bank to loan $25,000 to LLP. The man told the bank's loan officer that the funds would be used for ordinary maintenance of the apartment complex. This amount, though greater than LLP's previous borrowings from the bank for maintenance, was in line with loans made by the bank for maintenance to other similar apartment complexes.

When the loan officer asked the man if he had authority to borrow the money on behalf of LLP, the man handed the loan officer a copy of the partnership agreement. The man, however, did not give the officer a copy of the statement of partnership authority, nor did he tell the loan officer that it existed. The bank had no actual knowledge of the limitation on the man's authority to obtain the loan on behalf of LLP.

Without contacting the woman, the bank loaned $25,000 to LLP. The loan agreement was signed only by the man and the bank's loan officer. The woman, though she had knowledge of the earlier borrowings from the bank, had no knowledge of this loan.

The man then used the $25,000 to pay his personal gambling debts. LLP has not made any payments to the bank on the loan.

1. **Is LLP liable to the bank on the loan? Explain.**

2. **Is the woman personally liable to the bank on the loan? Explain.**

3.   Is the man liable for breaching his fiduciary duties and, if so, to whom is he liable? Explain.

MEE RELEASED ESSAY QUESTIONS

CONFLICT OF LAWS
February 1995

Although this question is from a very old exam, it is one of only two known MEE questions only testing Conflict of Laws (and no other subject). Therefore, it may be useful.

Foodco, a food processing company, has its place of incorporation and its principal place of business in State A. Foodco relies extensively on an independent distributor, located in State A, to sell its products to restaurants in State A and State B. In addition, the distributor arranges a monthly shipment of Foodco's sausage to a customer in State C. This sale amounts to less than 5% of Foodco's monthly sales.

Although it obtains most of its supplies from wholesalers in State A, Foodco frequently orders spices from Spiceco, located in adjoining State D, by telephoning Spiceco from State A. For several years, Foodco paid its account by check mailed at the end of each month to Spiceco's office in State D.

For the last three months, Foodco has failed to make payments to suppliers. Its balance with Spiceco has grown to $6,000. After making an unsuccessful demand for payment, Spiceco filed suit against Foodco in a State D trial court. Spiceco attached $5,000 worth of Foodco sausage that had been stored in a warehouse in State D by Foodco's distributor, pending shipment to the customer in State C. Spiceco then served process on Foodco in State A, informing it of the attachment and of the commencement of the action in State D.

State D statutes permit creditors like Spiceco to institute proceedings by attachment. The statutes permit State D courts 1) to adjudicate claims against nonresidents to the extent of any property located in the state and 2) to assert long--arm jurisdiction over nonresident corporations that "transact any business" in the state or fail to perform any contractual obligations with substantial ties to the state. State D courts construe these statutes as authorizing jurisdiction to the full extent permitted by the due process clause of the United States Constitution.

Foodco moved to dismiss the State D action for lack of jurisdiction. In addition to reciting the facts, Foodco supported its motion with an uncontradicted affidavit that no employee of Foodco has ever met with Spiceco in State D.

Should the court grant or deny Foodco's motion to dismiss? Explain.

MEE RELEASED ESSAY QUESTIONS

CONFLICT OF LAWS
July 1995

Although this question is from a very old exam, it is one of only two known MEE questions only testing Conflict of Laws (and no other subject). Therefore, it may be useful.

Petrol, a company incorporated in State X, purchased an insurance policy by mail from Insurer Inc. Insurer is incorporated and headquartered in State Y. The policy protected oil fields located in States X and Y against out-of-control oil wells and other risks. In early 1991, two wells, one in State X and one in State Y, went out of control, causing more than $50,000 damage to Petrol's fields. Petrol did not notify Insurer about these losses until 1993.

Insurer promptly rejected Petrol's two claims. Insurer relied on a clause in its policy with Petrol that denied coverage of any loss unless Petrol gave "written notice to Insurer in State Y of the loss as soon as practicable." This denial of coverage is valid under the law of State X. The denial of coverage, however, is not valid under the law of State Y, because Insurer cannot show prejudice caused by Petrol's delay in notifying it of a loss. There is no federal law on the subject and no choice-of-law clause in the insurance contract. State X courts apply First Restatement rules to resolve choice-of--law issues. State Y courts proceed first under governmental interest analysis; in the event of a true conflict, they also apply the First Restatement.

Petrol properly filed a diversity action against Insurer in the federal district court in State Y. After the court had determined the appropriate choice of law, Insurer successfully moved for a change of venue to the federal district court for State X. The case therefore is pending before the federal district court of State X.

Should the law of State X or the law of State Y be applied to determine the validity of the denial--of-coverage clause in the insurance contract? Explain.

Additional Conflict of Laws Questions

For additional questions testing Conflict of Laws issues, please see additional questions testing:

Family Law (e.g., July 2011)
Federal Civil Procedure (e.g., February 2012)

The National Conference of Bar Examiners has indicated that Conflict of Laws will not be the main subject of an essay question on the Multistate Essay Exam. If tested, Conflict of Laws will make up an issue or issues in an essay question primarily testing another subject. In the past, it has appeared as a minor part of questions testing Civil Procedure and Domestic Relations.

MBE SUBJECTS – RELEASED ESSAY QUESTIONS

CONSTITUTIONAL LAW
MEE Question - July 2009

Debate! is a local cable-TV program devoted to public affairs. Each program features a debate about a controversial public issue.

One year ago, a state official proposed legislation that would substantially increase tax rates. The proposal was very controversial, and the producers of *Debate!* invited two guests, Tax and Anti-Tax, to debate the proposal.

During a live broadcast, the following exchange took place:

Anti-Tax: Taxes are already much too high. If this ridiculous tax increase goes through, you'll have a revolution on your hands!

Tax: Don't be ridiculous. This tax increase is necessary and affordable.

Anti-Tax: You're a dishonest imbecile. The people have had enough! I call on all viewers to refuse to pay this proposed tax. And to make it clear that we mean business, I call on viewers to make Tax pay up. He lives at 224 Oak Street, right here in town. Let's show him what a taking really means.

At the conclusion of the program, Anti-Tax was arrested and charged with violating two state laws. One law, the "Sedition Statute," prohibits "any person from teaching the duty, necessity, or propriety of crime, violence, or unlawful acts of terrorism as a means of accomplishing political reform." The Sedition Statute has been construed to apply only to advocacy of imminent law-breaking.

The other law, the "Abusive Words Statute," punishes "directing any abusive word or term at another." This statute has not been interpreted by the state courts.

Two days after Anti-Tax's remarks, an unknown arsonist started a fire that destroyed Tax's home.

The proposed tax increase has not been enacted.

1.   **Assuming that Anti-Tax's statements fall within the scope of the Sedition Statute, what constitutional arguments can be made against convicting him for violating the statute? Explain.**

2.   **Assuming that Anti-Tax's statements fall within the scope of the Abusive Words Statute, what constitutional arguments can be made against convicting him for violating the statute? Explain.**

MBE SUBJECTS – RELEASED ESSAY QUESTIONS

CONSTITUTIONAL LAW
MEE Question - July 2010

The Church of Peace (the Church) is a religious organization that advocates "peace to everyone." Recently, a Church chapter (Chapter) was organized in the town of Homestead. Chapter members decided to spread the Church's message to the people of Homestead by handing out leaflets that proclaimed in bold letters, "PEACE TO ALL!" Chapter members who participated in passing out the leaflets stood on a public sidewalk and distributed the leaflets to pedestrians. The Chapter members did not block traffic or take any actions except passing out leaflets and remarking, "Peace to all!"

Many people who took the leaflets threw them onto the sidewalk, and Homestead employees spent several hours cleaning up these discarded leaflets. Chapter was fined $3,000 under a municipal anti-leafleting ordinance that prohibits any distribution of leaflets "in or on any public space, including roads, streets, and sidewalks." No Chapter member threw leaflets or other litter onto the ground.

Chapter members who attend High School, a public school in Homestead, recently formed the "Church of Peace Club" (Church Club) to pray together and to do good works. High School has a policy that permits student groups to meet in High School classrooms after scheduled classes. Under this policy, student groups must first obtain permission from Principal before using a classroom for a meeting. Pursuant to this policy, the Chess Club, the Drama Club, and the Future Lawyers Club all use classrooms for after-school meetings. Church Club officers asked Principal if they could meet in a classroom after school. Principal denied this request and stated that after-school use of a classroom by Church Club would be "a violation of the separation of church and state."

Father, a Chapter member and the parent of a Church Club officer, learned about Principal's decision and went to High School to see Principal. Outside Principal's office was a sign reading "No admittance without an appointment." Father, who had no appointment, threw open the closed door and marched into Principal's office, interrupting a meeting between Principal and another parent, and told Principal, "Your policy is unwise and unconstitutional. I believe that you are discriminating against members of my faith." Principal asked Father to leave the office until the meeting with the other parent was concluded, but Father refused. Principal called the police, who forcibly removed Father from Principal's office.

Father was convicted of trespassing on government property.

Does the First Amendment, as applied to state and local governments through the Fourteenth Amendment,

1. **Preclude Homestead's enforcement of its anti-leafleting ordinance against Chapter? Explain.**

2.   Preclude Principal's denial of Church Club's request to use classroom space for its meetings? Explain.

3.   Provide grounds to vacate Father's trespass conviction? Explain.

MBE SUBJECTS – RELEASED ESSAY QUESTIONS

CONSTITUTIONAL LAW
MEE Question - July 2011

There are two nursing schools in State A: Public Nursing School (Public) and Private Nursing School (Private). Public is an agency of the state government, and all its faculty and staff are state employees. Private is owned by a private corporation and receives no direct funding from the state. The State A Board of Education regulates the curriculum of each nursing school and certifies all graduates of the two nursing schools as eligible to become licensed nurses in State A.

Both Public and Private have a long-standing policy of restricting admission to women. Neither school has ever admitted a male applicant. There has been general discrimination against women in State A in the health care field. Historically, however, 95 percent of State A nurses have been female.

A male resident of State A wants to be a nurse. The man first applied to Private and was denied admission. His rejection letter from Private stated that he was "not eligible to enroll because Private was established as an all-female institution and does not admit or enroll male students."

The man next applied to Public and was again denied admission. His letter from Public stated that "you are not eligible to enroll because Public does not enroll male students. Mindful of the historical discrimination that women have faced in State A, our state has established Public to remedy this discrimination and provide opportunities for women who want to work in the growing field of health care as nurses." The letter continued, "Because your grades and test scores would have been sufficient to admit you if you were female, we offer you admission to our new Male Nursing Opportunity Program instead."

The Male Nursing Opportunity Program allows male residents of State A to become nurses by studying at a nursing school in an adjacent state. Graduates of the program are certified by the State A Board of Education as eligible to become licensed nurses in State A. However, the Male Nursing Opportunity Program facilities are not as modern as those at Public, the faculty is not as experienced, and graduates of the Male Nursing Opportunity Program do not enjoy the same employment opportunities as graduates of either Public or Private.

1. **Has Private violated the man's rights under the Equal Protection Clause of the Fourteenth Amendment? Explain.**

2. **Has Public violated the man's rights under the Equal Protection Clause of the Fourteenth Amendment? Explain.**

MBE SUBJECTS – RELEASED ESSAY QUESTIONS

CONSTITUTIONAL LAW
MEE Question - July 2012

Congress recently enacted the Violence at Work Act (the Act). Title I of the Act provides that an employee who has been injured in the workplace by the violent act of a coworker has a cause of action for damages against that coworker. Title II of the Act imposes several duties on employers subject to the Act and creates a cause of action against employers who do not fulfill those duties. Section 201 provides that all employers, "including all States, their agencies and subdivisions," who have more than 50 employees are subject to the Act. Section 202 requires employers subject to the Act to (i) train employees on certain methods of preventing and responding to workplace violence, (ii) conduct criminal background checks on job applicants, and (iii) establish a hotline to report workplace violence. Section 203 provides that if an employer subject to the Act does not fulfill the duties imposed by Section 202, an employee who has been injured by the violent act of a fellow employee may recover damages from the employer for the harm resulting from that violent act. Section 204 provides that any action brought pursuant to Section 203 may be brought in federal or state court and that "if brought in federal court against a State, its agencies or subdivisions, any defense of immunity under the Eleventh Amendment to the United States Constitution is abrogated."

The House and Senate committee reports on the Act note that Congress passed the Act under its power to regulate interstate commerce. To support its use of that power, Congress found that acts of workplace violence directly interfere with economic activity by causing damage to business property, injury to workers, and lost work time due to the violent acts and their aftermath. The House report estimated that total interstate economic activity is diminished by $5 to $10 billion per year as a result of losses associated with workplace violence.

After the Act's effective date, an employee of a state agency was injured in the workplace by the violent act of a disgruntled coworker. The state agency, which has over 100 employees, conceded that it had not implemented the measures required by Section 202 of the Act. Accordingly, the employee has sued the state agency in United States District Court to recover damages for the harm caused by the act of workplace violence. The state agency has moved to dismiss the lawsuit on three grounds: (1) Congress did not have the power to enact the Act, (2) Congress did not have the power to apply the Act to state agencies, and (3) the Eleventh Amendment bars the employee's lawsuit.

1.   **Is the Act a valid exercise of Congress's power to regulate interstate commerce? Explain.**

2.   **Assuming that the Act is a valid exercise of Congress's power, may the Act constitutionally be applied to state agencies as employers? Explain.**

3.   **Does the Eleventh Amendment bar the employee's lawsuit in federal court against the state agency? Explain.**

MBE SUBJECTS – RELEASED ESSAY QUESTIONS

CONSTITUTIONAL LAW
MEE Question – February 2013

AutoCo is a privately owned corporation that manufactures automobiles. Ten years ago, AutoCo purchased a five-square-mile parcel of unincorporated land in a remote region of the state and built a large automobile assembly plant on the land. To attract workers to the remote location of the plant, AutoCo built apartment buildings and houses on the land and leased them to its employees. AutoCo owns and operates a commercial district with shops and streets open to the general public. AutoCo named the area Oakwood and provides security, fire protection, and sanitation services for Oakwood's residents. AutoCo also built, operates, and fully funds the only school in the region, which it makes available free of charge to the children of its employees.

A family recently moved to Oakwood. The father and mother work in AutoCo's plant, rent an apartment from AutoCo, and have enrolled their 10-year-old son in Oakwood's school. Every morning, the students are required to recite the Pledge of Allegiance while standing and saluting an American flag. With the approval of his parents, the son has politely but insistently refused to recite the Pledge and salute the flag at the school on the grounds that doing so violates his own political beliefs and the political beliefs of his family. As a result of his refusal to say the Pledge, the son has been expelled from the school.

To protest the school's actions, the father walked into the commercial district of Oakwood. While standing on a street corner, he handed out leaflets that contained a short essay critical of the school's Pledge of Allegiance policy. Some of the passersby who took the leaflets dropped them to the ground. An AutoCo security guard saw the litter, told the father that Oakwood's anti-litter rule prohibits leaflet distribution that results in littering, and directed him to cease distribution of the leaflets and leave the commercial district. When the father did not leave and continued to distribute the leaflets, the security guard called the state police, which sent officers who arrested the father for trespass.

1. **Did the son's expulsion from the school violate the First Amendment as applied through the Fourteenth Amendment? Explain.**

2. **Did the father's arrest violate the First Amendment as applied through the Fourteenth Amendment? Explain.**

MBE SUBJECTS – RELEASED ESSAY QUESTIONS

CONSTITUTIONAL LAW
MEE Question – February 2014

A city ordinance required each downtown business to install high-powered halogen floodlights that would illuminate the property owned by that business and the adjoining sidewalks. A study commissioned by the city estimated that installation of the floodlights would cost a typical business about $1,000, but that increased business traffic due to enhanced public safety, especially after dark, would likely offset this cost.

A downtown restaurant applied to the city for a building permit to construct an addition that would increase its seating capacity. In its permit application, the restaurant accurately noted that its current facility did not have sufficient seating to accommodate all potential customers during peak hours. The city approved the permit on the condition that the restaurant grant the city an easement over a narrow strip of the restaurant's property, to be used by the city to install video surveillance equipment that would cover nearby public streets and parking lots. The city based its permit decision entirely on findings that the increased patronage that would result from the increased capacity of the restaurant might also attract additional crime to the neighborhood, and that installing video surveillance equipment might alleviate that problem.

The restaurant has challenged both the ordinance requiring it to install floodlights and the easement condition imposed on approval of the building permit.

1.   Under the Fifth Amendment as applied to the states through the Fourteenth Amendment, is the city ordinance requiring the restaurant to install floodlights an unconstitutional taking? Explain.

2.   Under the Fifth Amendment as applied to the states through the Fourteenth Amendment, is the city's requirement that the restaurant grant the city an easement as a condition for obtaining the building permit an unconstitutional taking?

MBE SUBJECTS – RELEASED ESSAY QUESTIONS

CONSTITUTIONAL LAW
MEE Question – February 2015

State A, suffering from declining tax revenues, sought ways to save money by reducing expenses and performing services more efficiently. Accordingly, various legislative committees undertook examinations of the services performed by the state. One service provided by State A is firefighting. The legislative committee with jurisdiction over firefighting held extensive hearings and determined that older firefighters, because of seniority, earn substantially more than younger firefighters but are unlikely to perform as well as their younger colleagues. In particular, exercise physiologists testified at the committee's hearings that, in general, a person's physical conditioning and ability to work safely and effectively as a firefighter decline with age (with the most rapid declines occurring after age 50) and that, as a result, firefighting would be safer and more efficient if the age of the workforce was lowered.

State A subsequently enacted the Fire Safety in Employment Act (the Act). The Act provides that no one may be employed by the state as a firefighter after reaching the age of 50.
A firefighter, age 49, is employed by State A. He is in excellent physical condition and wants to remain a firefighter. His work history has been exemplary for the last two decades. Nonetheless, he has been told that, as a result of the Act, his employment as a firefighter will be terminated when he turns 50 next month.

The firefighter is considering (a) challenging the Act on the basis that it violates his rights under the Fourteenth Amendment's Equal Protection Clause, and (b) lobbying for the enactment of a federal statute barring states from setting mandatory age limitations for firefighters.

1.   **Does the Act violate the Equal Protection Clause of the Fourteenth Amendment? Explain.**

2.   **Would Congress have authority under Section Five of the Fourteenth Amendment to enact a statute barring states from establishing a maximum age for firefighters? Explain.**

MBE SUBJECTS – RELEASED ESSAY QUESTIONS

CONSTITUTIONAL LAW
MEE Question – February 2016

State A, a leader in wind energy, recently enacted the "Green Energy Act" ("the Act").

Section 1 of the Act requires that 50% of the electricity sold by utilities in the state come from "environmentally friendly energy sources." Wind energy, which is produced in State A, is classified by the Act as an "environmentally friendly energy source." Natural gas, which is not produced in State A, is not classified by the Act as environmentally friendly. The preamble of the Act contains express findings that the burning of natural gas releases significant quantities of greenhouse gases into the atmosphere and requires the diversion of scarce water resources for use in gas-burning thermoelectric plants.

Section 2 of the Act prohibits the Public Service Commission of State A from approving any new coal-burning power plants in the state, unless it finds that "the construction of the plant is necessary to meet urgent energy needs of this state." A public utility in neighboring State B has applied for a permit to build a coal-burning power plant on property it owns across the border in State A. The Commission has denied the utility's application based on its finding that there is no evidence of any urgent energy needs in State A. The State B utility presented undisputed evidence of severe energy shortages in State B, but the Commission rejected this evidence as irrelevant to the statutory exception.

Section 3 of the Act requires State A, whenever possible, to buy goods and services only from "environmentally friendly vendors located within the state." To qualify as an "environmentally friendly vendor," a firm must meet specified standards concerning energy efficiency, chemical use, and use of recycled materials. A vendor located outside of State A meets all the standards to qualify as an environmentally friendly vendor. The vendor has sought to sell goods and services to State A. The relevant State A agencies have refused to purchase from this vendor, pointing out that the Act requires them to purchase, if possible, only from "environmentally friendly vendors located within the state," of which there are several.

There is no federal statute or regulation relevant to this problem.

Which provisions, if any, of the Green Energy Act unconstitutionally burden or discriminate   against interstate commerce? Explain.

MBE SUBJECTS – PRACTICE ESSAY QUESTIONS

CONSTITUTIONAL LAW
Question 1

A crop blight devastated the corn harvest of the State of Alpha causing tremendous economic harm to Alpha's farmers and straining the state's economy. Corn is Alpha's main cash crop. In response, the Alpha State Legislature authorized an emergency program to develop a strain of the crop that is resistant to the blight. Researchers at the Alpha State University developed a variety of corn that was immune to the blight.

The Alpha State Legislature authorized the Alpha Department of Agriculture to sell the blight-resistant corn to all farmers in the state at a substantial discount. Seed stocks began to run low in the second year of the program. It was alleged that large corporate farms – many of whose owners resided out of the state – were responsible for the shortages. It was projected that the State would be unable to fulfill all of the requests for the blight-resistant seeds. In response, the Alpha State Legislature authorized the Alpha Department of Agriculture to promulgate rules for the preservation of seed stocks in order to ensure that Alpha's farmers would be able to get the blight-resistant seeds.

Pursuant to this legislative authorization, the Alpha Department of Agriculture properly promulgated a rule under the Alpha Administrative Procedure Act requiring that requests for the blight-resistant seed made by farmers who were citizens of the State of Alpha be filled before any non-citizens who farmed in the state. In addition, the regulation prohibited the resale of the seed to anyone who was not a citizen of the State of Alpha.

Wickard is a citizen of the State of Beta which is adjacent to the State of Alpha. Wickard operates farms in both states as a sole proprietor. He has just been informed by the Alpha Department of Agriculture that it will be unable to fill his order for blight-resistant seed given the demand by in-state farmers. Wickard's corn crop faces ruin if he is unable to get the blight-resistant seed.

Wickard has come to you seeking advice about a possible legal challenge to the Alpha Department of Agriculture's regulation.

Write a memo analyzing possible challenges Wickard could make under the U.S. Constitution to the Department of Agriculture's regulation. Evaluate the chance of success of each. Assume that there is no extant federal legislation covering this area.

MBE SUBJECTS – PRACTICE ESSAY QUESTIONS

CONSTITUTIONAL LAW
Question 2

In September 2002, State adopted the State Sexual Responsibility Act. The first two sections of the Act state the following:

"1. Any unmarried person under 18 years old who possesses a contraceptive device or a contraceptive pill is guilty of a felony. This section does not apply to a married person who intends to use the contraceptive device or contraceptive pill during sexual intercourse with their husband or wife. The purpose of this section is to discourage sexual intercourse among unmarried minors, which leads to a number of social problems."

"2. No one may use a billboard located within State to advertise any contraceptive device or contraceptive pill. This section serves two purposes: 1) Proscribing advertisements that some state residents will find offensive; and 2) Advancing the state's esthetic interests by reducing the number of billboards."

Section 7 of the Sexual Responsibility Act specifically defines the terms "contraceptive device," "contraceptive pill," and "billboard." State does not have a statute that prohibits publication of information on billboards, other than Section 2 of the Sexual Responsibility Act.

After State adopts the Sexual Responsibility Act, a number of groups and individuals bring a constitutional challenge to the first two sections of the Act.

Analyze and discuss whether Section 1 and/or Section 2 of the Sexual Responsibility Act violates the United States Constitution.

MRE SUBJECTS – PRACTICE ESSAY QUESTIONS

CONSTITUTIONAL LAW
Question 3

You are an attorney working in the office of a state representative. Your job is to provide the representative with legal counsel.

A bill has been introduced in the state legislature that would amend current law regarding adoption procedures. The new law would require the state's child welfare agencies to "make placement decisions that are in the best interests of the child . . . taking the race of the prospective adoptive parents into account when making placement decisions." The prospective law also states with respect to adoption "that when possible, the race of the prospective parents should be the same as the child." This law would only apply when the state adoption agency can find no suitable blood relative.

Draft a memorandum for your state representative in which you analyze and discuss the U.S. constitutional law issues arising from this legislation, were it to become law.

MBE SUBJECTS – PRACTICE ESSAY QUESTIONS

CONSTITUTIONAL LAW
Question 4

You are counsel to the National Coalition Against Domestic Violence. The Coalition leadership has drafted a bill which it intends to introduce for adoption by the U.S. Congress. The bill is called the Domestic Violence Act.

The Act includes the following:

Language stating that domestic violence crimes often result in serious physical injury and economic losses, therefore this legislation is authorized by Congress' power to regulate interstate commerce.

- A definition of "domestic violence crime" as any battery committed by a person on his or her spouse or sexual partner.
- Section #1 stating that any person who intentionally or knowingly commits a domestic violence crime against his/her spouse or sexual partner is guilty of a felony.
- Section #2 stating that any person who knowingly possesses a gun after having been convicted of a felony domestic violence crime, is guilty of a felony.
- Section #3 stating that any person who transmits indecent or sexually explicit material in interstate commerce with the knowledge that the material will reach a person who has been convicted of a domestic violence crime, shall be guilty of a felony.

The Coalition asks for your legal opinion as to the constitutionality of this proposed Act. Prepare a memo in which you analyze and discuss whether the Domestic Violence Act may violate the United States Constitution.

MBE SUBJECTS – PRACTICE ESSAY QUESTIONS

CONSTITUTIONAL LAW
Question 5

In 2000, the U.S. Congress enacted a statute prohibiting all private elementary and secondary schools in the United States from discriminating in the admission of students on the basis of race, gender and religion.

Several schools filed suit in the appropriate federal district courts to enjoin on constitutional grounds, the enforcement of the statute as to their schools.

One suit was brought by the Wall Academy, a secondary high school that admits boys and girls of all religions, but only if they are white.

The second suit was brought by the Washington School for Boys, a secular high school that admits boys of all races and religions, but not girls.

The third suit was brought by the Grace Protestant School, a sectarian high school that admits boys and girls of all races, but only if they are of the Protestant faith.

All three schools are accredited by the state's department of education, but none receives any financial support from the state or federal government.

The U.S. Supreme Court will decide all three cases. Analyze and discuss the constitutionally relevant issues that will arise, even if the answer on one issue is dispositive of the case.

MBE SUBJECTS – PRACTICE ESSAY QUESTIONS

CONSTITUTIONAL LAW
Question 6

Congress enacted a statute (signed by the President) appropriating $20 billion to the Interior Department to purchase land on which unusual and interesting geological formations are located. The statute provided that if an owner refuses to sell, the Interior Department could take the land upon the payment of just compensation to the owner. The statute also appropriated $10 million apiece to each state so that the states could acquire land for the same purposes.

Alice Allen, as a federal income tax payer, filed suit asserting that the statute was unconstitutional because the purpose of the expenditure was beyond the powers of Congress.

The Interior Department also filed suit to appropriate the land of Billy Burton. Burton owned several hundred acres of land which was the site of an extremely unusual system of caverns that Billy was using as a very profitable tourist attraction. Billy had refused to sell his land for its fair market value to the federal government when requested to do so.

While these actions were pending, the President of the United States suddenly decided that it was time once again to reduce federal government spending. He issued an executive order directing the Secretary of the Interior to reduce the annual spending under the statute from $20 billion to $5 billion. The Secretary immediately ordered that no money be given to the states.

The State of Adam, to which $10 million had been allocated and then withdrawn, brought suit seeking a declaratory judgment that the President's order was unconstitutional. Standing is not an issue in this action.

Analyze and discuss how each of these actions might be decided if they were heard by the United States Supreme Court. Do not assume the existence of statutes not mentioned in this question.

MBE SUBJECTS – PRACTICE ESSAY QUESTIONS

CONSTITUTIONAL LAW
Question 7

In 1996, Congress enacted a statute requiring all motor vehicles engaged in or affecting interstate commerce to be equipped with a particular type of exhaust system (called a Clean Pipe) that would reduce the polluting effect of motor vehicles.

In 1997, Alice Alberts was arrested and subsequently convicted in federal court for driving on a two-lane dirt road between two small towns in the State of Adams in an old automobile not equipped with a Clean Pipe in compliance with the 1996 statute.

In 1998, the State of Adams enacted a statute requiring that all motor vehicles driven in the state be equipped with a different type of exhaust system called the Scrub Pipe. The Scrub Pipe was different from the device required by the federal government but was also designed to reduce pollution from motor vehicles.

In 1999, Barton drove his own tractor-trailer on a cross-country trip, hauling goods from New York to California. While in the State of Adams, Barton was arrested and subsequently convicted for driving a motor vehicle not equipped with a Scrub Pipe in compliance with 1998 state statute. Barton argued that his arrest under the state statute was inconsistent with the federal constitution and the federal statute.

Also in 1999, Charles Carter, a federal post office employee who drove a mail truck entirely within the State of Adams, was arrested and subsequently convicted in state court for violating the state's 1998 statute because the mail truck he drove was not equipped with the Scrub Pipe.

The United States Supreme Court ultimately reviewed the convictions of Alberts, Barton and Carter. What results and why? With respect to Barton and Carter, would your answers be different had the 1996 federal statute been repealed prior to their arrests in 1999?

MBE SUBJECTS – RELEASED ESSAY QUESTIONS

CONTRACTS
MEE Question - July 2008

Rancher conducts cattle roping clinics in various locations around the country. Rancher thought it would be more profitable to buy his own land and conduct the clinics there.

In March, Rancher bought the Bar-X Ranch (Ranch) with a large pasture on which Rancher could hold the roping clinics.

In April, before Rancher had offered any roping clinics on the property, Rancher agreed to allow Gasco, an oil and natural gas company, to explore for gas reserves on Ranch. Before the parties signed a contract, Gasco executives drove around Ranch, and Rancher pointed out to them the pasture where he planned to hold his roping clinics. Rancher told the Gasco executives, "I can't wait to start holding my clinics here so that I won't have to go on the road anymore. Every summer that I travel with my clinics costs me $50,000. It will cost me only $10,000 to work from Ranch."

In July, Rancher and Gasco signed a contract in which Gasco agreed to complete its gas exploration and restore Ranch to its pre-exploration condition by March 31 of the following year. Gasco immediately began exploring for gas on Ranch.

By March 31 of the following year, Gasco had completed its exploration but chose not to restore Ranch to its pre-exploration condition. Because of Gasco's failure to restore Ranch, the pasture was not usable, and Rancher had to cancel his plans to conduct roping clinics on Ranch that summer.

Rancher sued Gasco for breach of contract. At trial, an expert for Rancher testified that because of Gasco's failure to promptly restore Ranch to its pre-exploration condition, it would cost $500,000 and take three years to restore Ranch. Furthermore, during that time Ranch could not be used for roping clinics.

An expert for Gasco testified that Ranch was worth only $20,000 less in its unrestored condition than if it had been restored to its pre-exploration condition. There was no other expert testimony.

Rancher testified that Ranch could not be used for roping clinics for the next three summers. Rancher estimated that 50 people would have attended the roping clinics each year, and each person would have paid a fee of $2,000, for a total of $100,000 per year. Therefore, Rancher seeks $300,000 for his losses.

The trial court found that there was an enforceable contract between the parties and that Gasco had breached the contract by failing to restore Ranch. The court awarded Rancher $500,000 for the cost of restoring Ranch to its pre-exploration condition and $300,000 for his losses.

1. Did the court err in awarding Rancher the cost of restoring Ranch to its pre-exploration condition? Explain.

2. Did the court err in awarding Rancher $300,000 for damages resulting from Rancher's inability to conduct roping clinics on Ranch for three years? Explain.

MBE SUBJECTS – RELEASED ESSAY QUESTIONS

CONTRACTS
MEE Question - July 2009

Sam was walking down the sidewalk when he heard shouts coming from a burning house. Sam immediately called 911 on his cell phone and rushed into the house. Inside the house, Sam discovered Resident trying to coax Resident's frightened dog from behind a couch. Sam, at great risk to his safety, crawled behind the couch and pulled the dog from its hiding place. Sam, carrying the dog, and Resident then safely made their way outside.

Once outside, Resident thanked Sam and asked Sam about his work. Sam told Resident, "I was hoping to start training as a paramedic in the fall, but I don't think I'll be able to afford the cost of the program."

Resident responded, "We need all the good paramedics that we can get! If you are going to start paramedic training, I want to help you. Also, my dog means everything to me. I want to compensate you for your heroism. Give me your address, and I will send you a check for a thousand dollars."

Sam said, "Thank you so much! Here is my address. I'll apply to the paramedic program tomorrow."

Sam applied to the paramedic training program but was denied admission. Sam then applied for and was accepted into a cosmetology training program and owes that program $1,000. Sam cannot pay the $1,000 he owes because when Resident learned Sam was not attending the paramedic program, he refused to give Sam the $1,000.

Sam sued Resident to recover the $1,000.

What theories could Sam assert to recover all or some portion of the $1,000, and what is the likelihood of success on each theory? Explain.

MBE SUBJECTS – RELEASED ESSAY QUESTIONS

CONTRACTS
MEE Question – February 2011

Designer and Retailer entered into a legally binding contract for Designer to maintain Retailer's website. Under the terms of the written contract, Retailer was to pay Designer $20,000 per year. Retailer made timely payments for two years.

Eight months before the third year's payment was due, Designer learned of an investment opportunity. Designer called Retailer and said, "I need cash quickly to make an investment that will enable me to make a $35,000 profit. I know that you owe me $20,000, but if you promise now to pay me $15,000 in cash by the 25th of this month, I will accept that payment as satisfying your obligation under our contract for this year."

Retailer responded, "Thanks. That's a good deal. I don't have the cash to pay you now. I'll do it if I can get a loan."

"That will be great," responded Designer.

Because Designer assumed that Retailer would provide the cash Designer needed, Designer did not try to raise the cash from another source.

Retailer, however, was busy with other matters. He visited two banks and picked up loan applications, but he never bothered to submit them. Retailer did not take any other action to obtain a loan before the 25th of the month had passed.

When the 25th of the month passed without payment from Retailer, Designer telephoned Retailer. The moment that Retailer heard Designer's voice saying "Hello," Retailer quickly said, "Sorry, but I can't take you up on your offer to accept early payment."

Designer was shocked and angered. He had counted on that money. He can prove that he would have gained $35,000 had he been able to make the planned investment.

Designer has sued Retailer for actual damages plus punitive damages.

1.   **Is Retailer liable for breach of contract? Explain.**

2.   **Assuming that Retailer is liable, can Designer recover his actual damages from Retailer? Explain.**

3.   **Assuming that Retailer is liable, can Designer recover punitive damages? Explain.**

MBE SUBJECTS – RELEASED ESSAY QUESTIONS

CONTRACTS
MEE Question – February 2012

GreenCar owns a fleet of 10 identical energy-efficient, electric "green" cars that it rents out for special events. GreenCar is the only company that has such specialized cars available for rental. GreenCar needed all 10 of its cars to fulfill a contract to provide 10 identical green cars to carry dignitaries in the local Earth Day parade on April 22, but each of the cars needed repair to be operable for the parade.

In order to have all 10 cars repaired in time for the parade, GreenCar entered into a contract with RepairCo pursuant to which RepairCo promised to "repair all 10 cars and return them to GreenCar no later than April 21 for $1,000 per car, $10,000 total."

On April 21, RepairCo had completed repairs on only 6 of the 10 cars and returned those 6 cars to GreenCar. When RepairCo delivered the 6 cars, it informed GreenCar that the remaining 4 cars were not ready because RepairCo workers had walked off the job when salary negotiations broke down. RepairCo also explained to GreenCar that it planned to give its workers the raises they wanted, but it first wanted "to teach them a lesson." RepairCo estimated that the remaining 4 GreenCar cars (all still inoperable) would be repaired by April 30.

GreenCar demanded that RepairCo return the remaining 4 unrepaired cars immediately. RepairCo did so. GreenCar refused to pay RepairCo for any repairs to the other 6 cars.

RepairCo sued GreenCar, alleging that GreenCar's refusal to pay anything was a breach of contract.

Is RepairCo entitled to any payment from GreenCar, and if so, under what theory or theories? Explain.

MBE SUBJECTS – RELEASED ESSAY QUESTIONS

CONTRACTS
MEE Question – February 2013

On January 2, a boat builder and a sailor entered into a contract pursuant to which the builder was to sell to the sailor a boat to be specially manufactured for the sailor by the builder. The contract price was $100,000. The written contract, signed by both parties, stated that the builder would tender the boat to the sailor on December 15, at which time payment in full would be due.

On October 15, the builder's workers went on strike and there were no available replacements.

On October 31, the builder's workers were still on strike, and no work was being done on the boat. The sailor read a news report about the strike and immediately sent a letter to the builder stating, "I am very concerned that my boat will not be completed by December 15. I insist that you provide me with assurance that you will perform in accordance with the contract." The builder received the letter on the next day, November 1.

On November 25, the builder responded to the letter, stating, "I'm sorry about the strike, but it is really out of my hands. I hope we settle it soon so that we can get back to work."

Nothing further happened until December 3, when the builder called the sailor and said, "My workers are back, and I have two crews working overtime to finish your boat. Your boat is task one. Don't worry; we'll deliver your boat by December 15th." The sailor immediately replied, "I don't trust you. As far as I'm concerned, our contract is over. I am going to buy my boat from a shipyard." Two days later, the sailor entered into a contract with a competing manufacturer to buy a boat similar to the boat that was the subject of the contract with the builder.

The builder finished the boat on time and tendered it to the sailor on December 15. The sailor reminded the builder about the December 3 conversation in which the sailor had announced that "our contract is over," and refused to take the boat and pay for it.

The builder has sued the sailor for breach of contract.

1.   What was the legal effect of the sailor's October 31 letter to the builder? Explain.

2.   What was the legal effect of the builder's November 25 response to the sailor's October 31 letter? Explain.

3.   What was the legal effect of the sailor's refusal to take and pay for the boat on December 15? Explain.

MBE SUBJECTS - PRACTICE ESSAY QUESTIONS

CONTRACTS LAW
MEE Question - July 2013

On May 1, a manufacturer and a chef met at a restaurant trade show. The manufacturer showed the chef some carving knives that were on sale for $100 each. After examining the knives, the chef said, "I love these knives! I'll take 10 of them. Please send them to my restaurant within the month. As soon as I receive them, I'll send you a check for $1,000." The manufacturer said, "I'll ship the 10 knives to your restaurant in a few weeks," and he took the chef's address for shipping purposes.

On May 15, the manufacturer sent six knives to the chef. Enclosed in the shipping box was a document on the manufacturer's letterhead that stated in its entirety: "It is a pleasure to do business with you. Enclosed, pursuant to our agreement, are six knives. Please remit $600 at your earliest convenience."

On May 17, the chef sent the manufacturer a check for $600 and included in the envelope an unsigned note to the manufacturer, handwritten on plain paper, requesting the remaining four knives. The manufacturer did not respond to the note.

The knives were particularly well-suited for the chef's uses, and the $100 price was a bargain, so the chef was very eager for the manufacturer to deliver the remaining four knives. On June 17, the chef wrote to the manufacturer claiming that the manufacturer was contractually bound to sell the chef 10 knives and that the manufacturer had breached that contract by furnishing only 6 knives. The manufacturer did not reply to the chef's letter.

Is there an enforceable contract against the manufacturer that binds him to sell 10 knives to the chef?

MBE SUBJECTS - PRACTICE ESSAY QUESTIONS

CONTRACTS
MEE Question - July 2014

A music conservatory has two concert halls. One concert hall had a pipe organ that was in poor repair, and the other had no organ. The conservatory decided to repair the existing organ and buy a new organ for the other concert hall. After some negotiation, the conservatory entered into two contracts with a business that both repairs and sells organs. Under one contract, the business agreed to repair the existing pipe organ for the conservatory for $100,000. The business would usually charge a higher price for a project of this magnitude, but the business agreed to this price because the conservatory agreed to prepay the entire amount. Under the other contract, the business agreed to sell a new organ to the conservatory for the other concert hall for $225,000. As with the repair contract, the business agreed to a low sales price because the conservatory agreed to prepay the entire amount. Both contracts were signed on January 3, and the conservatory paid the business a total of $325,000 that day.

Two weeks later, before the business had commenced repair of the existing organ, the business suffered serious and unanticipated financial reversals. The chief financial officer for the business contacted the conservatory and said,

> Bad news. We had an unexpected liability and as a result are in a real cash crunch. In fact, even though we haven't acquired the new organ from our supplier or started repair of your existing organ, we've already spent the cash you gave us, and we have no free cash on hand. We're really sorry, but we're in a fix. I think that we can find a way to perform both contracts, but not at the original prices. If you agree to pay $60,000 more for the repair and $40,000 more for the new organ, we can probably find financing to finish everything. If you don't agree to pay us the extra money, I doubt that we will ever be able to perform either contract, and you'll be out the money you already paid us.

After receiving this unwelcome news, the conservatory agreed to pay the extra amounts, provided that the extra amount on each contract would be paid only upon completion of the business's obligations under that contract. The business agreed to this arrangement, and the parties quickly signed documents reflecting these changes to each contract. The business then repaired the existing organ, delivered the new organ, and demanded payment of the additional $100,000.

The conservatory now has refused to pay the business the additional amounts for the repair and the new organ.

1. **Must the conservatory pay the additional $60,000 for the organ repair? Explain.**

2. **Must the conservatory pay the additional $40,000 for the new organ? Explain.**

MBE SUBJECTS - PRACTICE ESSAY QUESTIONS

CONTRACTS
MEE Question - July 2015

A seller and a buyer both collect antique dolls as a hobby. Both live in the same small city and are avid readers of magazines about antique dolls. The seller placed an advertisement in an antique doll magazine seeking to sell for $12,000 an antique doll manufactured in 1820.

On May 1, the buyer saw the advertisement and telephoned the seller to discuss buying the doll. During this conversation, the seller and the buyer agreed to a sale of the doll to the buyer for $12,000 and also agreed that the seller would deliver the doll to the buyer's house on May 4, at which time the buyer would pay the purchase price.

The next day, May 2, the buyer changed his mind and decided not to buy the doll. He signed and mailed a letter to the seller, which stated in relevant part:

> I have decided not to buy the 1820 doll that we agreed yesterday you would sell to me.

The seller received the letter on May 3, immediately telephoned the buyer, and said, "I consider your letter of May 2 to be the final end to our deal. I will sell the doll to someone else and will hold you responsible for any loss."

On May 4, the seller received a telephone call from another antique doll collector. The collector had seen the seller's advertisement for the doll and expressed interest in buying it. After some discussion, the seller and the collector agreed to a sale of the doll to the collector for $11,000. Because the collector lived in a distant part of the state, the agreement provided that the seller, at her expense, would arrange for delivery of the doll by an express delivery service. The express delivery service that they selected charges $150 for deliveries of this type. The sale, the method of delivery, and the fee were all commercially reasonable. The seller acted in good faith in entering into this agreement with the collector.

On May 5, the buyer telephoned the seller and said, "I made a mistake when I sent the letter, and I will buy the doll from you on the terms we agreed to. Come to my house tomorrow—I'll have the $12,000 for you." The seller replied, "You're too late. I've already sold the doll to someone else." The seller then took the doll to the delivery service and paid the $150 delivery fee. The delivery service delivered the doll to the collector, who immediately wired the $11,000 payment to the seller. Two weeks later, the seller sued the buyer for breach of contract.

1.   **Is there a contract for the sale of the doll that is enforceable against the buyer? Explain.**

2. Assuming that there is a contract enforceable against the buyer, did the buyer breach that contract? Explain.

3. Assuming that there is a contract enforceable against the buyer and that the buyer breached that contract, how much can the seller recover in damages? Explain.

5/1 - agreed via phone for doll $12K and deliver to B's house 5/4.

5/2 - B did mind - sent letter revoking

5/3 - S rec'd ltr

5/4 - DC doll for $11K + $150 @ S expense

5/5 - B called S and wanted to buy doll @ $12K S refused and sued B.

Sale of goods - UCC Art. 9 -
① No contract - UCC sale of goods > $500 must be in writing to satisfy S/F. S - argue mailed ltr from B is evidence that there was an agreement but still violated S/F. Even if both merchants, need a writing

② No breach. Breach of a K occurs when a party to the K does not perform after performance comes due. Therefore, if performance has not come due, there cannot be a breach

③ $1,150 - expectation & incidental damages.

MBE SUBJECTS - PRACTICE ESSAY QUESTIONS

CONTRACTS
MEE Question - July 2016

A homeowner and his neighbor live in houses that were built at the same time. The two houses have identical exteriors and are next to each other. The homeowner and his neighbor have not painted their houses in a long time, and the exterior paint on both houses is cracked and peeling. A retiree, who lives across the street from the homeowner and the neighbor, has complained to both of them that the peeling paint on their houses reduces property values in the neighborhood.

Last week, the homeowner contacted a professional housepainter. After some discussion, the painter and the homeowner entered into a written contract, signed by both of them, pursuant to which the painter agreed to paint the homeowner's house within 14 days and the homeowner agreed to pay the painter $6,000 no later than three days after completion of painting. The price was advantageous for the homeowner because, to paint a house of that size, most professional housepainters would have charged at least $8,000.

The day after the homeowner entered into the contract with the painter, he told his neighbor about the great deal he had made. The neighbor then stated that her parents wanted to come to town for a short visit the following month, but that she was reluctant to invite them. "This would be the first time my parents would see my house, but I can't invite them to my house with its peeling paint; I'd be too embarrassed. I'd paint the house now, but I can't afford the going rate for a good paint job."

The homeowner, who was facing cash-flow problems of his own, decided to offer the neighbor a deal that would help them both. The homeowner said that, for $500, the homeowner would allow the neighbor to take over the homeowner's rights under the contract. The homeowner said, "You'll pay me $500 and take the contract from me; the painter will paint your house instead of mine, and when he's done, you'll pay him the $6,000." The neighbor happily agreed to this idea.

The following day, the neighbor paid the homeowner $500 and the homeowner said to her, "The paint deal is now yours." The neighbor then invited her parents for the visit that had been discussed. The neighbor also remembered how annoyed the retiree had been about the condition of her house. Accordingly, she called the retiree and told him about the plans to have her house painted. The retiree responded that it was "about time."

Later that day, the homeowner and the neighbor told the painter about the deal pursuant to which the neighbor had taken over the contract from the homeowner. The painter was unhappy with the news and stated, "You can't change my deal without my consent. I will honor my commitment to paint the house I promised to paint, but I won't paint someone else's house."

There is no difference in magnitude or difficulty between the work required to paint the homeowner's house and the work required to paint the neighbor's house.

1. **If the painter refuses to paint the neighbor's house, would the neighbor succeed in a breach of contract action against the painter? Explain.**

2. **Assuming that the neighbor would succeed in the breach of contract action against the painter, would the retiree succeed in a breach of contract action? Explain.**

3. **If the painter paints the neighbor's house and the neighbor does not pay the $6,000 contract price, would the painter succeed in a contract claim against the neighbor? Against the homeowner? Explain.**

MBE SUBJECTS – PRACTICE ESSAY QUESTIONS

CONTRACTS
Question 1

While at the bank, John saw a notice posted which said the following:

> **"For Sale - Prime Recreational Property. Only 1 hour from town. Call Mary - 555-2345"**

John called Mary and asked if she would be willing to sell the property for $250,000. Mary responded that she would have to get at least $300,000. John stated that Mary's offer sounded interesting and asked if he might have a 30-day option. Mary said that was fine and gave John the following writing:

> **"In consideration of $1.00 (one dollar) paid by John, Mary will sell her recreational property to John for $300,000. This option good for 30 days."**

> **(signed) Mary**

John never paid the $1.00 to Mary but two weeks later, after John had inspected the property, he wrote to Mary:

> **"I really like the property, but I still think your price is too high. Will you take $270,500?"**

> **(signed) John**

Mary received the letter but did not send a reply. The next week John was informed by Tim that Mary either had sold the property or was offering to sell it to Bob. John immediately went back to the office and sent Mary the following letter:

> **"Accept your offer to buy recreational property. Enclosed is my check for $300,000."**

> **(signed) John**

After the letter and check were mailed, but before they arrived, Mary died in a skiing accident. The next day, John's letter and check were duly delivered to Mary's mailbox.

Analyze and discuss whether there is a contract between John and Mary. Discuss the legal effect of the various communications between the parties.

MBE SUBJECTS – PRACTICE ESSAY QUESTIONS

CONTRACTS
Question 2

On June 1, Builder agreed in writing to build a house for Owner on a lake front lot owned by Owner. The house was to be built according to plans supplied by Builder and the agreed price for the work was $300,000. The agreement contained a clause excluding modification or rescission except by a signed writing.

Before Builder began construction, the threat of a nationwide brick shortage significantly increased Builder's cost for bricks, resulting in an increase in the cost of the house to $350,000. Builder notified Owner about the cost increase in the bricks, and after some discussion about that cost increase, Builder and Owner orally agreed to increase the contract price to $350,000. Thereupon, Builder immediately began construction.

On September 1, Builder informed Owner that construction was complete. Upon inspection, however, Owner discovered that Builder had failed to furnish kitchen cabinets, gutters and downspouts, and sidewalks. It will cost $17,000 to remedy these deficiencies. It was also discovered that a wall between the family room and the kitchen had been misplaced. The cost of tearing down this wall and rebuilding it is $60,000. The market value of the house has been diminished by $5,000 due to the misplaced wall. Owner refuses to accept the house, and Builder brings suit for $350,000.

Thoroughly analyze and discuss the following: What should the total contract price be? Should Owner be required to pay the contract price? What remedies, if any, is it likely that Owner is entitled to?

MBE SUBJECTS – PRACTICE ESSAY QUESTIONS

CONTRACTS LAW
Question 3

Ben, the owner of a private day care center for pre-school children, purchased two air purifiers for use in his day care center from Silent Air, a company that manufactures and distributes air cleaners for use in offices and homes. Before the purchase, Silent Air's salesperson, Stella, met Ben at the day care center and discussed his air purification needs. Ben told Stella that he needed an exceptionally high level of indoor air quality because many of the children at the day care center had asthma and/or severe allergies. Stella assured him that Silent Air's premier model, the SuperCleanser, would clean and purify the air in the day care center to the highest level of purity recognized by the State Environmental Protection Agency (EPA). She also told him that the SuperCleanser ran efficiently and noiselessly.

After meeting with Stella, Ben sent Silent Air a letter in which he ordered "two Silent Air SuperCleansers, designed to purify air to Level 1 quality as specified by the State EPA; price: $600 each, for a total of $1,200." Silent Air's written response provided for "two Silent Air SuperCleansers at a price of $600 each, plus a $50 delivery charge; full amount due upon delivery."

Silent Air delivered two SuperCleansers to Ben's day care center. Ben paid the $1,200 purchase price plus a $50 delivery charge upon receipt of the goods. Along with the goods, Silent Air included an owner's manual, which Ben did not read. The manual contained a section that read: "there are no warranties, express or implied, given by the seller in conjunction with the sale of these goods."

Ben immediately set up the air purifiers in the two rooms of his day care center. They ran only a few days at a time before malfunctioning. Silent Air tried to effect repairs but was unsuccessful in getting the air purifiers to operate properly. In addition, one of the purifiers made an annoying rasping sound that frightened the children. Also, Ben hired an indoor air quality consultant who came to the day care center to measure the air quality on the days that the purifiers were operating. The consultant found that the air quality was never any better than Level 2 under the State EPA standards.

Now three months later, Ben has demanded that Silent Air supply him with two functioning air purifiers that meet his expectations -- providing efficient, reliable, noiseless operation and Level 1 air quality. Silent Air responded that it has done as much as it can for Ben and that it never gave any warranties in conjunction with the transaction.

Ben is very upset about this situation, especially since two families have removed their children from the day care center because of their concerns about the air quality.

Fully analyze and discuss what claims Ben can bring against Silent Air, and what remedies are available to him.

MBE SUBJECTS – PRACTICE ESSAY QUESTIONS

CONTRACTS
Question 4

On May 2, Grandpa Smith wrote to Mary, his unemployed adult granddaughter, and said the following:

> If you will come to Smallville and take care of me and my estate, Tara, for the rest of my life, I will leave Tara to you in my will.
>
> (s) Grandpa

On May 3, Mary moved to Smallville and began to take care of Grandpa and the estate, Tara.

On May 10, Mary met with Tom and offered, in writing, to sell Tara to Tom for $100,000 when she received title to the property. Tom was delighted with this offer since it would allow him to re-acquire Tara which was the home his great grandparents had lived in.

On May 21, upon returning from the local pub with a new friend, Stella, Grandpa told Mary he no longer wanted her to take care of him. When Mary protested, Grandpa ordered Mary, at gunpoint, to leave the property immediately.

On May 22, Grandpa was thrown from his horse, struck his head and died instantly.

On May 23, Tom wrote to Mary accepting her offer to sell Tara for $100,000. The letter, although properly mailed, was never received by Mary.

In his will dated May 22, Grandpa left his entire estate including Tara, to the local historical society.

What, if any, are Mary's rights against Grandpa's estate and the historical society? As part of your answer, discuss whether there is an enforceable contract and why. Also discuss what remedies, if any, might be available. What, if any, are Tom's rights against Mary? Fully discuss your answers.

MBE SUBJECTS – PRACTICE ESSAY QUESTIONS

CONTRACTS
Question 5

Becky, the owner of a retail clothing store, submitted an order to Samz Furniture Store for a desk, desk chair and credenza for use in Becky's place of business. Becky's written order described the items ordered by the manufacturer and model number. She agreed to pay Samz' list price of $700 for the desk, $300 for the chair, and $500 for the credenza. A few days later, Samz sent Becky its own form confirming the order. Samz' form repeated all of the items on Becky's form, but added the clause, "Buyer must make any complaints concerning defects in or non-conformity of the goods delivered within a reasonable period after delivery."

A month later, Samz delivered the specified furniture to Becky's place of business. Becky immediately had her old desk and chair removed and put the new desk and chair into place and began using them. She set aside the credenza and kept it in its original plastic wrapping. A week after delivery, she called Samz and notified the store manager that she wanted to return the credenza. The manager asked her why, and she responded, "I realized that I don't really need it in my office." The manager told her that all sales were final and that she was obligated to pay for all three pieces of furniture. She said that she did not want the credenza and expected Samz to pick it up immediately. The manager said that he would have a truck pick up the credenza the next day, but that he expected her to pay for all three items.

The next day, Samz picked up the credenza. Samz sold the same credenza to Bob a week later for $450 – a slight discount off the list price of $500. Samz had paid $350 to acquire the credenza from the manufacturer and added a coat of wax to the piece at its store for a cost of $25.

Becky has not yet paid for any of the furniture despite repeated demands by Samz.

Fully discuss Samz' litigation options as well as the likelihood of success. If Samz is successful, what will Samz' damages be?

MBE SUBJECTS – PRACTICE ESSAY QUESTIONS

CONTRACTS
Question 6

Jane Addams is a real estate broker who owns a successful brokerage business. In the year preceding the current year, Ms. Addams sold fifteen (15) homes for a total of $3,000,000. Several lawyers have been providing her with legal representation. She fears that she has been paying these lawyers too much.

Addams has contacted Jacob Jones, a local lawyer, and has told him that she has been paying fees between $200 and $300 per hour. She explains to Jones the nature of her business and the type of work she would like him to do. She and Jones have negotiated the following agreement: Addams will give Jones all of her legal work for a three-month period during which he promises to provide her with all of the legal services she needs at a flat fee of $150 per hour.

Jones then prepared a written memorandum of the agreement outlining the terms stated above. Both Jones and Addams signed the memorandum.

During the first month, Addams sent Jones all of her legal work and Jones billed Addams $15,000 for his hours.

In the middle of the second month, Addams sent Jones a particularly difficult mortgage to draft for a customer and told Jones that he had to complete the document within 24 hours. She told him that if he did not have the document ready in that time period she would lose a $500,000 sale.

Upon receiving this request, Jones telephoned Addams and told her that he could only do what she asked in the time period she requested for a higher fee, i.e. $300 per hour. Addams objected vigorously to this. Jones then told her that if she did not agree, he would not do the work.

Addams realized at that point that she had no choice but to agree to Jones' demand for a higher fee since she did not have the time to hire another lawyer. She then agreed.

Jones completed the mortgage as requested. He then sent Addams a bill for this work at the higher hourly rate. Addams refused to pay the bill. In addition, she ceased to send Jones any further work.

Subsequently, Jones learned that Addams had hired another local lawyer to do her work and that this lawyer had billed 100 hours to Addams during the remainder of the three-month period. Jones then telephoned Addams and explained his position and demanded that she pay him both for the mortgage work at $300 per hour and for the additional 100 hours of work she had had the other lawyer complete at a rate of $150 per hour as per their written memorandum.

When Addams finished the telephone call with Jones, she immediately telephoned you and asked whether Jones was correct that she owed him both for the mortgage work at $300 per hour and the other work which he had not done (payable at the memorandum rate of $150 per hour). She also asked whether what Jones had done was permissible under the rules of professional conduct for lawyers and whether it would be a good idea to file a complaint against him.

What would you advise Addams as to her contract rights and liabilities in regard to Jones? How would you answer Addams regarding filing a professional conduct complaint?

MBR SUBJECTS – PRACTICE ESSAY QUESTIONS

CONTRACTS
Question 7

On March 15th Owner sent Buyer the following letter:

> "I offer to sell you Happyacres for $200,000, closing to take place within 10 days of acceptance. In exchange for $10, I agree that this offer will remain open for 30 days from the date hereof."

> Signed: Owner

On March 25[th,] Owner wrote Buyer that the offer of March 15th was withdrawn. Buyer received the March 25th letter on March 26th. On March 27th, Buyer wrote Owner the following letter:

> "Please be advised that I hereby accept your offer of March 15th."

> Signed: Buyer

Owner received this letter on March 28th.

Thereafter, Owner and Buyer had several telephone discussions. On April 10th, Buyer, in a telephone conversation, told Owner that he would pay $250,000 if closing could take place on or before April 13th. Owner reluctantly orally agreed to Buyer's terms.

Owner owed Creditor $100,000 on an old debt which was barred by the statute of limitations. On April 12th, Owner called Creditor and stated that he would pay Creditor $100,000 for the debt if Owner received that amount from the proceeds of the sale of Happyacres. Buyer knew nothing of the arrangement between Owner and Creditor.

On April 12th, when Owner tendered the deed to Happyacres, Buyer refused to pay more than $200,000.

Analyze and discuss whether the original agreement, the oral agreement and the promise to pay Creditor are enforceable.

MBE SUBJECTS – RELEASED ESSAY QUESTIONS

CORPORATIONS
MEE Question- February 2003

Corn Corp was properly incorporated in 1980 with $500,000 of initial capital. Its shares are owned equally by Alan, Bruce, and Kathy, who are also the sole directors and officers. Corn Corp produces and sells corn under the brand name "Super Corn." Until 2000, it was a profitable corporation.

In the late 1990s, Kathy, who has a Ph.D. in genetics and is in charge of product development, was experimenting with genetically engineered corn. She created a new strain of corn that was more resistant to disease than regular corn. Corn Corp patented the new strain of corn. In order to be the first to bring genetically engineered corn to market, Kathy, without the knowledge of Alan and Bruce, negligently omitted several tests that would normally be applied to a new strain of corn, including tests to establish whether it would cause allergic reactions.

Alan, president of Corn Corp, was concerned that some food processors might not want genetically engineered corn. Therefore, on December 31, 1999, Corn Corp properly incorporated Gen-Corn, Inc. (GCI), a wholly owned subsidiary, to produce and sell the new strain of corn. In exchange for all of GCI's stock, Corn Corp contributed to GCI the patent to the new strain of corn and $6,000, just enough to produce the seed for the first crop. Alan, Bruce, and Kathy were the sole directors and officers of GCI.

In 2000, GCI, operating out of the offices of Corn Corp, started marketing the genetically engineered corn under the name "Super Corn Plus." While Kathy scrupulously maintained minute books for Corn Corp, she kept no minute books for GCI. Corn Corp kept meticulous records of all of its business transactions, but GCI did not keep separate records. Although each corporation had its own bank account, Corn Corp often made informal "emergency loans" to GCI to help with cash flow problems. Unfortunately, GCI never became profitable.

Shortly after the first harvest of "Super Corn Plus," Stuart, a young business executive, died from an allergic reaction after eating cornbread made from "Super Corn Plus." GCI immediately pulled "Super Corn Plus" from the market and soon after filed for bankruptcy. Because of the similar product names, Corn Corp's sales of "Super Corn" plummeted, and Corn Corp can no longer pay its bills.

Assuming Stuart's estate obtained a wrongful death judgment against GCI, can it recover the judgment from Corn Corp or any of Corn Corp's shareholders? Explain.

MBE SUBJECTS – RELEASED ESSAY QUESTIONS

CORPORATIONS
MEE Question- July 2003

Corp owns 95% of the outstanding stock of Sub. Pat and Dale own the remaining 5% of Sub stock, and they are also two of the three directors of Sub. Both Corp and Sub are properly incorporated and have only one class of stock outstanding. Corp's board of directors is composed of five directors; none of them is Pat or Dale.

Corp's board of directors voted unanimously, for valid business reasons, to merge Sub into Corp and to adopt a plan for a cash-out merger. Pursuant to the plan of merger, each Sub shareholder would receive $20 per share, which is $4 per share above the current book value. No changes to Corp's articles of incorporation are required as a result of this merger, and Corp shareholders will not experience a change in their shareholder rights. Corp did not submit the plan of merger to its shareholders for a vote.

At a regularly scheduled meeting of Sub's board of directors, Corp announced its intent to merge with Sub. Sub's board voted against the merger by a 2 to 1 vote, with Pat and Dale voting against it. Corp decided to proceed with the merger in spite of the vote against it by Sub's board and subsequently filed articles of merger with the Secretary of State. Shortly thereafter, Pat and Dale each received a check for $20 per share, a copy of the plan of merger, and a notice including all other statutorily required information.

Pat and Dale sued to unwind the merger. They claim the merger was improper because (a) Sub's board of directors did not approve the merger, (b) Corp's shareholders did not vote on the merger, and (c) Sub's shareholders did not vote on the merger.

Further, Pat and Dale claim that, even if the merger stands, they are entitled to receive more than the $20 per share paid by Corp. They claim the true value of their shares is $25 per share. Pat and Dale base this valuation on their knowledge of the financial condition of Sub, which they acquired while serving as directors of Sub, and the advice they received from an independent financial advisor. The independent financial advisor is willing to testify that the value of Sub is between $21 and $26 per share.

1.   **Should the court unwind the merger for any of the reasons asserted by Pat and Dale? Explain.**

2.   **Assuming that the merger is allowed to stand, do Pat and Dale have any legal basis for asserting the right to receive more than the $20 per share offered by Corp? Explain.**

MBE SUBJECTS – RELEASED ESSAY QUESTIONS

CORPORATIONS
MEE Question- February 2004

Zeta, Inc., is a corporation with 80,000 shares outstanding. Its articles of incorporation provide for a nine-person board of directors, with staggered three-year terms. Three directors are elected each year. Zeta's articles require cumulative voting. Therefore, when electing the three directors, each share is entitled to three votes, meaning that there are 240,000 votes eligible to be cast. Accordingly, a person who receives at least 60,001 votes would be elected a director. Neither the articles nor Zeta's bylaws contain any other provisions concerning elections, voting, or removal of directors.

Diane is one of Zeta's directors. Although Diane's term does not expire for another two years, at the request of a group of shareholders, Zeta has scheduled a special shareholders' meeting on September 1 to consider removing Diane from office. Proper notice of that meeting has been given to all of Zeta's shareholders.

Sam owns 16,000 of the 80,000 outstanding Zeta shares. On August 1, Sam gave Arnie a proxy to vote Sam's shares at the special meeting. The proxy signed by Sam stated that it was "irrevocable."

On August 15, Betty, another Zeta shareholder, convinced Sam that giving a proxy to Arnie was a mistake. Sam then signed another proxy, dated August 15, which revoked the proxy to Arnie and gave Betty the right to vote Sam's 16,000 shares.

At the special shareholders' meeting on September 1, the shareholders in favor of Diane's removal argued that Diane was too critical of the company's management at board meetings and was "rocking the boat." No one alleged any breach of duty or other wrongdoing by Diane. Both Arnie and Betty attempted to vote Sam's shares by proxy. Counting Arnie's vote of Sam's shares, the result was 117,000 votes to remove Diane and 123,000 votes not to remove her. Counting Betty's vote of Sam's shares, the result was 165,000 votes to remove Diane and 75,000 votes not to remove her.

Zeta's corporate secretary ruled that Diane was not removed as a director because: (1) no valid cause was shown for removing Diane and showing cause was required to remove her; (2) Arnie was entitled to vote Sam's shares and removal therefore failed by a vote of 117,000 votes to remove Diane and 123,000 votes not to remove her; and (3) even if Betty had the right to vote Sam's shares, the resulting vote of 165,000 votes to remove Diane and 75,000 votes not to remove her was insufficient to remove Diane.

Was each of these three rulings correct? Explain.

MBE SUBJECTS – RELEASED ESSAY QUESTIONS

CORPORATIONS
MEE Question- February 2005

Corp, a corporation validly incorporated in State A, manufactures computer desks and sells them to furniture stores in State A and several nearby states. The board of directors of Corp consists of three members. The board of directors appointed Presley as the president of Corp. The bylaws of Corp provide that "the president, as the chief executive officer of the corporation, shall manage the business of the corporation and perform such other duties as the board of directors may from time to time direct."

Furniture Store (FS) owes Corp $11,000 for computer desks it purchased last year. Presley learned that FS was on the verge of bankruptcy and retained an attorney to file suit against FS to collect payment. The attorney filed suit as directed.

Presley believes that Corp should pay a dividend to its shareholders. Consequently, Presley sent a letter to all shareholders declaring a dividend of 10 cents per share to be paid at the end of the month.

Large Corp (Large), a large national furniture chain, contacted Presley and offered to sell its local manufacturing plant to Corp for what Presley considers a very reasonable price. Further, Large is willing to accept payment of the purchase price over 10 years. Acquiring this plant would triple Corp's manufacturing capacity. Presley signed a purchase agreement for the plant on behalf of Corp without consulting the board.

1.   **Did Presley, as president, have the authority to retain an attorney to file suit against FS on behalf of Corp? Explain.**

2.   **Did Presley, as president, have the authority to declare a dividend payable to Corp's shareholders? Explain.**

3.   **Did Presley, as president, have the authority to enter into a purchase agreement with Large to acquire its local manufacturing plant on behalf of Corp? Explain.**

MBE SUBJECTS – RELEASED ESSAY QUESTIONS

CORPORATIONS
MEE Question- July 2005

Peg, an entrepreneur, decided to develop a widget manufacturing business. Widget production requires the use of a chemical called chromite. Because the market price for chromite has fluctuated between $150 and $200 per ton over the past year, the first thing Peg did was contact numerous chemical companies to find a long-term supplier for chromite.

On May 20, Peg received a quote from Chem Corp. stating that it could supply Peg's corporation with all of its chromite at $145 per ton for the next three years. Chem Corp. indicated that the quote would expire at the end of the week. Peg informed Chem Corp. that her corporation, to be called "Acme, Inc.," would not be formed by that time. Peg further indicated that, "The deal should be between Acme, Inc. and Chem Corp. If Chem Corp. does not care if I sign for a non-existent corporation, you have a deal." Chem Corp. responded: "No problem. We know with whom we are dealing and what the chromite's for. Do not waste our time. If you are serious, lock in the deal."

On May 26, Peg and Chem Corp. signed a three-year requirements contract for Chem Corp. to supply her soon-to-be-formed corporation with all of its chromite at a price of $145 per ton. Peg signed the contract "Peg, as agent for Acme, Inc., a corporation to be formed." The requirements contract was valid under state law. It contained a valid and substantial liquidated damages clause in the event Acme purchased chromite from any other supplier.

On August 1, Peg formed Acme, Inc. Peg was a shareholder, but not an officer or a director. Neither the board of directors nor the officers of Acme, Inc. formally reviewed or approved the contract with Chem Corp.

On August 15, Chem Corp. made its first delivery of chromite to Acme, Inc. at the contract price of $145 per ton. Vic, an Acme employee, acting pursuant to the direction of Acme's board of directors, accepted delivery and approved payment of the invoice after checking the contract and determining that the invoice agreed with the contract price. Acme, Inc. immediately began widget production.

In September and October, Chem Corp. made deliveries of chromite to Acme and charged Acme according to the contract. Acme promptly paid each invoice. During the fall, the market price for chromite fell. By November, the market price for chromite was $100 per ton. The Acme board of directors, seeking a cheaper supply of chromite, entered into an agreement with Supply, Inc. to provide Acme with its monthly requirements of chromite at $95 per ton.

Acme immediately contacted Chem Corp. and instructed it not to ship Acme any more chromite. When Chem Corp. demanded payment under the liquidated damages clause, Acme refused.

1.   **Is Peg personally liable to Chem Corp. under the contract? Explain.**

2.   **Is Acme, Inc. liable to Chem Corp. under the contract? Explain.**

MBE SUBJECTS – RELEASED ESSAY QUESTIONS

CORPORATIONS
MEE Question- February 2006

Green Corporation (Green) was properly incorporated in State A. Green's articles of incorporation authorize 100 shares of common stock (Common) and 300 shares of Class A non-voting cumulative preferred stock (Class A Preferred). Each Class A Preferred share is entitled to a quarterly dividend of $1. Green's articles provide that, if Green fails to pay this dividend for four consecutive quarters, each Class A Preferred share becomes entitled to one vote on all matters voted on at shareholders' meetings until all arrearages have been paid.

Deb owns all 100 shares of the Common and 100 shares of the Class A Preferred. Ed owns the remaining 200 shares of the Class A Preferred. Neither Deb nor Ed is a director or officer of Green.

Green has been experiencing financial difficulties for some time and has not paid the Class A Preferred dividends for more than four consecutive quarters. On September 2, Green's board unanimously adopted a proposal to dissolve the corporation. The board then called a special meeting of the shareholders to vote on this proposal. The notice of the special meeting indicated that a special meeting would be held at the corporation's principal office on October 15. The notice did not state the purpose of the meeting. The notice was sent to Deb. She received it on September 10.

On October 13, two days before the special meeting, Deb and Ed met for dinner. At dinner, Deb asked Ed to serve as her proxy at the special meeting because she could not attend. Ed was surprised because he had not received any notice of the special meeting from Green. Nonetheless, Ed told Deb that he would attend the meeting and vote her shares.

On October 15, at breakfast before the meeting began, Ed first learned of the proposed dissolution of Green. Ed immediately called Deb to inform her of the proposal. Deb directed Ed to vote all of her shares in favor of the proposal. Ed went to the meeting, voted Deb's shares in favor and his own shares against the proposal to dissolve Green.

1. **Was the special shareholder meeting called to dissolve Green properly held? Explain.**

2. **Was the proposal to dissolve Green properly adopted by its shareholders? Explain.**

MBE SUBJECTS – RELEASED ESSAY QUESTIONS

CORPORATIONS
MEE Question- July 2006

Until early this year, Parensco, Inc. (Parensco) owned 75% of the outstanding shares of Subco Corp. (Subco). The remaining 25% of the outstanding shares of Subco were held by numerous other shareholders. The president of Parensco is Carr, who is also a director of Parensco.

Several months ago, the president of Aster, Inc. (Aster) approached Carr, expressed an interest in acquiring control of Subco, and stated that Aster would consider a purchase price in the range of $200 per Subco share. After Carr's conversation with Aster, the board of directors of Parensco decided to merge Subco into Parensco. The purchase price for the 25% of the outstanding shares of Subco not owned by Parensco was set at $120 per share.

After its board duly authorized this transaction, Parensco issued the following press release:

> The board of Parensco announced today that it seeks to acquire the 25% of Subco that it does not own. Subject to the approval of the Subco board, Parensco will pay $120 for each share of Subco in a cash-out merger, for a total cost to Parensco of $200 million.

Shortly after this press release was issued, the board of directors of Subco (Subco board), consisting solely of officers and directors of Parensco, but not including Carr, met to consider the merger offer.

At the meeting, the Subco board heard a brief presentation from Carr and reviewed a report from Banker, an investment banker. Banker's report advised that, after undertaking a review of Subco, a fair valuation of Subco was $800 million and the price of $120 per share was generous for a minority interest in the corporation. Neither the Subco board nor Banker was aware of the discussion between Carr and Aster. After hearing Carr's presentation and reviewing Banker's report, the Subco board voted to approve the merger after a brief discussion and without any further investigation.

Parensco and Subco then issued a proxy statement to the Subco shareholders, which was complete and accurate except for its failure to mention the Aster proposal.

The merger was approved by a vote of 90% of the outstanding Subco shares, consisting of the 75% of the outstanding shares held by Parensco and 15% of the outstanding shares held by minority shareholders. The merger was then consummated and Parensco sent checks to the Subco shareholders in payment for their stock. A few months later, Parensco announced the sale for $3 billion of the division of its business consisting almost exclusively of assets acquired in the Subco merger.

1. **Did Parensco breach any of its fiduciary duties by failing to disclose the Aster proposal to the minority shareholders of Subco? Explain.**

2.   Did the Subco board breach its duty of care in approving the merger? Explain.

3.   Did Parensco breach any duty to the minority shareholders of Subco by offering them only $120 per share? Explain.

MBE SUBJECTS – RELEASED ESSAY QUESTIONS

CORPORATIONS
MEE Question- July 2007

Last July Art, Brett, and Chad formed LeaseAll, Limited Liability Company (LLC), to lease personal property to individuals and businesses. Art, Brett, and Chad had equal ownership interests in LLC and entered into a written operating agreement (OA). Under the OA, only Art had authority to manage the business, to hire and fire employees, and to buy and sell real and personal property. Art contributed a business plan and his expertise to the leasing business, and Brett and Chad each contributed $50,000 to the capital of LLC.

Over the next year, Brett and Chad did not participate in the business. No meetings were held, and Art did not provide Brett or Chad with any information about LLC. In accordance with the business plan, Art purchased, in the name of LLC, a building and inventory for the leasing business.

Things have not gone well for LLC. Its initial capital is exhausted, and the cash generated by operations is inadequate to allow it to pay its debts as they come due. Additionally, one of LLC's customers, Peter, was badly injured when a chainsaw he rented from LLC malfunctioned. Peter sued LLC and obtained a judgment of $500,000. LLC does not have liability insurance because Art forgot to sign the check when he sent the premium payment to the insurance company and, as a result, the company did not issue the policy. LLC cannot pay Peter's judgment from its current capital.

1.   If Brett and Chad bring an action against Art to recover damages claiming that Art mismanaged LLC, should that action be direct or derivative and what corporate law requirements must they meet before bringing an action? Explain.

2.   Did Art breach his fiduciary duty in managing LLC? Explain.

3.   Can Peter recover the $500,000 judgment against LLC from Art, Brett, and/or Chad personally? Explain.

MBE SUBJECTS – RELEASED ESSAY QUESTIONS

CORPORATIONS
MEE Question- February 2008

Cal is the CEO and chairman of the 12-member board of directors of Prime, Inc. (Prime). Three other members of Prime's board of directors (the Board) are also senior officers of Prime. The remaining eight members of the Board are wholly independent directors.

Recently, the Board decided to hire a consulting firm to help Prime market a new product. The Board met to consider whether to hire Wiseman Consulting (Wiseman) or Smart Group (Smart). The Board first heard from a representative of Wiseman. The Wiseman representative described some of the projects Wiseman had completed for other clients and outlined the work it proposed to do for Prime for $500,000. The Board then heard from a representative of Smart, another consulting firm. The Smart representative described a similar work plan and stated that Smart's proposed fee was $650,000. Either of these amounts would be a significant outlay for Prime.

After the Board heard both presentations, Cal disclosed to the Board that he had a 25% partnership interest in Smart. Cal stated that he would not be involved in any work to be performed by Smart for Prime. He knew but did not disclose to the Board that Smart's proposed fee for this consulting assignment was substantially higher than it normally charged for comparable work. The Board did not ask about the basis for Smart's proposed fee.

After receiving all of this information, and no other information, the Board discussed the relative merits of the two proposals for 10 minutes. The Board then voted unanimously (Cal abstaining) to hire Smart, even though hiring Smart would cost Prime approximately 30% more than hiring Wiseman. Cal was present throughout the meeting but did not participate except to the extent indicated above.

1.   **Did Cal violate his duty of loyalty to Prime? Explain.**

2.   **Assuming Cal breached his duty of loyalty to Prime, does he have any defense to liability? Explain.**

3.   **Did the directors of Prime, other than Cal, violate their duty of care? Explain.**

MBE SUBJECTS – RELEASED ESSAY QUESTIONS

CORPORATIONS
MEE Question- February 2009

Corporation has 20 shareholders. Its largest shareholder, Major, owns just over 30 percent (30%) of Corporation's shares. No other shareholder owns more than five percent (5%) of the shares.

Major is also the president and one of the five directors of Corporation. The other four directors are also shareholders of Corporation.

Over the past two years Major, acting in his capacity as president of Corporation, has persuaded Corporation's board of directors (Board) to approve the purchase of a number of valuable items of Major's personal property appropriate for Corporation's business. Corporation paid vastly inflated prices for Major's property.

Major always informed Board of each proposed purchase before it was made. In each case, Minor, another member of Board, asked Major whether the purchase price was "fair." Major always replied: "I have investigated the value of my property to be purchased by Corporation and I assure you that the purchase price represents its fair market value." Board, relying on this statement and undertaking no further inquiry, always approved the purchases, with Major abstaining from voting.

Corporation's articles of incorporation contain a provision that exculpates the directors of the corporation for liability to the corporation for money damages "to the fullest extent permitted" by the applicable corporation-law statute.

A shareholder derivative suit has been properly brought against Corporation's directors seeking money damages for breach of their fiduciary duties as directors with regard to the transactions between Corporation and Major.

1. **Will the directors (other than Major) be protected from liability by the business judgment rule? Explain.**

2. **Will Major be protected from liability by the business judgment rule? Explain.**

3. **Will Major be protected from liability by Board's approval of the transactions? Explain.**

4. **Will the directors (other than Major) be protected from liability by the exculpatory provision in the articles of incorporation? Explain.**

5. **Will Major be protected from liability by the exculpatory provision in the articles of incorporation? Explain.**

MBE SUBJECTS – RELEASED ESSAY QUESTIONS

CORPORATIONS
MEE Question- February 2010

Smith owns 10% of the common shares of Omega, Inc., a closely held corporation. Baker and Jones each own 45% of Omega's common shares. Baker and Jones also serve on Omega's board of directors and are paid corporate officers.

Omega has not paid a dividend on its common shares for several years. Smith, who is not an officer of the corporation and has never received a salary from the corporation, is very unhappy that no dividends are being paid.

When Smith complained to Baker and Jones about nonpayment of dividends, they said that while Omega could legally pay dividends, it has not done so in order to retain the corporation's earnings for expansion of the business. They also pointed to data showing that Omega's business has expanded considerably in the past several years, financed entirely through undistributed earnings, and told Smith that he should "go away and let us run the show." Smith complained that "only you are enjoying the fruits of Omega's success." In response to an inquiry from Smith, Baker and Jones refused to reveal the amounts of their salaries, even though those salaries are within industry range.

Baker and Jones each offered to purchase all of Smith's shares for $35 per share. Smith suspects that the shares are worth more than $35 per share. Smith has asked to inspect Omega's corporate books and records in order to determine the value of his shares, but Jones and Baker have refused to give Smith access to any corporate records.

Smith has asked your law firm the following questions:

1. **Does Smith have a right to inspect Omega's corporate books and records to determine whether $35 per share is a fair price for his shares? Explain.**

2. **If Smith brings a suit to compel the payment of a dividend, must Smith first make a demand on the corporation? Explain.**

3. **If Smith brings a suit to compel the payment of a dividend, is that suit likely to be successful? Explain.**

MBE SUBJECTS – RELEASED ESSAY QUESTIONS

CORPORATIONS
MEE Question- July 2010

On December 30, X Corporation's legal record date, X Corporation had 100 shares of issued and outstanding common stock. Fifty shares were owned by Amy, 25 shares were owned by Brian, and 25 shares were owned by Carter. X Corporation also had 50 shares of stock that it previously had issued to, but later repurchased from, Amy.

On January 30, X Corporation's annual shareholders' meeting was validly held. Before the meeting, X Corporation's staff prepared a list of shareholders entitled to vote at the meeting and mailed proper notice to them. That notice stated that a proposal requiring shareholder approval would be voted on at the annual shareholders' meeting.

Before the annual shareholders' meeting and in a timely manner, Amy mailed in her duly executed proxy, directing the secretary of X Corporation to vote her 50 shares in favor of the proposal. However, before the annual shareholders' meeting date, Zach called the secretary of X Corporation and truthfully told the secretary that Amy's shares belonged to Zach because he had bought the shares from Amy on December 31. Zach then mailed the secretary a duly executed proxy directing the secretary of X Corporation to vote his 50 shares against the proposal.

Prior to the annual shareholders' meeting, Brian duly executed a proxy in favor of Dell. The proxy stated in its entirety, "I, Brian, hereby grant Dell full authority to vote my 25 shares of X Corporation at the January 30th annual shareholders' meeting." Dell timely mailed a duly executed proxy directing the secretary of X Corporation to vote Brian's 25 shares against the proposal. Dell also sent the secretary a copy of the proxy given to Dell by Brian. Brian, however, attended the annual meeting and voted his 25 shares in favor of the proposal.

Carter personally appeared at the annual shareholders' meeting and voted his 25 shares against the proposal.

X Corporation's president attended the annual meeting and, on behalf of X Corporation, voted the 50 shares that X Corporation had repurchased from Amy against the proposal.

X Corporation's Articles of Incorporation require an affirmative vote by the holders of two-thirds of the shares entitled to be voted to approve any proposal at a shareholders' meeting. The bylaws, on the other hand, require a unanimous vote of such shares to approve any proposal.

Your law firm represents X Corporation. You have been asked to advise the firm's senior partner on whether the proposal received sufficient votes to be approved. Explain your conclusion.

MBE SUBJECTS – RELEASED ESSAY QUESTIONS

CORPORATIONS
MEE Question- February 2011

On September 1, Adam, Baker, and Clark formed a shoe manufacturing business called Delta Incorporated (Delta). Each was to be a shareholder. Adam was named president of Delta.

Adam agreed to prepare and file articles of incorporation and bylaws for Delta, in accordance with the state's corporation statute, which is identical to the Model Business Corporation Act (1984, with 2000 amendments). Adam, Baker, and Clark agreed to include a provision in Delta's articles of incorporation stating that the corporation's existence would begin on September 1.

On October 1, Adam, acting on behalf of Delta, entered into a contract with Mega Stores Corporation (Mega) pursuant to which Mega was to purchase shoes from Delta for $3,000. Following delivery of the shoes and after Mega had paid in full, Mega discovered that the shoes did not conform to the contract specifications and returned the shoes to Delta. It is undisputed that Delta owes Mega the $3,000 purchase price.

On October 15, Baker learned that Delta's articles of incorporation had not been filed.

On November 1, Adam, acting on behalf of Delta, entered into a contract with Sole Source, Inc. (Sole), a supplier of shoe soles, pursuant to which Delta purchased shoe soles from Sole for $100,000. The soles were delivered to Delta, and it is uncontested that Delta owes Sole the $100,000 purchase price. Adam learned of the opportunity to contract with Sole from Baker, who had worked with Sole in the past. Baker helped Adam negotiate the contract with Sole.

On November 15, Adam filed Delta's articles of incorporation with the appropriate state official.

When Delta did not pay either Mega or Sole the amounts it owed them, each company sued Delta, Adam, Baker, and Clark for the amounts owed.

At all times, Clark believed that Delta's articles of incorporation had been filed.

1.   **When did Delta's corporate existence begin? Explain.**

2.   **Is Adam, Baker, or Clark personally liable on the Mega contract? Explain as to each.**

3.   **Is Adam, Baker, or Clark personally liable on the Sole contract? Explain as to each.**

MBE SUBJECTS – RELEASED ESSAY QUESTIONS

CORPORATIONS
MEE Question- February 2012

A corporation's articles of incorporation state that the corporation shall have a seven-member board of directors. Neither the articles of incorporation nor the corporation's bylaws contain any special provisions regarding the board of directors.

On March 1, the corporation's president told its secretary to convene a special meeting of the board of directors. Accordingly, the secretary prepared a Notice of Special Meeting (Notice) and sent it by overnight mail to six of the seven directors. The secretary did not send the Notice to the seventh director — Claire — because Claire had recently moved and the corporation did not have a current mailing address for her.

The Notice stated only that a special meeting of the corporation's board of directors would be held on March 31 at 10 a.m., at the corporate headquarters.

On March 2, each member of the board of directors except Claire received the Notice. Directors Alan and Barb, both of whom had vacation plans for March 31, made arrangements with the secretary to participate in the special meeting by telephone.

On March 30, Alan called Claire and informed her that a special meeting of the board of directors was going to be held on March 31.

On March 31, five members of the board of directors (including Claire but neither Alan nor Barb) gathered in the corporation's conference room. Alan and Barb called in from their vacation homes. The five directors present in the conference room could hear both Alan and Barb. Alan and Barb could each hear the five directors in the conference room but could not hear each other.

After a lengthy discussion, the board of directors voted 4–3 to approve the corporation's purchase of a major asset. Alan and Barb both voted to approve the purchase.

Claire, who voted against the purchase, is very upset and has brought an action seeking an injunction to prevent the purchase of the asset. Claire asserts that the board of directors did not properly approve the purchase of the asset.

Did the board of directors properly approve the purchase of the asset? Explain.

MBE SUBJECTS – RELEASED ESSAY QUESTIONS

CORPORATIONS
MEE Question - July 2012

Acme Inc. manufactures building materials, including concrete, for sale to construction companies. To create a market for its building materials, Acme enters into agreements with construction companies under which Acme and the construction company agree to form a member-managed limited liability company (LLC). The LLC builds the project, purchasing building materials from Acme and contracting for construction services with the construction company.

The operating agreements for these LLCs always provide that Acme has a 55% voting interest, that Acme and the construction company contribute equally to the capital of the venture, and that the parties share in profits at a negotiated rate. The agreements are silent as to the allocation of losses.

Acme entered into such a relationship with Brown Construction Co. LLC (Brown), forming Acme-Brown LLC (A-B LLC) to build 50 homes. The operating agreement for A-B LLC gives Acme a 55% voting interest and provides for a 20%/80% division of profits in favor of Brown.

A-B LLC built all 50 homes and sold them to homeowners. The members received a distribution of profits from the sales, split between them according to their agreement on the division of profits. However, all the concrete manufactured by Acme and sold to A-B LLC for the foundations of the homes proved to be defective. After a year, the concrete dissolved, collapsing the homes and rendering them worthless. In a class action by the homeowners against A-B LLC, the plaintiffs were awarded a $15 million judgment. The LLC has no assets with which to pay the judgment.

Although Acme would be liable to A-B LLC for the loss caused by the defective concrete, A-B LLC has not brought a claim against Acme. Acme has the financial resources to pay damages equal to the amount of the $15 million judgment in the homeowners' lawsuit and to fully cover A-B LLC's liability.

Brown has sent a letter to A-B LLC demanding that A-B LLC bring a claim against Acme to recover those damages and pay the judgment to the plaintiffs, after which A-B LLC would be dissolved. But Acme, as the manager of A-B LLC, has refused to do so.

Acme's lawyer has sent a letter to Brown stating the following:

> (1) Acme has no fiduciary obligations to either A-B LLC or Brown that require it to have A-B LLC bring the concrete claim against Acme.

> (2) Brown cannot bring a claim against Acme.

> (3) Brown does not have sufficient grounds to seek the judicial dissolution of A-B LLC.

(4) Because the A-B LLC agreement provides for a 20%/80% division of profits, the losses arising from the judgment obtained by the plaintiffs against the LLC should also be allocated 20% to Acme and 80% to Brown.

Is Acme's lawyer correct? Explain.

MBE SUBJECTS – RELEASED ESSAY QUESTIONS

CORPORATIONS
MEE Question - July 2013

On February 2, Alice, Bob, and Carla formed ABC Hospitality, LLC (ABC), a member-managed limited liability company, for the purpose of building, owning, and running a 100-room luxury hotel in their hometown. ABC soon began to experience unexpected financial problems, prompting Bob to look for other investment opportunities. On March 10, Bob told Alice and Carla that, although he would remain as a member of ABC, he would no longer contribute any capital to ABC, and he was also becoming a co-owner of the Metro Inn, an existing 200-room hotel in the same town near the ABC hotel project. Alice and Carla objected to Bob's plan, fearing that he might put the interests of the Metro Inn ahead of his existing obligations to ABC. In response, Bob cited § 5.1 of ABC's Operating Agreement, which states as follows:

> Members of ABC shall not in any way be prohibited from or restricted in managing, owning, or otherwise having an interest in any other business venture that may be competitive with the business of ABC.

Shortly after Bob became a co-owner of the Metro Inn, ABC's financial situation worsened. Alice and Carla worried that ABC would not be able to pay a bill it owed to its concrete supplier. Alice proposed to pay the concrete supplier's bill from her own personal funds and then obtain reimbursement from ABC once the hotel project was completed. Alice wanted to do this so that she could file a personal financial statement which underreported her assets and so enable her son to qualify for student financial aid. Carla agreed to this proposal. Alice and Carla also agreed to alter ABC's financial records so that it would appear as if ABC had paid the concrete supplier's bill out of its own accounts, without showing the obligation to reimburse Alice for that amount.

In the weeks following Alice's payment to the concrete supplier, several other of ABC's bills became due. Alice tried to pay as many of these bills as she could using her personal funds, but despite her best efforts, it soon became clear that ABC was rapidly approaching insolvency. On August 15, the hotel's designer left a message for Carla seeking payment of an overdue bill. Alice and Carla were concerned about the solvency of the company. Without responding to the designer, Alice and Carla, acting with Bob's consent, sold all of ABC's property and remaining assets. Alice and Carla each kept one-third of the sale proceeds and gave the remaining one-third to Bob. They did not file articles of dissolution with the state. When the designer later called Carla again about the bill, she responded that ABC had been "dissolved" and that no payment would be forthcoming.

1. **Did Alice and Carla have any legal basis to object to Bob's co-ownership of the Metro Inn? Explain.**

2. **Under what theory or theories could Alice, Bob, or Carla be personally liable to the designer? Explain.**

MBE SUBJECTS – RELEASED ESSAY QUESTIONS

CORPORATIONS
MEE Question - July 2014

Mega Inc. is a publicly traded corporation incorporated in a state whose corporate statute is modeled on the Model Business Corporation Act (MBCA). Mega's articles of incorporation do not address the election of directors or amendment of the bylaws by shareholders.

Well within the deadline for the submission of shareholder proposals for the upcoming annual shareholders' meeting, an investor, who was a large and long-standing shareholder of Mega, submitted a proposed amendment to Mega's bylaws. The proposal, which the investor asked to be included in the corporation's proxy materials and voted on at the upcoming shareholders' meeting, read as follows:

> Section 20: The Corporation shall include in its proxy materials (including the proxy ballot) for a shareholders' meeting at which directors are to be elected the name of a person nominated for election to the Board of Directors by a shareholder or group of shareholders that beneficially have owned 3% or more of the Corporation's outstanding common stock for at least one year.

> This Section shall supersede any inconsistent provision in these Bylaws and may not be amended or repealed by the Board of Directors without shareholder approval.

Mega's management decided to exclude the investor's proposal from the corporation's proxy materials and explained its reasons in a letter to the investor:

> The investor's proposed bylaw provision would be inconsistent with relevant state law because the Board of Directors has the authority to manage the business and affairs of the Corporation. Generally, shareholders lack the authority to interfere with corporate management by seeking to create a method for the nomination and election of directors inconsistent with the method chosen by the Board of Directors.

> Furthermore, at its most recent meeting, the Board of Directors unanimously approved an amendment to the Corporation's bylaws that provides for proxy access for director nominations by a shareholder or a group of shareholders holding at least 10% of the Corporation's voting shares for at least three years. This procedure takes precedence over any nomination methods that might be sought or approved by shareholders.

The investor is considering bringing a suit challenging management's refusal to include the investor's proposed bylaw provision and challenging the board's amendment of the bylaws at its recent meeting.

1.   **Is the investor's proposed bylaw provision inconsistent with state law? Explain.**

2.   If the investor's proposed bylaw provision were approved by the shareholders, would the bylaw amendment previously approved by the board take precedence over the investor's proposed bylaw provision? Explain.

3.   Must the investor make a demand on Mega's board of directors before bringing suit? Explain.

MBE SUBJECTS – RELEASED ESSAY QUESTIONS

CORPORATIONS
MEE Question - July 2015

The board of directors of a commercial real estate development corporation consists of the corporation's chief executive officer (CEO) and three other directors, who are executives at various other firms.

The corporation owns a commercial office tower, the value of which is approximately 10 percent of the corporation's total holdings. The corporation uses one floor of the tower as its corporate headquarters, but it wants to vacate that floor as soon as it locates suitable replacement space.

Two years ago, the board obtained an independent appraisal of the tower, which indicated a fair market value of between $12 and $15 million. After considering that appraisal, the board authorized the corporation's CEO to seek a purchaser for the tower.

The CEO immediately showed the tower to several sophisticated real estate investors and received offers ranging from $8 million to $13 million. The CEO decided that these offers were insufficient, and after he reported back to the board, no further action to sell the tower was taken.

Two months ago, the CEO and the other three directors of the corporation formed a limited liability company (LLC) in which each holds a 25 percent ownership interest.

One month ago, the corporation's board unanimously authorized the corporation's sale of the tower to LLC for $12 million. The minutes of the board's meeting at which the tower sale was authorized reflect that the meeting lasted for 10 minutes and that the only document reviewed by the corporation's directors was the two-year-old appraisal of the tower.

The minutes of the board's meeting further state that the transaction was to be carried out with "a friendly company so that the corporation will have time to relocate to a new headquarters" and that the board "authorized the transaction because the $12 million price is toward the high end of the range of offers received in the past from sophisticated real estate investors and is within the range of fair market values listed in the appraisal."

After the board's authorization of the tower sale, the corporation entered into a contract to sell the tower to LLC. The board did not seek shareholder approval of the transaction.

A non-director shareholder of the corporation is upset with the board's decision authorizing the sale of the tower to LLC. The shareholder believes that the corporation could have obtained a higher price for the tower.

1.   Does the business judgment rule apply to the board's decision to have the corporation sell the tower to LLC? Explain.

2.   Did the directors breach their fiduciary duties by authorizing the tower sale? Explain.

MBE SUBJECTS – RELEASED ESSAY QUESTIONS

CORPORATIONS
MEE Question - July 2016

Two siblings, a brother and a sister, decided to start a bike shop with their cousin. They filed a certificate of organization to form a limited liability company. The brother and the sister paid for their LLC member interests by each contributing $100,000 in cash to the LLC. Their cousin paid for his LLC member interest by conveying to the LLC five acres of farmland valued at $100,000; the LLC then recorded the deed.

Neither the certificate of organization nor the members' operating agreement specifies whether the LLC is member-managed or manager-managed. However, the operating agreement provides that the LLC's farmland may not be sold without the approval of all three members.

Following formation of the LLC, the company rented a storefront commercial space for the bike shop and opened for business.

Three months ago, purporting to act on behalf of the LLC, the brother entered into a written and signed contract to purchase 100 bike tires for $6,000 from a tire manufacturer. When the tires were delivered, the sister said that they were too expensive and told her brother to return the tires. The brother was surprised by his sister's objection because twice before he had purchased tires for the LLC at the same price from this manufacturer, and neither his sister nor their cousin had objected. The brother refused to return the tires, pointing out that the tires "are perfect for the bikes we sell." The sister responded, "Well, pay the bill with your own money; you bought them without my permission." The brother responded, "No way. I bought these for the store, I didn't need your permission, and the company will pay for them." To date, however, the $6,000 has not been paid.

One month ago, purporting to act on behalf of the LLC, the cousin sold the LLC's farmland to a third-party buyer. The buyer paid $120,000, which was well above the land's fair market value. Only after the cousin deposited the sale proceeds into the LLC bank account did the brother and sister learn of the sale. Both of them objected.

One week ago, the brother wrote in an email to his sister, "I want out of our business. I don't want to have anything to do with the bike shop anymore. Please send me a check for my share." What type of LLC was created—member-managed or manager-managed? Explain.

1.   **Is the LLC bound under the tire contract? Explain.**

2.   **Is the LLC bound by the sale of the farmland? Explain.**

3.   **What is the legal effect of the brother's email? Explain.**

MBE SUBJECTS – RELEASED ESSAY QUESTIONS

CRIMINAL LAW AND PROCEDURE
MEE Question - February 2008

On April 10, a convenience store was robbed by someone carrying a gun. The store's video camera caught the robbery on tape. The tape was shown on the evening news.

On April 11, an anonymous caller contacted the police saying, "I saw that tape of the robbery. The robber kind of looks like Student. He's an 18-year-old student at the high school."

On April 12, two police officers took the tape to the high school and showed it to the principal, who said, "It could be Student. It's hard to tell because the tape is not clear." The tape was also shown to Student's homeroom teacher, who said, "It might be him, but I couldn't say for sure."

Later that day, the police officers went to the store where Student works after school. They asked the manager if they could talk with Student, who was called to the manager's office. The police introduced themselves to Student and said, "We'd like to talk to you." They walked with Student into the manager's office and shut the door. One police officer sat behind the manager's desk; the other, in full uniform with his revolver visible, sat near the door. Student sat between them. The manager's office measures eight feet by ten feet.

The police officers told Student they wanted to ask him some questions about the convenience store robbery on April 10. Student said he knew nothing about a robbery. He continued to deny that he had any knowledge of the robbery for about 20 minutes. Student did not ask to leave, and neither police officer told Student he was free to leave.

After about 20 minutes, the police officers told Student that they had a videotape of the robbery and that they had shown it to three people, all of whom positively identified Student as the robber.

Student said nothing for a few minutes. One of the police officers then said, "You know, if we can tell the prosecutor that you cooperated, she might go a lot easier on you. I'd hate to see you end up doing a long stretch in prison. Let's just say it's not a nice place." Student then blurted out, "I did the robbery. I used a little air gun."

Immediately after Student made that statement, the police officers informed Student that he was under arrest for the robbery of the convenience store. They read him his *Miranda* rights. Student stated he understood his *Miranda* rights and told the police officers that he was not going to say anything more to them. The police officers placed Student in handcuffs and took him to the police station where he was booked for armed robbery.

Student had had two earlier brushes with the law. When he was 16, he had been found delinquent in juvenile court for auto theft and had been placed on supervision for one year. When he was 17, he had received a ticket for underage drinking and had paid a fine of $150. He is a "C" student, but his teachers believe he is an "underachiever."

Student's defense attorney has filed a motion to suppress Student's statements on three grounds:

(1)   Student's statements were obtained in violation of Student's Fourth Amendment rights.

(2)   Student's statements were obtained in violation of his *Miranda* rights.

(3)   Student's confession was not voluntary.

How should the trial court rule on each of the grounds in the motion to suppress? Explain.

MBE SUBJECTS – RELEASED ESSAY QUESTIONS

CRIMINAL LAW AND PROCEDURE
MEE Question - July 2009

John, age 18, and Crystal, age 14, walked into the Minit Mart, a convenience store. They wandered around the store for a few minutes and then walked up to the counter. John had his hand in a leather bag. He stared at the store clerk for about 10 seconds and started to sweat. At this point, Crystal began to cry. She said, "I don't want to do this," and ran out of the store. John remained for a few more seconds and then ran out of the store himself. The store clerk immediately called 911 and nervously said, "Two kids were about to rob me, but I guess they changed their minds."

Three days later, the police came to Crystal's home, where she lives with her parents. The police told Crystal's mother that Crystal was a suspect in an attempted robbery and that they wanted to search for evidence. Crystal's mother asked the police if they had a warrant. They said, "No, but we can get one." Crystal's mother let the police in.

When the police searched Crystal's room, they found John's zipped leather bag in Crystal's closet. Without first obtaining a search warrant, or asking Crystal's mother who owned the bag, the police opened the bag and found a gun and printouts of e-mails from John to a friend. The police read the e-mails, which described John's plans to rob the Minit Mart with the help of his girlfriend, Crystal.

Crystal later confessed that she and John had planned to rob the Minit Mart, but that she got scared and ran out of the store. She also said that John gave her the leather bag with the gun after they had left the Minit Mart and told her to "get rid of it."

John was charged with attempted armed robbery of the Minit Mart store. His lawyer filed a motion to suppress the leather bag and its contents on the grounds that the bag was seized and searched in violation of John's Fourth Amendment rights. The trial court denied the motion, and the issue was properly preserved for appeal.

At John's trial for attempted armed robbery, the Minit Mart clerk testified to the facts that he had told the police earlier. Crystal also testified for the prosecution, repeating what she had previously told the police. She also said that the leather bag belonged to John, that she and John had planned the robbery together, that she saw John load the gun and put it in his leather bag before they entered the Minit Mart, and that John's hand was in the leather bag with the gun for the entire time that they were in the Minit Mart. She testified that she "got scared" when she and John were standing at the counter, which is why she ran from the store. She said that when John got into the car after running out of the store, he said, "Well, that went bad," and then drove away from the store.

After Crystal's testimony, the prosecution introduced the leather bag, the e-mails, and the gun into evidence. The court admitted all of the evidence over the objection of John's lawyer.

John presented no evidence.

At the close of the case, the trial court denied both John's motion for judgment of acquittal and his request for a jury instruction on the defense of abandonment.

The jury convicted John of attempted armed robbery. Did the trial court err:

1.   **In denying John's motion to suppress the leather bag and its contents? Explain.**

2.   **In denying John's motion for judgment of acquittal? Explain.**

3.   **In failing to instruct the jury on the defense of abandonment? Explain.**

MBE SUBJECTS – RELEASED ESSAY QUESTIONS

CRIMINAL LAW AND PROCEDURE
MEE Question - July 2010

Customer went to Star Computers (Star) to buy a refurbished computer. Upon arrival, Customer was approached by Owner, who identified himself as the owner of Star. Owner directed Customer to a refurbished desktop computer and told Customer, "We have the best refurbished computers in town. We send used computers to a computer technician who always installs new hard drives and replaces any defective parts." Owner made these claims because Owner believed that they would be effective in persuading Customer to buy a refurbished computer. In fact, Customer was persuaded by Owner's claims and purchased a computer for $250 cash.

At the time of this transaction, Owner did not believe that Star had the best refurbished computers in town. Owner was aware of at least two other computer stores in town and believed that the refurbished computers sold by these other stores were better than those sold by Star. Owner also thought it was very likely that the computer technician used by Star did not actually install new hard drives in the refurbished computers. Owner had never raised the issue with the technician because the technician offered much faster service and lower rates than those of any other technician in the area.

After Customer's purchase, a local news station conducted an investigation into the computer technician used by Star and reported that the technician did not install new hard drives in any of the computers she refurbished. After the report aired, the computer technician acknowledged that no new hard drives had been installed in the computers she had refurbished for Star.

Owner has been charged with larceny by false pretenses in connection with the computer sale to Customer.

Is Owner guilty of larceny by false pretenses? Explain.

MBE SUBJECTS – RELEASED ESSAY QUESTIONS

CRIMINAL LAW AND PROCEDURE
MEE Question - July 2011

A police officer (Officer) on routine traffic patrol watched Suspect drive by. Suspect was in compliance with all applicable traffic laws except the state seat belt law. The state motor vehicle code provides that police officers have discretion to make an arrest for any traffic infraction, including violation of the state seat belt law. Officer had never stopped a driver merely for violating the seat belt law. However, Officer knew that Suspect was a reputed drug dealer and stopped Suspect's vehicle, hoping to uncover evidence of a more serious crime.

Officer directed Suspect to get out of his vehicle, handcuffed Suspect, and told Suspect that he was under arrest for violating the seat belt law. Immediately afterward, Officer looked through the driver's-side car window and noticed a clear plastic bag containing white powder on the front seat of Suspect's car. Officer asked Suspect, "Are those drugs yours?" Suspect responded, "No, that cocaine isn't mine!" Officer then opened the car door and removed the bag of white powder.

Officer transported Suspect to the police station for booking. An hour later, Detective visited Suspect in the police station holding cell to attempt an interview. Detective read Suspect his *Miranda* rights. Suspect stated that he understood his *Miranda* rights but nonetheless would answer Detective's questions. Suspect voluntarily answered Detective's questions for about five minutes and then said, "I'm not sure about this. Maybe I need a lawyer." Detective did not seek clarification of Suspect's statement but continued to question Suspect, who ultimately confessed to possessing the cocaine found in his car.

The state charged Suspect with misdemeanor violation of the seat belt law and felony drug possession. Suspect has moved to suppress all the state's evidence, alleging an unlawful stop, an unlawful arrest, an unlawful seizure of evidence, and multiple *Miranda* violations.

1.   **Did the traffic stop and subsequent arrest violate Suspect's constitutional rights? Explain.**

2.   **Did Officer's seizure of evidence from Suspect's car violate Suspect's constitutional rights? Explain.**

3.   **Did Officer's questioning of Suspect violate Suspect's *Miranda* rights? Explain.**

4.   **Should Suspect's confession to Detective be suppressed? Explain.**

MBE SUBJECTS – RELEASED ESSAY QUESTIONS

CRIMINAL LAW AND PROCEDURE
MEE Question - July 2012

At 9:00 p.m. on a Sunday evening, Adam, age 18, proposed to his friend Bob, also age 18, that they dump Adam's collection of 2,000 marbles at a nearby intersection. "It'll be funny," Adam said. "When cars come by, they'll slip on the marbles and they won't be able to stop at the stop sign. The drivers won't know what happened, and they'll get really mad. We can hide nearby and watch." "That's a stupid idea," Bob said. "In the first place, this town is deserted on Sunday night. Nobody will even drive through the intersection. In the second place, I'll bet the cars just drive right over the marbles without any trouble at all. It'll be a total non-event." "Oh, I'll bet someone will come," Adam replied. "And I'll bet they'll have trouble; maybe there will even be a crash. But if you're not interested, fine. You don't have to do anything. Just give me a ride to the intersection—these bags of marbles are heavy."

At 10:00 p.m. that same night, Bob drove Adam and his bags of marbles to the intersection. Adam dumped several hundred marbles in front of each of the two stop signs at the intersection. Adam and Bob stayed for 20 minutes, waiting to see if anything happened. No one drove through the intersection, and Adam and Bob went home.

At 2:00 a.m., a woman drove through the intersection. Because of the marbles, she was unable to stop at the stop sign. Coincidentally, a man was driving through the intersection at the same time. The woman crashed into the side of the man's car. The man's eight-year-old child was sitting in the front seat without a seat belt, in violation of state law. The child was thrown from the car and killed. If the child had been properly secured with a seat belt, as required by state law, he would likely not have died.

Adam has been charged with involuntary manslaughter as defined at common law, and Bob has been charged with the same crime as an accomplice. State law does not recognize so-called "unlawful-act" involuntary manslaughter.

1.   **Could a jury properly find that Adam is guilty of involuntary manslaughter? Explain.**

2.   **If a jury did find Adam guilty of involuntary manslaughter, could the jury properly find that Bob is guilty of involuntary manslaughter as an accomplice? Explain.**

MBE SUBJECTS – RELEASED ESSAY QUESTIONS

CRIMINAL LAW AND PROCEDURE
MEE Question – February 2014

A defendant was charged under state law with felony theft (Class D) and felony residential burglary (Class C). The indictment alleged that the defendant entered his neighbors' home without their consent and stole a diamond ring worth at least $2,500.

Defense counsel filed a pretrial motion to dismiss the charges on the ground that prosecuting the defendant for both burglary and theft would constitute double jeopardy. The trial court denied the motion, and the defendant was prosecuted for both crimes. The only evidence of the ring's value offered at the defendant's jury trial was the owner's testimony that she had purchased the ring two years earlier for $3,000.

At trial, the judge issued the following jury instruction on the burglary charge prior to deliberations:

> If, after consideration of all the evidence presented by the prosecution and defense, you find beyond a reasonable doubt that the defendant entered the dwelling without the owners' consent, you may presume that the defendant entered with the intent to commit a felony therein.

The jury found the defendant guilty of both offenses.

At the defendant's sentencing hearing, an expert witness called by the prosecutor testified that the diamond ring was worth between $7,000 and $8,000. Over defense objection, the judge concluded, by a preponderance of the evidence, that the value of the stolen ring exceeded $5,000. The judge sentenced the defendant to four years' incarceration on the theft conviction. On the burglary conviction, the defendant received a consecutive sentence of seven years' incarceration.

In this state, residential burglary is defined as "entry into the dwelling of another, without the consent of the lawful resident, with the intent to commit a felony therein." Residential burglary is a Class C felony for which the minimum sentence is five years and the maximum sentence is ten years of incarceration.

In this state, theft is defined as "taking and carrying away the property of another with the intent to permanently deprive the owner of possession." Theft is a Class D felony if the value of the item(s) taken is between $2,500 and $10,000. The sentence for a Class D felony theft is determined by the value of the items taken. If the value is between $2,500 and $5,000, the maximum sentence is three years' incarceration. If the value of the items exceeds $5,000, the maximum sentence is five years' incarceration.

This state affords a criminal defendant no greater rights than those mandated by the United States Constitution.

1.   Did the trial court err when it denied the defendant's pretrial motion to dismiss on double jeopardy grounds? Explain.

2.   Did the trial court err in its instruction to the jury on the burglary charge? Explain.

3.   Did the trial court err when it sentenced the defendant to an additional year of incarceration on the theft conviction based on the expert's testimony? Explain.

MBE SUBJECTS – RELEASED ESSAY QUESTIONS

CRIMINAL LAW AND PROCEDURE
MEE Question – July 2014

While on routine patrol, a police officer observed a suspect driving erratically and pulled the suspect's car over to investigate. When he approached the suspect's car, the officer detected a strong odor of marijuana. The officer immediately arrested the suspect for driving under the influence of an intoxicant (DUI). While the officer was standing near the suspect's car placing handcuffs on the suspect, the officer observed burglary tools on the backseat.

The officer seized the burglary tools. He then took the suspect to the county jail, booked him for the DUI, and placed him in a holding cell. Later that day, the officer gave the tools he had found in the suspect's car to a detective who was investigating a number of recent burglaries in the neighborhood where the suspect had been arrested.

At the time of his DUI arrest, the suspect had a six-month-old aggravated assault charge pending against him and was being represented on the assault charge by a lawyer.

Early the next morning, upon learning of her client's arrest, the lawyer went to the jail. She arrived at 9:00 a.m., immediately identified herself to the jailer as the suspect's attorney, and demanded to speak with the suspect. The lawyer also told the jailer that she did not want the suspect questioned unless she was present. The jailer told the lawyer that she would need to wait one hour to see the suspect. After speaking with the lawyer, the jailer did not inform anyone of the lawyer's presence or her demands.

The detective, who had also arrived at the jail at 9:00 a.m., overheard the lawyer's conversation with the jailer. The detective then entered the windowless interview room in the jail where the suspect had been taken 30 minutes earlier. Without informing the suspect of the lawyer's presence or her demands, the detective read to the suspect full and accurate Miranda warnings. The detective then informed the suspect that he wanted to ask about the burglary tools found in his car and the recent burglaries in the neighborhood where he had been arrested. The suspect replied, "I think I want my lawyer here before I talk to you." The detective responded, "That's up to you."

After a few minutes of silence, the suspect said, "Well, unless there is anything else I need to know, let's not waste any time waiting for someone to call my attorney and having her drive here. I probably should keep my mouth shut, but I'm willing to talk to you for a while." The suspect then signed a Miranda waiver form and, after interrogation by the detective, made incriminating statements regarding five burglaries. The interview lasted from 9:15 a.m. to 10:00 a.m.

In addition to the DUI, the suspect has been charged with five counts of burglary.

The lawyer has filed a motion to suppress all statements made by the suspect to the detective in connection with the five burglaries.

The state supreme court follows federal constitutional principles in all cases interpreting a criminal defendant's rights.

1. **Did the detective violate the suspect's Sixth Amendment right to counsel when he questioned the suspect in the absence of the lawyer? Explain.**

2. **Under Miranda, did the suspect effectively invoke his right to counsel? Explain.**

3. **Was the suspect's waiver of his Miranda rights valid? Explain.**

MBE SUBJECTS – RELEASED ESSAY QUESTIONS

CRIMINAL LAW AND PROCEDURE
MEE Question – July 2015

On his way to work one morning, a man stopped his car at a designated street corner where drivers can pick up passengers in order to drive in the highway's HOV (high-occupancy vehicle) lanes. When the man, who was driving alone, opened his car door and announced his destination, a woman (a stranger) jumped into the front seat.

As soon as the man drove his car onto the busy highway, the woman took a knife from her backpack and held it against the man's throat. She said to him, "I am being followed by photographers from another planet where I am a celebrity. Pictures of me are worth a fortune, so I never give them away for free. Forget the speed limit and get me out of here fast, or else."

With the woman holding the knife at his neck, the man sped up to 85 miles per hour (30 mph over the posted speed limit of 55 mph), weaving in and out of traffic to avoid other cars, while the woman urged him to drive faster. While attempting to pass a motorcycle at a curve in the highway, the man lost control of the car, which struck and killed the motorcyclist before crashing into a railing.

A police car arrived at the scene a few minutes later. The man and the woman were treated for minor injuries at the scene and then arrested and taken to the police station.

While in custody, the woman was examined by two psychiatrists. Both psychiatrists submitted written reports stating that the woman suffers from schizophrenia and that, at the time of the accident, her delusions about alien photographers were caused by her schizophrenia.

The State A prosecutor has charged the woman with felony murder for the motorcyclist's death based on her kidnapping of the man, but is not sure whether to charge the man with any crime.

In State A, the rules governing crimes and affirmative defenses follow common law principles. However, in State A the Not Guilty by Reason of Insanity ("NGRI") defense is defined by statute as follows:

> To establish the defense of NGRI, the defendant must show that, at the time of the charged conduct, he or she suffered from a severe mental disease or defect and, as a result of that mental disease or defect, he or she did not know that his or her conduct was wrong. The defendant has the burden to prove all elements of the defense by a preponderance of the evidence.

Assume that the two psychiatric reports will be admitted into evidence.

1.   **Can the woman establish an NGRI defense?
Explain.**

2.   With what crimes, if any, can the man be charged as a result of the motorcyclist's death? Explain.

3.   What defenses, if any, will be available to the man if he is charged with a crime related to the motorcyclist's death? Explain.

MBE SUBJECTS – PRACTICE ESSAY QUESTIONS

CRIMINAL LAW AND PROCEDURE
Question 1

A credible, reliable informant tells police that Ruth Rogers was involved in a burglary that had occurred a couple of days earlier, in which valuable jewelry was stolen.

Officer Stevens located and transported Rogers to the stationhouse and placed her in an interrogation room. Counsel for Rogers and the State's Attorney stipulate that Rogers was in custody from this point on.

Officer Stevens then gave Rogers *Miranda* warnings. Upon hearing the warnings, Rogers said: "I think I want a public defender. I probably shouldn't talk to you at all. I think you're trying to get me in big trouble."

Officer Stevens said, "Well, you're asking me whether it's in your best interests to talk to me, and it's only right that I tell you what's what. The fact is, once we get you a lawyer I won't be able to help you. My hands will be tied. This is your last chance to let me help you."

Rogers then asked, "What do you mean? How can you help me? What do I need to do to get help?"

Officer Stevens replied, "If you want my help, you have to tell me you don't want to exercise your *Miranda* rights, and then explain your role in the burglary."

Rogers then stated that she understood her rights and wanted to waive them and talk to Officer Stevens. She proceeded to confess to the burglary. No electronic recording was made of any part of the conversation.

As part of her confession, Rogers informed the police that she had hidden the stolen jewelry in a dresser drawer in her bedroom. This information gave police probable cause to obtain a warrant to search Rogers' bedroom. They obtained the warrant, conducted the search, and found the jewelry. Rogers was charged with burglary.

Prior to trial, her attorney filed a motion to suppress her confession, and also to suppress the jewelry. Rogers stipulates that she had no sixth amendment right to counsel at any relevant time, so this issue should not be addressed.

Analyze and discuss all other arguments for suppression of Rogers' confession and the jewelry. Offer your opinions as to the likelihood of the success of the suppression motions.

MBE SUBJECTS – PRACTICE ESSAY QUESTIONS

CRIMINAL LAW AND PROCEDURE
Question 2

Officer Jones received a reliable tip establishing probable cause to believe that Jimmy held up a liquor store and escaped on foot with $1,000, the contents of the store's cash register. Officer Jones knew Jimmy from previous encounters. About two hours after receiving the tip, Officer Jones recognized Jimmy driving a car that Officer Jones knew was Jimmy's car.

The car also contained two passengers, a man in the front passenger seat (Leonard) and a woman in the backseat (Lana). Officer Jones pulled the car over and placed Jimmy under arrest. She ordered Jimmy, Leonard and Lana out of the car. Lana was wearing a backpack, which Officer Jones told Lana to take off and leave on the back seat of the car. She handcuffed Jimmy and performed a full body search of his person, in the course of which she discovered in his pants pocket, a baggie containing a white powder which she believed, based on her experience in narcotics enforcement, to be cocaine.

Officer Jones proceeded to search the car. She had no warrant. She began with the glove compartment, which contained a small satchel. She unzipped the satchel, and found it contained the full $1,000 proceeds of the cash register. She continued to search, coming across the backpack on the back seat. She cut the combination lock off the backpack, unzipped the backpack, and searched its contents, finding inside, a baggie of what appeared to be marijuana. She proceeded to search the trunk of the car, in which she found another two bags that appeared to contain cocaine. At that point she arrested Lana and Leonard, performing full body searches on both of them. She found more marijuana in Leonard's pants pocket.

Jimmy is charged with robbery and possession of cocaine, and Lana and Leonard are each charged with possession of marijuana. Jimmy seeks to suppress the $1,000 and the cocaine and Leonard and Lana seek to suppress the marijuana, as fruits of an illegal search.

Assuming that there is probable cause for Jimmy's arrest, analyze and discuss all defendants' arguments for suppression. Offer your opinion as to the likelihood of the success of the suppression motions.

MBE SUBJECTS – PRACTICE ESSAY QUESTIONS

CRIMINAL LAW AND PROCEDURE
Question 3

Police Officers Jones and Adams approached the home of Jack Smith and knocked on the door. As they later conceded, they had no probable cause to suspect any wrongdoing at this point, and no warrant. They were acting on an unsubstantiated hunch that Smith was using drugs.

Smith opened the door and, when Jones and Adams identified themselves, said, "No way am I letting you in. I'm asking you to get off my property now." However, Jones was able to see into the living room, where about an ounce of a powdery substance that looked like cocaine was lying on the coffee table.

At this point Jones and Adams pushed past Smith into the home and seized the cocaine. They turned to Smith, who was still standing near the front door, and placed him under arrest. They performed a full body search, and discovered a small bag of cocaine in Smith's shirt pocket. They then handcuffed him, and while Jones guarded him, Adams searched the rest of the room.

In the corner of the room farthest from the front door Adams noticed a card table with a cloth covering it. He lifted the cloth, and found a young woman, later identified as Smith's friend Jane Spencer, crouching under the table. He noticed that she was clutching a pipe in her hand. He could see that the pipe contained a small amount of cocaine. The officers then arrested Spencer as well.

Smith and Spencer were both charged with possession of cocaine. Smith was charged with possession of the cocaine on his person, Spencer with possession of the cocaine on her person, and both with possession of the cocaine on the coffee table.

At their trial for possession of cocaine, Smith sought to suppress the evidence against him, and Spencer sought to suppress the evidence against her. Analyze and discuss their arguments for suppression. Offer your opinion as to the likelihood of the success of their suppression motions.

MBE SUBJECTS - PRACTICE ESSAY QUESTIONS

CRIMINAL LAW AND PROCEDURE
Question 4

Officer Sarah, in uniform, was patrolling the perimeter of a high school when she heard what sounded like an argument happening a block away in a quiet residential area. Sarah walked briskly over to investigate. She came around a street corner and saw two young men, shouting at each other in anger. They appeared to be arguing over something contained in a student backpack. Sarah approached them and said: "Is everything OK?" When they saw her, one of them, Jerry, spun around and began walking away from Sarah, carrying the backpack with him.

The other young man ran away.

Sarah began walking quickly after Jerry. When she got close to him, Jerry broke into a run. When Sarah began to give chase, Jerry threw the backpack in an open dumpster behind an apartment building. Moments later, Sarah caught up to Jerry, put her hand on Jerry's shoulder and commanded him to stop.

Sarah quickly patted Jerry down. In Jerry's pocket, she found a sealed envelope. Tearing it open, she discovered what appeared to be (and was later found to be) cocaine. Sarah immediately placed Jerry under arrest. She then retrieved the backpack from the dumpster and opened it. In it she found a portable DVD player. "Well, I wonder who this belongs to," Sarah said aloud. "That DVD player belongs to me!" Jerry said. A later check at the police station showed the DVD player to be stolen.

Jerry is charged with the crime of possession of a controlled substance and possession of a stolen item. Jerry denies having possessed the DVD player or the backpack.

Under the federal constitution, will the cocaine, the DVD player and Jerry's statement be admissible in his trial? Fully analyze and discuss your answer.

MBE SUBJECTS - PRACTICE ESSAY QUESTIONS

CRIMINAL LAW AND PROCEDURE
Question 5

Dennis and Vickie lived together for 10 years in their home. Dennis regularly abused alcohol, and when he was intoxicated he would often beat Vickie. Vickie usually suffered such beatings without resisting, but sometimes she fought back and occasionally she started fights.

One night when Dennis and Vickie were extremely intoxicated, Vickie announced that she was tired of living with Dennis and she was going to leave him. Dennis replied, "I will kill you first." In response, Vickie went to the kitchen, returned with a large knife and started packing her belongings. When Dennis saw the knife he went to a back room and returned with a gun.

Vickie raised the knife and demanded that Dennis leave the room. When Dennis refused, Vickie threw the knife at Dennis, missing him. Furious, Dennis aimed the gun at Vickie and pulled the trigger twice. The gun did not fire because it was not loaded. Dennis did not know it was unloaded when he pulled the trigger.

Bob, their neighbor, heard the disturbance and called the police. The police arrived and arrested Dennis. He was subsequently charged with attempted first-degree murder.

At trial, Dennis' attorney tried to introduce evidence that Dennis was so intoxicated he lacked the intent required for first-degree murder. The trial court sustained the state's objection and excluded all evidence of the defendant's intoxication. Instead, the trial court instructed the jury, over the defendant's objection, that "the law presumes that a person intends the natural and probable consequences of his or her actions."

Dennis' attorney also raised the defense of self-defense. The trial court instructed the jury that the defendant bore the burden of proving self-defense by a preponderance of the evidence. Dennis' attorney objected to the burden being placed on the defendant, arguing that this was contrary to state law and violated the United States Constitution. The trial court further instructed the jury, over defendant's objection, that the defendant had the duty to retreat before employing force in self-defense.

At the conclusion of the trial, Dennis was convicted of attempted first-degree murder.

Based on the trial court's rulings, prepare a memorandum addressing the sufficiency of the evidence to convict Dennis and identifying possible errors to raise on appeal.

MBE SUBJECTS - PRACTICE ESSAY QUESTIONS

CRIMINAL LAW AND PROCEDURE
Question 6

Dave lives in a small town and is the owner of several businesses, including a security camera business and a real estate development business. On April 1, Dave was indicted by a grand jury for criminal fraud as a result of his selling parcels of real estate without making legally required disclosures.

On April 2, Dave received a call from Local Grocery Store to check out a malfunctioning security camera. Dave went to Local Grocery Store to repair the camera and stayed until after the store was closed to the public. While in the store, Dave had access to the holding area where the bags of cash were stored until a security shipper came to transfer the cash to the bank.

Dave did not know that an undercover police officer (Petra) had been hired by the store to observe all cash movements. On April 2, Officer Petra was observing the holding area through a one-way glass in a back room.

Thinking that he was not being observed, Dave picked up one of the bags, put it in his briefcase, and then casually started to walk out of the store.

Just as Dave opened the door, Officer Petra stepped out of the back room and said "What are you doing, Dave?" Dave recognized Officer Petra.

Not realizing that Officer Petra had seen him through the glass, Dave replied jokingly, "Just a peaceful robbery, Petra."

Officer Petra then placed Dave under arrest for robbery and read him his Miranda warnings. "Maybe I should ask for a lawyer," said Dave after hearing his rights.

Officer Petra hit a silent alarm for assistance from additional officers, and while she was waiting said to Dave, "So, are you in trouble again for selling some of that swamp land without giving the proper disclosures?" Dave answered casually: "I sold another parcel of swamp yesterday."

"I want a lawyer," Dave added. Officer Petra suggested that Dave would be more comfortable if he sat down.

Dave broke a brief silence by saying: "You know, one of my best friends is a rich real estate broker."

"Really," said Officer Petra, "Does he help you sell the real estate?" Dave replied, "Yes, and he always knows the best way to cut corners."

Officer Petra again read Dave his Miranda rights and then said: "Does your partner help you cut corners?" Dave answered, "I already told you – he does help me."

Dave continued, "I want a lawyer."

Then Officer Petra said, "Dave, you were indicted yesterday for fraud involving your real estate sales."

"What? Indicted?" said a surprised Dave. "I don't know anything about that. I can't believe not completing a couple of forms could lead to that!"

Dave is charged both with robbery and fraud and the case has gone to trial. Under federal constitutional law, which of Dave's statements will be admissible against him? Fully explain your answer.

MBE SUBJECTS - PRACTICE ESSAY QUESTIONS

CRIMINAL LAW AND PROCEDURE
Question 7

Smallville Police Officer James Miller prided himself on the fact that he knew everyone in town. One day he spotted a late model Camaro driving down Main Street. He began watching the car carefully, as he did not recognize either it or the people in it. He also noted that the driver and passenger wore leather jackets, had unkempt hair, and looked to him "like druggies." He followed the car for a short time, and soon noted that the license plate on the car was expired, in violation of a state traffic ordinance.

Officer Miller knew that there were no state or local rules limiting the types of offenses for which he could make a custodial arrest. Miller pulled the car over and ordered the driver to step out. He informed the driver, Andy, that he was under arrest for driving with an expired license plate and would be taken into custody. He proceeded to perform a full body search of Andy, incident to the arrest. In the course of the search, he found a baggie containing marijuana in Andy's waistband. Andy immediately stated, "I just want to say that my friend had nothing to do with this."

Officer Miller observed that Beth, sitting in the passenger seat, was wearing a backpack. He told Beth to take the backpack off and leave it on the seat, and ordered her to step out of the car. He proceeded to search the entire car, including the backpack. He found an ounce of marijuana in the zipper compartment of the backpack, and a small bag of cocaine in the trunk of the car.

Andy and Beth were both charged with possession of marijuana and cocaine. Both seek to suppress the marijuana and cocaine as fruits of an illegal search.

Analyze and discuss the 4th and 5th Amendment arguments that Andy and Beth should raise. Offer your opinion as to the likelihood of success of their suppression motions.

MEE RELEASED ESSAY QUESTIONS

DECEDENTS' ESTATES
July 2002

On February 10, 2000, Testator signed her last will, which was witnessed by two witnesses Testator's nephew, Nephew, and Testator's next-door neighbor. Testator died on May 10, 2000, after a brief hospitalization.

During the six months before she died, Testator experienced frequent episodes of forgetfulness. For example, Testator often missed appointments with her physicians and her bank trust officer. Testator had also become increasingly forgetful about matters of personal hygiene. On the other hand, throughout that six-month period, Testator maintained all of her financial records and visited in person and by telephone with each of her 20 living relatives, all of whom she easily recognized and identified. On April 3, she contacted her broker to advise him to sell her shares in Able Corporation because she had lost complete faith in the corporation's management following the release of its poor quarterly earnings report.

Testator's will bequeathed $100,000 to Nephew and the residue of her estate to Charity, a charitable organization with which Testator had been associated for more than 35 years. Nephew had no knowledge of the $100,000 bequest until after Testator died. She left no bequest to her three nieces, who are Nephew's three sisters. None of Testator's other living relatives was as closely related to her as Nephew and her three nieces.

Contemporaneous with the execution of her last will, Testator signed a durable health care power of attorney designating Nephew as her agent to make all health care decisions for her in the event she could no longer make them for herself. Nephew and Testator's next-door neighbor also witnessed this document.

One week before she died, Testator was admitted into a local hospital following a massive stroke causing severe brain damage. The following day, she lapsed into a coma and was connected to a life-support system. Four days later, Testator's physician advised Nephew that there was nothing medical science could do for Testator. After considering this advice, Nephew directed the physician to remove Testator from all life-support systems. The following day, Testator was removed from the life-support system and she died. She left an estate in excess of $1 million.

Testator's three nieces argue that Testator's durable health care power was not valid and that as a result Nephew should be liable in wrongful death for causing Testator's death because Nephew directed Testator's physician to withdraw Testator's life-support systems. Furthermore, they claim that either Testator's will is invalid or that, at minimum, the bequest to Nephew should be forfeited.

1. **Is Nephew liable in wrongful death for causing Testator's death? Explain.**

2. **Is Testator's will invalid because of incapacity? Explain.**

3. **Assuming Testator's will is valid, is the bequest to Nephew valid? Explain.**

MEE RELEASED ESSAY QUESTIONS

DECEDENTS' ESTATES
February 2003

Testator was an 80-year-old mentally alert widow. Testator retained Lawyer to prepare her will naming Charity, a charitable organization, as the sole beneficiary of her estate. One week later, Testator received a photocopy of a proposed will that Lawyer had prepared for her.

A few days later, on October 1, 1998, Lawyer called Testator to inquire whether the proposed will conformed with her wishes. When Testator responded that it did, Lawyer suggested that Testator make an appointment to come to his office so that she could execute the original, which was in his possession. Testator responded that, because of her arthritic condition, it would not be convenient for her to do so, and she told him, "Just go ahead and sign the will for me." Lawyer said, "OK."

Later that day, Lawyer inserted "October 1, 1998" as the date of execution on the original will and signed Testator's name on the will in front of three secretaries who acted as witnesses. The secretaries then signed their names in the spaces provided on the will. All of them saw Lawyer sign Testator's name, and each of them saw the others sign their own names. Lawyer then called Testator and told her the will had been signed and witnessed. Testator replied, "Good, now it's done. Please keep the will for me."

A year later, Testator decided that she wanted to change the will to give her diamond ring to her niece, Nora. Deciding to make the change herself, she asked a friend to type up a document, which was identified as "a codicil to my existing last will." This document was then validly executed and stated, "I leave my diamond ring to my niece, Nora. In all other respects I hereby affirm my existing last will, executed on October 1, 1998."

A year later, Testator had a falling out with Nora. Remembering that she had devised her diamond ring to Nora, she gave the ring to another niece, Betty, as a gift. Testator died a few months later. Her closest surviving relatives were her two nieces, Nora and Betty. At the time of her death, her only asset was a parcel of real estate known as "Blackacre."

Who is entitled to Blackacre and to the diamond ring? Explain.

MEE RELEASED ESSAY QUESTIONS

DECEDENTS' ESTATES
July 2003

In 1988, Testator duly executed a will devising Blackacre to Adam, $100,000 to Carrie, and the residue of her estate to Doris. However, in 1992, Testator telephoned her lawyer, Lawyer, who had possession of the 1988 will, and asked her to destroy it because Testator had changed her mind. Lawyer agreed. Immediately after hanging up the phone, Lawyer found the will, shredded it, and threw it away.

In 1996, Testator signed and dated a wholly handwritten document that stated: "I devise Blackacre to Earl and $2,500,000 to my good friend, Fred."

Testator died in 2002, a domiciliary of State A. She was survived by Greg, age 30, who was her child and only heir. Adam, Carrie, Doris, Earl, and Fred also survived Testator. There was no surviving spouse. Testator's net probate estate (after taxes, debts, and expenses) consisted of $5,000,000 plus Blackacre.

The 1996 document, together with an unexecuted copy of the 1988 will, the original of which Lawyer had shredded, were found among Testator's valuable papers. Both documents were offered for probate.

Under State A law, holographic wills are valid.

1.   **Which documents, if any, govern the distribution of Testator's estate? Explain.**

2.   **What are the respective shares, if any, in Testator's estate of each of the following: Adam, Carrie, Doris, Earl, Fred, and Greg? Explain.**

MEE RELEASED ESSAY QUESTIONS

DECEDENTS' ESTATES
February 2004

In 1995, Testator, age 85, executed a will in the presence of two witnesses. Immediately before signing the document, Testator's attorney asked Testator if she declared the instrument to be her will. Testator responded: "You bet it is. I want Charity to have everything. My family has enough." Then the attorney had Testator sign the document on the line provided for her signature. The two witnesses signed immediately below Testator's signature without any further direction or comment from Testator.

When Testator executed this will, she was suffering from cancer and her medications made it very difficult for her to remember facts. For example, when she executed her will she knew, correctly, that her estate was worth $500,000 and that she had previously made large gifts to her child and some of her grandchildren. However, she could neither remember the name of her stockbroker nor recount the names of her stocks under her stockbroker's management. Also, she had no difficulty correctly naming her child and all of her grandchildren, but she could not recall that she had a great-grandchild. She also knew she owned both a home and a condominium but could not recall the precise street address for either residence.

Testator died in 2002 survived by her only child, Mary, and by three grandchildren and one great-grandchild, all of whom are descendants of Mary. Testator's will, which devised her entire estate to Charity, was timely offered for probate by Bank, the executor named in the will. Mary and one of her children, Grandchild, have initiated a timely contest of the will.

Governing state law provides that a will is properly executed if the testator signs the will in the presence of two witnesses after having (a) declared the instrument to be her will, and (b) requested the witnesses to act in such capacity.

1. **Do Mary and Grandchild each have standing to contest Testator's will? Explain.**

2. **On what theory or theories, other than undue influence, might a person with standing contest Testator's will, what defenses might Bank, as executor, assert, and what is the likely outcome? Explain.**

MEE RELEASED ESSAY QUESTIONS

DECEDENTS' ESTATES
July 2004

Decedent and his only child, Clara, died as the result of an accident when Clara's car was struck from the rear by a truck. Clara was driving and Decedent was riding in the back seat directly behind her. The emergency medical team that arrived at the accident scene found no evidence that either of them was alive. The emergency room physician examined their bodies as they were being removed from the ambulance. She first pronounced Decedent dead and then pronounced Clara dead.

Clara was survived by her spouse, Son-in-Law, who was named as the sole beneficiary of her estate under her duly probated will. Clara had no descendants.

Decedent died intestate leaving an estate of approximately $300,000. Decedent left no surviving spouse. Decedent's parents had predeceased him by many years. Decedent's closest surviving relatives are:

1.   A brother, Brother;

2.   A half-sister, Half-Sister, who is related to Decedent through a common mother;

3.   An adopted sister, Adopted-Sister, who was adopted by Decedent's parents; and

4.   His paternal grandfather, Gramps.

Three years before Decedent died, he gave Brother a check for $90,000 to enable Brother to buy a new home.

Among Son-in-Law, Brother, Half-Sister, Adopted-Sister, and Gramps, who will share in Decedent's estate, and what is the value of the share each will receive? Explain.

MEE RELEASED ESSAY QUESTIONS

DECEDENTS' ESTATES
February 2005

In 1991, Testator validly executed a typewritten will. Its dispositive provision provided that:

1.   I give $10,000 to Cousin.

2.   I give Blackacre, my family home, to Sister.

3.   I give the residue of my estate to University, my alma mater.

Three months after executing this will, Testator, desiring to increase the bequest to Cousin, scratched out Item 1 in its entirety and immediately above it wrote in by hand:

"I give $100,000 to Cousin."

This handwritten $100,000 bequest was not witnessed.

In 1994, Testator sold Blackacre, the family home, and reinvested the entire sales proceeds in Whiteacre, which became Testator's new family home.

In 1994, one month after buying Whiteacre and following a heated argument with Cousin, Testator validly executed two copies of a new typewritten will that left his entire estate to University. Testator then put both executed copies of the 1994 will in his safe deposit box, where the 1991 will was also located.

In 1999, Testator and Cousin reconciled. Immediately thereafter, Testator went to the safe deposit box and removed one of the executed copies of the 1994 will. In the course of reviewing it, Testator had second thoughts about leaving nothing to Cousin. However, rather than executing a new will, he tore up that copy of the 1994 will in the presence of his neighbor and stated: "I feel better now. Cousin is taken care of."

Last year, Testator, a domiciliary of State A, died leaving a substantial estate, including Whiteacre. Both the 1991 will with the handwritten changes and the remaining executed copy of the 1994 will were found in Testator's safe deposit box.

Both Cousin and Sister survived Testator. Under State A intestacy law, Sister would be Testator's only heir. State A also has a statute providing: "The revocation of a will that revoked an earlier will revives the earlier will in the absence of a contrary intention." State A does not permit holographic wills.

What, if anything, are Cousin and Sister entitled to receive from Testator's estate? Explain.

MEE RELEASED ESSAY QUESTIONS

DECEDENTS' ESTATES
July 2005

Ten years ago, Testator purchased an insurance policy on his life from Insurer. The policy provided that Insurer would pay the proceeds only to the person named on a beneficiary form filed with Insurer. Testator filed such a form with Insurer, naming his son Sam as the sole beneficiary.

A year later, Testator, concerned about his failing physical health, opened Account #1 at Bank in the name of "Testator and Sam" as joint tenants with right of survivorship, not as tenants in common. Testator thereafter gave Sam checks that would enable him to withdraw funds from Account #1. Testator was the only person who deposited funds into Account #1, and he received all statements relating to it.

Five years ago, Testator duly executed a will containing the following dispositive clauses:

1. I give the proceeds of my Insurer life insurance policy to my daughter, Doris.
2. I give Account #1 at Bank to my daughter, Doris.
3. I give the balance of my estate to the children of my son Sam, to be divided equally among them.

Three months ago, Testator died and his will was duly probated. Testator was survived by Sam, Doris, and one of Sam's three children. Two of Sam's children predeceased Testator. One of the predeceased children, Ann, died seven years ago, and the other, Bill, died two years ago. Ann had a child who survived Testator, and Bill had a child who survived Testator.

Testator was a domiciliary of State A. State A law provides that, "if a beneficiary who is a descendant of the testator predeceases the testator, the beneficiary's surviving issue take the share the deceased beneficiary would have taken had the beneficiary survived."

To whom should the life insurance proceeds, Account #1, and the balance of Testator's estate be distributed? Explain.

MEE RELEASED ESSAY QUESTIONS

DECEDENTS' ESTATES
February 2006

Dorothy had three children, Abel, Brandon, and Carrie. Abel had two children, Grandchild 1 and Grandchild 2; Brandon had three children, Grandchild 3, Grandchild 4, and Grandchild 5; and Carrie had one child, Grandchild 6.

Following the deaths of all three of her children, Dorothy was judicially appointed the guardian of all six grandchildren. Dorothy raised all of the grandchildren in her home and loved them all equally.

Five years ago, Dorothy gave $60,000 to Grandchild 6 to help Grandchild 6 buy a new home. The only statement Dorothy ever made regarding this payment was a contemporaneous statement to Grandchild 6: "This is for you because I love you." Dorothy made no other transfers to her grandchildren.

One year ago, Dorothy executed a valid will providing: "I give my entire estate to my heirs, said heirs to take the same shares thereof that they would have taken had I died intestate."

Three months ago, Dorothy was visiting Grandchild 1's home. While Dorothy was working in the front yard, Grandchild 1 backed a car out of the garage and, inadvertently, albeit negligently, struck Dorothy. Dorothy later died from the injuries.

Dorothy's only survivors are all six grandchildren and one great-grandchild, who is a child of Grandchild 1. Dorothy left a probate estate of $120,000.

To whom should Dorothy's $120,000 probate estate be distributed, and what is the amount of each person's share? Explain.

MEE RELEASED ESSAY QUESTIONS

DECEDENTS' ESTATES
July 2006

In 1995, Husband and Wife duly executed a joint will which provided, in relevant part:

> Each of us agrees that, when one of us dies, all of our property shall be distributed to the survivor. Furthermore, upon the death of the survivor we agree that: (1) $1,000 shall be distributed to the person who is then the pastor of the First Avenue Church; (2) $1,000 shall be distributed to the person named in a memorandum that the survivor shall leave in our safe deposit box at the Main Street Bank; and (3) at the survivor's death, the remainder of the survivor's property, however acquired, shall be distributed to our child, Child.

When this joint will was executed, George was the pastor of the First Avenue Church.

In 2000, Husband died. His estate of $150,000 was distributed to Wife pursuant to the joint will.

In 2001, Wife inherited $200,000 from her sister.

In 2002, Wife duly executed a new will providing in relevant part:

> Upon my death I give: (1) $1,000 to the person who is then the pastor of the First Avenue Church; (2) $1,000 to the person named in a memorandum to be left in my safe deposit box; (3) $100,000 to my child, Child; and (4) the balance of my estate to my boyfriend, John, who has provided me with loving companionship since my late husband died.

In late 2003, Wife died leaving an estate valued at $400,000. A memorandum, dated February 2, 2003, and signed by Wife, was found in Wife's safe deposit box directing that $1,000 be distributed to her friend, Robin. Wife was survived by John, Robin, Child, George, and Ted, who had been appointed pastor of the First Avenue Church one week before Wife died. Wife's 2002 will was duly admitted to probate.

To whom should Wife's estate be distributed? Explain.

MEE RELEASED ESSAY QUESTIONS

DECEDENTS' ESTATES
February 2007

In 2000, Testator executed a valid will. The will provided:

1. I give my 100 shares of stock in XYZ Company to Brother.
2. I give $3,000 to Sister.
3. I give $5,000 to Uncle.
4. I give $10,000 to Cousin.
5. I give the residue of my estate to my alma mater, Polytech.

In 2001, XYZ Company issued its annual dividend in stock. For each 100 shares held, the dividend was 6 shares of XYZ stock.

In 2002, Testator gave $5,000 to Uncle on Uncle's birthday.

In 2005, Testator died, survived by Brother, Sister, Uncle, and Cousin. Testator's estate consists of the following assets: 106 shares of XYZ Company stock (worth $1 per share) and $9,000. Sister made a valid disclaimer of her interest in Testator's estate.

How should Testator's estate be distributed? Explain.

MEE RELEASED ESSAY QUESTION

DECEDENTS' ESTATES
February 2008

Six years ago, Testator retired from his work as a business executive but he continued to serve as a trustee of several nonprofit organizations and manage all of his own financial affairs. He maintained these activities until his death. Five years ago, Testator hired a housekeeper, Harriet.

Four years ago, Harriet began to ask Testator to provide for her in his will. She also began to interfere with Testator's relationship with his daughter, Doris. When Doris called, Harriet sometimes falsely told her that Testator was sleeping and could not talk on the phone. When Doris came to visit Testator, Harriet often stayed in the room to overhear their conversations. Harriet also made critical remarks about Doris to Testator and told him that Doris should visit him more regularly.

On a number of occasions, Harriet threatened to quit if Testator did not provide for her in his will. These threats made Testator fearful, particularly during the last year of his life when his declining health made him increasingly dependent on Harriet.

Six months ago, Harriet again threatened to quit if Testator did not provide for her in his will and told Testator that he should see her attorney. Testator told Harriet: "Stop bugging me. I'll see my own attorney."

Three months ago, Testator executed a will in accordance with the applicable statute of wills. The will was drafted by Testator's attorney pursuant to Testator's handwritten instructions.

The will specified as follows:
"I leave my estate in equal shares to my housekeeper, Harriet, and my daughter, Doris."

This is the only will Testator ever executed. Testator recently died at age 78. Testator left a substantial estate.

Both Harriet and Doris survived Testator. Testator was also survived by a son (Sam), a grandchild (Ella), who was the child of Doris, and a grandchild (Fred), who was the child of Testator's son, Bob. Both Testator's spouse and Bob predeceased Testator. Testator and Sam had been estranged for several years prior to the time of Testator's death.

1. **Is the will invalid in whole or in part? Explain.**

2. **Assuming the will is invalid in whole, to whom and in what shares should Testator's estate be distributed? Explain.**

3. **Assuming the will is invalid in part, to whom and in what shares should Testator's estate be distributed? Explain.**

MEE RELEASED ESSAY QUESTIONS

DECEDENTS' ESTATES
February 2009

In 2004, Testator duly executed a will providing as follows:

1.   I give my 100 shares of XYZ common stock to my cousin Andy.

2.   I give my home at 4 Cypress Garden to my cousin Ben.

3.   I give my automobile to my friend Carrie.

4.   I give $10,000 to my friend Donna.

5.   I give the residue of my estate to my friend Ed.

In 2006, Testator sold her home at 4 Cypress Garden and, with the entire sales proceeds, purchased a condominium as her new home.

In 2007, Testator traded the white automobile that she owned when her will was executed for a blue automobile.

In 2008, Testator died. At the time of her death, Testator owned 200 shares of XYZ common stock, having acquired an additional 100 shares as the result of a dividend paid by XYZ to its shareholders in its own stock. Testator also owned the condominium, the blue automobile, and a $50,000 bank account.

Testator was survived by Andy, Ben, Carrie, Donna, and Ed. She was also survived by Donna's daughter. Three months after Testator died, Donna made a valid disclaimer of any rights to the $10,000 bequest to which she might otherwise be entitled. Testator's will was admitted to probate.

To whom should Testator's probate estate be distributed? Explain.

MEE RELEASED ESSAY QUESTIONS

DECEDENTS' ESTATES
July 2009

Two years ago, Testator, age 70, met Friend, age 50, through a dating service. Testator was a successful businessman and a widower. Friend worked for low-income wages. Friend showered Testator with affection and appeared to enjoy sharing his interests.

Three months ago, Testator proposed marriage to Friend, and Friend accepted. Thereafter, Testator decided to consult Friend's Brother, an attorney, about executing a will that would provide for Friend after Testator's death.

Without Testator's knowledge, Friend promised Brother that she would "be very generous" to him if Testator left her everything.

Testator consulted Brother and told him that he would like to leave his entire estate to a testamentary trust that would give Friend all trust income during her lifetime and give Charity the remaining trust assets after Friend's death. Brother told Testator that he would draft a will in accordance with these instructions. Brother instead drafted a will in which Testator bequeathed all of his assets to a trust, named Friend the beneficiary of "all trust income during her lifetime," gave Friend a "general power of appointment exercisable by deed or will" over trust assets, and named Charity the taker in default of appointment. After Brother advised Testator that the will reflected Testator's instructions, Testator properly executed the will drafted by Brother.

Shortly thereafter, Friend properly executed a will leaving her entire residuary estate to her Sister. Neither the residuary clause nor any other clause in Friend's will made reference to the power of appointment in Testator's will.

On the way to their wedding, Testator and Friend were in an automobile accident. Testator died immediately, and Friend died one week later.

Testator left a substantial estate. He was survived by his elderly Uncle and his Niece, both of whom he had not seen in several years. Friend is survived by Sister and Brother.

1. **Is Testator's will invalid on the basis of undue influence? Explain.**

2. **Is Testator's will invalid on the basis of fraud? Explain.**

3. **If Testator's will is valid, to whom should Testator's estate be distributed? Explain.**

4. **If Testator's will is invalid, to whom should Testator's estate be distributed? Explain.**

MEE RELEASED ESSAY QUESTIONS

DECEDENTS' ESTATES
July 2010

Three years ago, Testator told his attorney to draft a will leaving $20,000 to his Sister and the balance of his estate to his children. Testator told his attorney that he was divorced and that he had two children, Abby and Bruce, both biological children born during Testator's first marriage. Testator did not tell the attorney that he had adopted his stepchild, Carl, when Carl was two years old.

The attorney prepared a typed will based on Testator's instructions. When Testator came to the attorney's office to execute the will, the attorney placed the three unstapled pages of the will on her desk and said to Testator, "Please sign your will."

Page 1 of the will included introductory clauses and two bequests reading: "I give $20,000 to Sister. I give the balance of my estate to my children, in equal shares." Pages 2 and 3 of the will contained clauses relating to the responsibilities of the executor. At the bottom of page 3, there were lines for Testator's and his witnesses' signatures and an attestation clause.

Testator, in the presence of two witnesses, read the three pages, declared the document on the attorney's desk to be his will, and signed it on the line provided on page 3. Both witnesses, who were able to see all three pages, signed their names underneath Testator's signature and again under the attestation clause. The attorney thereafter folded the three pages together and gave them to Testator. Two years ago, Testator decided that he wanted to leave more money to Sister. To accomplish this, Testator crossed out the bequest reading "I give $20,000 to Sister" on page 1 of the will and wrote above the crossed-out phrase, "I give $40,000 to Sister."

Last month, Testator died. Testator's will, all three pages folded together, was found in a night table in Testator's bedroom. Abby, Bruce, Carl, and Sister survived Testator. In addition, Don claims to be Testator's nonmarital child.

The only relevant state statutes provide:

    I.   "No will or codicil thereto is valid unless signed by the testator and two attesting witnesses."

    II.   "A will may be revoked, in whole or in part, by destruction or cancellation."

    III.   "If a decedent dies intestate survived by children and no spouse, the decedent's entire estate passes to his children, in equal shares."

1.   Is Testator's will valid? Explain.

2.   To whom should Testator's estate be distributed? Explain.

MEE RELEASED ESSAY QUESTIONS

DECEDENTS' ESTATES
February 2011

Two years ago, Testator purchased a $50,000 life insurance policy and named Niece as beneficiary.

One year ago, Testator invited three friends to dinner. After dessert had been served, Testator brought a handwritten document to the table and stated, "This is my will. I would like each of you to witness it." Testator then signed and dated the document. The three friends watched Testator sign her name, and immediately thereafter, they signed their names below Testator's name.

One month ago, Testator died. Testator was survived by Niece, Cousin, and Son. Son is Testator's child from her first marriage. Testator's second husband, Husband, died six months before Testator. Husband's daughter from a prior marriage also survived Testator.

The handwritten document that Testator signed and that the three friends witnessed was found in Testator's desk. Its dispositive provisions provide in their entirety:

> *I, Testator, hereby make my Last Will and Testament.*
> *I give my life insurance proceeds to Cousin.*
> *I give the items listed in a memorandum to be found in my safe-deposit box to Niece.*
> *I give $25,000 each to Church, Library, and School.*
> *I give $40,000 to Husband.*
> *I give the remainder of my assets to Son.*

At Testator's death, she owned the following assets:

1. The $50,000 life insurance policy, payable on Testator's death "to Niece"
2. Jewelry worth $15,000
3. A bank account with a balance of $60,000

The jewelry was found in Testator's safe-deposit box with a handwritten memorandum signed and dated by Testator the day before she signed her will. The memorandum lists each piece of jewelry and states, "I want Niece to have all the jewelry here."

The terms of Testator's life insurance contract provide that the beneficiary may be changed only by submitting the change on the insurer's change-of-beneficiary form to the insurance company.

State law explicitly disallows "all holographic wills and codicils." To be valid, a will must be "acknowledged by the testator to the witnesses and signed by the testator in the presence of at least two attesting witnesses, who shall sign their names below that of the testator within 30 days."

1.   Is Testator's will valid? Explain.

2.   Assuming that Testator's will is valid, who is entitled to

     (a) Testator's life insurance policy? Explain.

     (b) Testator's jewelry? Explain.

     (c) Testator's bank account? Explain.

MEE RELEASED ESSAY QUESTIONS

DECEDENTS' ESTATES
February 2012

Five years ago, Testator asked her attorney to draft a will that would leave Testator's entire estate to Nephew. One week later, the attorney mailed to Testator a document captioned "Last Will and Testament." Although the document complied with Testator's instructions, Testator did not sign it or have it witnessed.

Three years ago, Testator called her attorney and said, "I want my 400 shares of XYZ Corporation common stock to go to Aunt instead of Nephew." Testator added, "I also want my home to go to Cousin. The house has five bedrooms, and Cousin has such a large family." Testator told the attorney that her home was located at 340 Green Avenue, Springfield, State A.

Subsequently, the attorney sent Testator a document stating in its entirety:

> I, Testator, being of sound and disposing mind, give my home, located at 340 Green Avenue, Springfield, State A, to Cousin and my 400 shares of XYZ Corporation common stock to Aunt. In all other respects, I republish my will.

Upon receipt of this document, Testator properly executed it.

Two years ago, Testator sold her five-bedroom house at 340 Green Avenue and used the proceeds to purchase a two-bedroom house located at 12 Elm Street in Springfield. The same year, Testator received 200 shares of XYZ common stock from XYZ Corporation in the form of a "dividend paid in stock."

Three weeks ago, Testator died. Her probate estate consists of $200,000, her house at 12 Elm Street, and 600 shares of XYZ Corporation common stock, consisting of Testator's original 400 shares and the 200-share stock dividend.

Testator is survived by Daughter, Daughter's child (Grandson), Nephew, Cousin, and Aunt.

Fifteen years ago, Daughter was convicted of murdering her father, Testator's husband. Testator and Daughter have had little contact since Daughter's conviction, and Daughter remains in prison.

Testator is a resident of State A, and all of Testator's assets are located in State A.

How should Testator's probate assets be distributed? Explain.

MEE RELEASED ESSAY QUESTIONS

DECEDENTS' ESTATES
July 2012

Zach died a domiciliary of State A. At Zach's death, he owned a house located in State A. Zach also owned a farm located in State B and had a savings account at a bank in State B.

Zach left a handwritten document containing instructions for the disposition of his assets. The only words on this document were the following:

> I, Zach, being of sound and disposing mind, leave my entire estate to my alma mater, University. I appoint Bank as executor of my estate.

Zach's wife predeceased him. Zach was survived by three children, Alex, Brian, and Carrie. Alex was the biological child of Zach and his deceased wife. Brian was the biological child of Zach's deceased wife and her first husband, but Zach adopted Brian when Brian was 12. Carrie was the biological child of Zach and a woman whom Zach never married. Zach's paternity of Carrie was adjudicated during Zach's lifetime.

State A law provides that a holographic will "entirely handwritten and signed at the end by the testator" is valid. State A law also provides that if a decedent dies intestate and leaves no surviving spouse, the decedent's estate passes in equal shares to the decedent's "surviving children." The phrase "surviving children" is defined to exclude "nonmarital children." There are no other relevant statutes in State A.

State B law provides that (1) the will of a nonresident that bequeaths real property located in State B must comply with the law of State B; (2) a will is invalid unless it was signed by the testator and two witnesses; and (3) the estate of an intestate decedent who leaves no surviving spouse passes to the decedent's "biological and adopted children, in equal shares." There are no other relevant statutes in State B.

How should Zach's three assets be distributed? Explain.

MEE RELEASED ESSAY QUESTIONS

DECEDENTS' ESTATES
July 2013

Twenty years ago, John and Mary were married. One month before their wedding, John and Mary signed a valid prenuptial agreement in which each of them waived "any property rights in the estate or property of the other to which he or she might otherwise be legally entitled upon the termination of their marriage by death or divorce."

Seventeen years ago, John executed a valid will, which provided as follows:

> I, John, leave my entire estate to my wife, Mary. However, if I should hereafter have children, then I leave three-fourths of my estate to my wife, Mary, and one-fourth of my estate to my children who survive me, in equal shares.

Fifteen years ago, John had an extramarital affair with Beth, who gave birth to their child, Son. Both Beth and John consented to Son's adoption by Aunt. At the time of the adoption, Beth, John, and Aunt agreed that Son would not be told that he was the biological child of Beth and John.

Three years ago, Aunt died, and Son moved into John and Mary's home. At that time, John admitted to Mary that he had had an extramarital affair with Beth which had resulted in Son's birth.

Three months ago, Mary filed for divorce. Nonetheless, she and John continued to live together.

One month ago, before John and Mary's divorce decree was entered, John was killed in a car accident. John's will, executed 17 years ago, has been offered for probate. John's will did not designate anyone to act as the personal representative of his estate.

John was survived by Mary, Son, and John's mother.

1.   **To whom should John's estate be distributed? Explain.**

2.   **Who should be appointed as the personal representative of John's estate? Explain.**

MEE RELEASED ESSAY QUESTIONS

DECEDENTS' ESTATES
February 2015

A husband and wife were married in 2005.

In 2009, the husband transferred $600,000 of his money to a revocable trust. Under the terms of the properly executed trust instrument, upon the husband's death all trust assets would pass to his alma mater, University.

In 2012, the husband properly executed a will, prepared by his attorney based on the husband's oral instructions. Under the will, the husband bequeathed $5,000 to his best friend and the balance of his estate "to my wife, regardless of whether we have children." The husband failed to mention the revocable trust to his attorney during the preparation of this will, and the attorney did not ask the husband whether he had made any significant transfers in prior years.
In 2013, the husband and wife had a daughter.

In 2014, the husband was killed in an automobile accident. After his death, the wife found the husband's will and the revocable trust instrument on his desk. On the first page of the will, beginning in the left-hand margin and extending over the words setting forth the bequests to the husband's best friend and his wife, were the following words: "This will makes no sense, as most of my assets are in the trust for University and neither my wife nor my daughter seems adequately provided for. Estate plan should be changed. Call lawyer to fix." The statement was indisputably in the husband's handwriting. The wife also found a voice message on the phone from the husband's lawyer, which said, "Calling back. I understand you have concerns about your will."

The husband is survived by his wife, their daughter, and the husband's best friend. The assets in the revocable trust are now worth $900,000. The husband's probate estate is worth $300,000. He owed no debts at his death.

All the foregoing events occurred in State A, which is not a community property state. State A has enacted all of the customary probate statutes, but of particular relevance to the wife are the following:

(i) If a decedent dies intestate survived by a spouse and issue, the decedent's surviving spouse takes one-half of the estate and the decedent's surviving issue take the other half.

(ii) A revocable trust created by a decedent during the decedent's marriage is deemed illusory and the decedent's surviving spouse is entitled to receive one-half of the trust's assets.

1.   **How should the assets of the husband's probate estate be distributed? Explain.**
2.   **How should the assets of the revocable trust be distributed? Explain.**

MEE RELEASED ESSAY QUESTIONS

DECEDENTS' ESTATES
February 2016

Last year, a patient, age 80, was diagnosed with cancer. Shortly after receiving the cancer diagnosis, the patient signed a durable health-care power of attorney (POA) designating her son as her "agent to make all health-care decisions on my behalf when I lack capacity to make them myself." The POA contained no other provisions relevant to the commencement or duration of the agent's authority. The patient thereafter underwent several cancer therapies which were so successful that, two months ago, the patient's doctor said that, in his opinion, the patient's cancer was in "complete remission."

Last week, the patient was struck by an automobile, suffered serious injuries to her head and neck, and underwent emergency surgery for those injuries. Following surgery, the patient's doctor explained to her son that there was a more than 50% risk that the patient would not regain consciousness and would need to be maintained on life-support systems to provide her with food, hydration, and respiration. The doctor also noted that, during the next few days, there was a large risk of a stroke or cardiac arrest, which would substantially increase the risk that the patient would never regain consciousness, and which could be fatal.

The patient's son was confident that his mother would not want to be kept on life support if she were permanently unconscious but believed that she would want to be maintained on life support until her status was clear. He thus instructed the doctor to put the patient on life support but not to resuscitate her if she were to experience a stroke or cardiac arrest. The son issued these instructions after conferring with the doctor and with his two sisters. The sisters disagreed with their brother's decision and told the doctor to ignore the instructions "because we have as much right to say what happens to Mom as he does, and we want her resuscitated in all events." Nonetheless, the doctor thereafter placed a "do not resuscitate" (DNR) order in the patient's chart.

Four days ago, the patient, who had not regained consciousness, suffered a cardiac arrest. Following the DNR order, the nursing staff did not attempt to resuscitate the patient, and she died.

The patient's valid will devised her estate to her three children in equal shares. All three children survived the patient.

This jurisdiction has a typical statute authorizing durable health-care powers of attorney. This jurisdiction also has a statute providing that "[n]o person shall share in the estate of a decedent when he or she intentionally caused the decedent's death."

The patient's two daughters have consulted an attorney, who has advised them that (1) the patient's son had no authority to instruct the doctor to write the DNR order; (2) in a wrongful death action, the son would be liable for the patient's death; and (3) the son is barred from taking under the patient's will because his actions intentionally caused her death.

Is the attorney correct? Explain.

MBE SUBJECTS – RELEASED ESSAY QUESTIONS

EVIDENCE
MEE Question - February 2009

Plaintiff, an employee of Contractor, was injured while using a table saw manufactured by Defendant and owned by Contractor. Plaintiff sued Defendant in federal court to recover damages for his injuries.

At trial, Defendant called Witness, another employee of Contractor. Neither Witness nor Contractor is a party to Plaintiff's action against Defendant. On direct examination, Witness testified that he saw Plaintiff remove a safety guard from the table saw on the morning of the accident.

During cross-examination by Plaintiff's Counsel, Witness testified as follows:

> PLAINTIFF'S COUNSEL: At the time you applied for your job with Contractor, you had three years of previous construction experience, didn't you?

> WITNESS: Yes.

> PLAINTIFF'S COUNSEL: Didn't you lie about how much construction experience you had when you applied for the job with Contractor?

> DEFENSE COUNSEL: Objection, inadmissible character evidence.

> PLAINTIFF'S COUNSEL: We are impeaching this witness with a specific instance of untruthful conduct under Rule 608(b), Your Honor.

> COURT: Overruled.

> PLAINTIFF'S COUNSEL: I'll repeat my question—didn't you lie about how much construction experience you had?

> WITNESS: No, I did not.

> PLAINTIFF'S COUNSEL: Isn't Plaintiff's Exhibit 37 a genuine copy of your job application?

> WITNESS: Yes, it is.

> PLAINTIFF'S COUNSEL: Didn't you lie on that application?

> WITNESS: No.

> PLAINTIFF'S COUNSEL: We offer Plaintiff's Exhibit 37.
> DEFENSE COUNSEL: Objection, inadmissible character evidence.

> COURT: Approach the bench. (The following occurred outside the hearing of the jury.)

PLAINTIFF'S COUNSEL: Judge, this is a copy of Witness's job application in which he represented that he had twelve years of construction experience when he actually had only three.

COURT: Sustained.

Plaintiff's Counsel then asked Witness to review Plaintiff's Exhibit 37 to refresh his recollection about whether he had lied. Witness did so and then testified: "I didn't lie."

Plaintiff's Counsel thereafter re-offered Exhibit 37, claiming that it was admissible under Rule 612 to refresh Witness's recollection. Defense Counsel objected, and the Court sustained the objection.

Later, Plaintiff's Counsel called Contractor to testify. During direct examination, Plaintiff's Counsel asked Contractor, "Did Witness tell you that he had twelve years of construction experience during his job interview?" Defense Counsel objected that this was inadmissible character evidence, and the Court sustained the objection.

Did the Court err in:

1.   **Overruling Defense Counsel's objection to cross-examination about an alleged lie by Witness? Explain.**

2.   **Sustaining Defense Counsel's objection to the introduction of Exhibit 37 as inadmissible character evidence? Explain.**

3.   **Sustaining Defense Counsel's objection to the introduction of Exhibit 37 to refresh the recollection of Witness? Explain.**

4.   **Sustaining Defense Counsel's objection to Contractor's testimony? Explain.**

MBE SUBJECTS – RELEASED ESSAY QUESTIONS

EVIDENCE
MEE Question - February 2010

Driver was driving an automobile that struck Pedestrian in the crosswalk of a busy street. Pedestrian suffered painful fractures and a concussion that affected her memory of the accident.

Pedestrian filed a negligence action against Driver, who responded with a general denial and an assertion that Pedestrian's negligence caused her injuries. The parties have stipulated to the severity of Pedestrian's injuries, to Pedestrian's pain and suffering, and to the total value of Pedestrian's damages. The parties are scheduled for a jury trial on the issues of both Driver's and Pedestrian's negligence.

Pedestrian plans to call Witness to testify at trial. Witness did not see the collision occur. However, Witness will testify that he walked past Pedestrian no more than five seconds before the collision, at which time Witness saw that Pedestrian was deeply engrossed in a cell phone conversation. Witness will also testify that he saw Driver's distinctive sports car as it approached the intersection in which Pedestrian was hit. Witness, who has no specialized training, experience, or education, will also offer the opinion that the car was speeding just prior to the collision because it was traveling noticeably faster than the cars near it, all of which appeared to be traveling at the same slower speed.

Pedestrian plans to call her Spouse to testify that Pedestrian is very cautious and risk-averse.

Pedestrian also plans to testify at trial. She will not deny having been on the cell phone when Witness walked by, but will claim to have lowered the cell phone and looked for traffic just prior to entering the intersection. In fact, Pedestrian intends to testify that she has used a cell phone for many years, that she talks on it while walking almost every day, and that she invariably ends a call or lowers the cell phone when preparing to cross a street in order to look both ways before entering the intersection.

Driver intends to undermine Pedestrian's credibility by introducing evidence of her memory loss. Pedestrian counters that if the jury hears about some of Pedestrian's injuries, then it must hear about all of them, and so Pedestrian seeks to introduce evidence on the full nature and extent of her other injuries.

At the final pretrial motion hearing, Driver's counsel argued that the court should grant these four motions *in limine*:

(1)   to exclude Witness's opinion that Driver was speeding;

(2)   to exclude Spouse's testimony;

(3)   to exclude evidence of Pedestrian's cell phone use at any time other than the day of the collision;

(4)   to admit evidence of Pedestrian's memory loss, but to exclude evidence of Pedestrian's other injuries.

The evidence rules of this jurisdiction are identical to the Federal Rules of Evidence.

How should the court rule on each of these motions? Explain.

MBE SUBJECTS – RELEASED ESSAY QUESTIONS

EVIDENCE
MEE Question - February 2011

On May 5, at 2 p.m. in City Park, Victim was hit from behind and temporarily knocked unconscious. Upon regaining consciousness moments later, Victim discovered that his bag containing valuables had been stolen.

While investigating the crime later that day, Police Officer interviewed Witness. Witness told Police Officer that she had seen the robbery of Victim and had recognized Defendant, a resident of the neighborhood, as the perpetrator. Witness also told Police Officer that Defendant had a reputation in the neighborhood for violence, that everyone was afraid of him, and that she shouldn't be talking to the police at all. Nevertheless, Witness agreed to accompany Police Officer to police headquarters, where she looked at photographs of suspects and signed a written statement. The statement read, "I was walking in City Park on May 5, at 2 p.m., when I saw Defendant. I saw Defendant attack Victim and then run away with Victim's bag. I know Defendant from the neighborhood and recognized Defendant as suspect number 1 on the 12-person photograph display shown to me today by Police Officer."

Defendant was subsequently arrested and charged with robbery and assault.

At Defendant's trial, Prosecutor called Witness to the stand. In response to questions from Prosecutor, Witness testified that she had no memory of the incident. She stated that she did not remember seeing anyone in City Park at the time of the alleged robbery. When Prosecutor asked Witness whether her sudden memory loss was because she was afraid of Defendant, Witness said that she had never seen Defendant before in her life and was not afraid of him because she did not know him. When Witness was asked whether she had told Police Officer that Defendant had robbed Victim, Witness denied ever making that statement.

Immediately after this testimony, Prosecutor offered Witness's signed statement into evidence to impeach Witness's credibility and to prove that Defendant was in City Park and attacked Victim. An authenticated copy of Witness's statement was provided to Defense Counsel. Defense Counsel raised no constitutional challenges to Witness's identification of Defendant at police headquarters. However, Defense Counsel objected to Prosecutor questioning Witness about the statement and to admission of the copy of the statement. The judge sustained both objections.

After the prosecution had rested, Defense Counsel called Buddy to the stand. Buddy testified that he had never met Defendant. He also testified that some of his friends had recently met Defendant a few times, and that they think that Defendant is an honest and gentle person who would never hurt anyone. Prosecutor objected to this testimony. The judge sustained the objection and excluded Buddy's testimony.

The rules of evidence in this jurisdiction are identical to the Federal Rules of Evidence.

1.   **Should the judge have permitted Prosecutor to question Witness about Witness's written statement and admitted the copy of the statement to impeach Witness's**

credibility? Explain.

2.   Should the judge have admitted Witness's written statement to prove that Defendant was in City Park and attacked Victim? Explain.

3.   Should the judge have admitted Buddy's testimony to prove Defendant's character for honesty and gentleness? Explain.

MBE SUBJECTS – RELEASED ESSAY QUESTIONS

EVIDENCE
MEE Question - February 2012

Six months ago, a woman was taken to a hospital following what she alleged was a sexual assault by a man during a fraternity party. The woman and the man were both seniors attending the college where the party was held.

At the time of the alleged assault, the hospital's policy required that "in all cases of alleged or suspected sexual assault, non-emergency patients must be interviewed by a victim counselor before receiving medical treatment." The woman was deemed a non-emergency patient and was told to wait in the waiting room to see a victim counselor. Three hours later, the victim counselor finally interviewed the woman. Thereafter, hospital personnel treated the woman for her injuries and sent her home.

There was no contact between the woman and the man until one week later, when the man sent the woman a text message on her cell phone. The text message said, "If you are upset about what happened, I can send you a check for $10,000 to help you forget the whole thing. I can also pay any medical expenses." The woman did not respond.

Four months after the alleged assault, the woman contacted a lawyer and filed a civil action against the man and the hospital. She sought damages from the man for physical injuries resulting from the alleged assault. She also sought damages from the man for psychological injuries. According to the woman, these injuries were especially traumatic because of her belief in sexual abstinence before marriage and her lack of prior sexual experience. She sought damages from the hospital for exacerbating her injuries by negligently delaying her medical treatment.

The man filed an answer admitting that he had had sexual relations with the woman but asserting that they were consensual. In its answer, the hospital denied that its conduct had exacerbated the woman's injuries.

Immediately after filing its answer, the hospital contacted the woman and offered to settle the claim for $5,000. The woman refused the hospital's offer.

Five weeks after the woman filed her suit, the hospital changed its policy on dealing with sexual assault victims to provide that "in all cases of alleged or suspected sexual assault, immediate medical care will be provided to emergency and non-emergency patients."

The woman's suit against the man and the hospital is now set for trial. The following properly filed motions are before the court:

1.   **The hospital's motion to exclude evidence of its new policy providing immediate medical treatment to emergency and non-emergency patients in all cases of alleged or suspected sexual assault.**

2.   **The hospital's motion to exclude evidence of its offer to settle with the woman.**

3.   **The man's motion to exclude evidence of**

     (a) his offer to pay the woman $10,000.

(b) his offer to pay the woman's medical expenses.

4.   The man's motion to admit evidence that the woman had sexual relations with another student during her junior year.

The rules of evidence in this jurisdiction are identical to the Federal Rules of Evidence.

How should the court rule on each of these motions? Explain.

MBE SUBJECTS – RELEASED ESSAY QUESTIONS

EVIDENCE
MEE Question - February 2013

A woman who owns a motorized scooter brought her scooter to a mechanic for routine maintenance service. As part of the maintenance service, the mechanic inspected the braking system on the scooter. As soon as the mechanic finished inspecting and servicing the scooter, he sent the woman a text message to her cell phone that read, "Just finished your service. When you pick up your scooter, you need to schedule a follow-up brake repair. We'll order the parts."

The woman read the mechanic's text message and returned the next day to pick up her scooter. As the woman was wheeling her scooter out of the shop, she saw the mechanic working nearby and asked, "Is my scooter safe to ride for a while?" The mechanic responded by giving her a thumbs-up. The woman waved and rode away on the scooter.

One week later, while the woman was riding her scooter, a pedestrian stepped off the curb into a crosswalk and the woman collided with him, causing the pedestrian severe injuries. The woman had not had the scooter's brakes repaired before the accident.

The pedestrian has sued the woman for damages for his injuries resulting from the accident. The pedestrian has alleged that (1) the woman lost control of the scooter due to its defective brakes, (2) the woman knew that the brakes needed repair, and (3) it was negligent for the woman to ride the scooter knowing that its brakes needed to be repaired.

The woman claims that the brakes on the scooter worked perfectly and that the accident happened because the pedestrian stepped into the crosswalk without looking and the woman had no time to stop. The woman, the pedestrian, and the mechanic will testify at the upcoming trial.

The pedestrian has proffered an authenticated copy of the mechanic's text message to the woman.

The woman plans to testify that she asked the mechanic, "Is my scooter safe to ride for a while?" and that he gave her a thumbs-up in response.

The evidence rules in this jurisdiction are identical to the Federal Rules of Evidence.

Analyze whether each of these items of evidence is relevant and admissible at trial:

1.   **The authenticated copy of the mechanic's text message;**

2.   **The woman's testimony that she asked the mechanic, "Is my scooter safe to ride for a while?" and**

3.   **The woman's testimony describing the mechanic's thumbs-up.**

MBE SUBJECTS - RELEASED ESSAY QUESTIONS

EVIDENCE
MEE Question - July 2013

The city police department received a 911 call regarding a domestic violence incident. The caller said that she was staying with her sister and her sister's boyfriend. The caller said that she had called the police because her sister's boyfriend was becoming violent. The police department records all 911 calls. The relevant portions of the 911 recording are as follows:

> Caller: My sister's boyfriend is out of control right now. He just threw a broken beer bottle at my sister. It hit her on the arm. Now he's holding a chair like he's going to throw that at her, too.
> Police Dispatcher: Where is your sister?
> Caller: She's running toward the bathroom.
> Police Dispatcher: Is she injured?
> Caller: I see some blood on her arm.
> Police Dispatcher: Does he have a gun?
> Caller: I don't see a gun.

A nearby police officer arrived on the scene five minutes after the caller telephoned 911. The police officer found the boyfriend pacing in the front yard and ordered him to sit in the rear seat of the patrol car. The boyfriend sat in the patrol car, and the officer locked the door from the outside so that the boyfriend would stay in the car while the officer spoke to the sister.

When the sister saw that her boyfriend was locked in the patrol car, she came out on the porch to speak with the officer. The sister was in a highly agitated and emotional state, and she had several fresh cuts on her right arm. The officer asked her how she got the cuts. The sister replied, "My boyfriend threw a bottle at me which cut my arm." The sister declined the officer's offer of medical assistance but said that she wanted to press charges against her boyfriend. The sister was in tears throughout her conversation with the officer.

The boyfriend was charged in state court with battery and disorderly conduct. The prosecutor made every effort to secure the appearance of both the sister and the caller at trial, but when the trial began, the sister and the caller did not appear.

The prosecutor is attempting to convict the boyfriend without trial testimony from the sister or the caller. The prosecutor plans to introduce the caller's statements to the police dispatcher and to call the officer to testify and to repeat the statements the sister made to him at her house to prove that the boyfriend attacked the sister.

The 911 recording containing the caller's statements to the police dispatcher has been properly authenticated. Defense counsel has objected to the admission of (1) the caller's statements to the police dispatcher on the 911 recording and (2) the officer's testimony repeating the sister's statements to the officer (at her house). Defense counsel asserts the following:

a)   The caller's statements to the police dispatcher are inadmissible hearsay.

b) Admission of the caller's statements to the police dispatcher would violate the boyfriend's constitutional rights.

c) The officer's testimony repeating the sister's statements is inadmissible hearsay.

d) Admission of the officer's testimony repeating the sister's statements would violate the boyfriend's constitutional rights.

This jurisdiction has adopted rules of evidence identical to the Federal Rules of Evidence and interprets the provisions of the Bill of Rights in accordance with relevant United States Supreme Court precedent.

How should the trial court rule on each defense objection? Explain.

MBE SUBJECTS - RELEASED ESSAY QUESTIONS

EVIDENCE
MEE Question - July 2014

A prison inmate has filed a civil rights lawsuit against a guard at the prison, alleging that the guard violated the inmate's constitutional rights during an altercation. The inmate and the guard are the only witnesses to this altercation. They have provided contradictory reports about what occurred.

The trial will be before a jury. The inmate plans to testify at trial. The guard's counsel has moved for leave to impeach the inmate with the following:

> (a) Twelve years ago, the inmate was convicted of felony distribution of marijuana. He served a three-year prison sentence, which began immediately after he was convicted. He served his full sentence and was released from prison nine years ago.
> (b) Eight years ago, the inmate pleaded guilty to perjury, a misdemeanor punishable by up to one year in jail. He paid a $5,000 fine.
> (c) Seven years ago, the inmate was convicted of felony sexual assault of a child and is currently serving a 10-year prison sentence for the crime. The victim was the inmate's daughter, who was 13 years old at the time of the assault.

The inmate's counsel objects to the admission of any evidence related to these three convictions and to any cross-examination based on this evidence.

The guard also plans to testify at trial. The inmate's counsel has moved for leave to impeach the guard with the following:

> Last year, the guard applied for a promotion to prison supervisor. The guard submitted a résumé to the state that indicated that he had been awarded a B.A. in Criminal Justice from a local college. An official copy of the guard's academic transcript from that college indicates that the guard dropped out after his first semester and did not receive a degree.

The guard's counsel objects to the admission of this evidence and to any cross-examination based on this evidence.

The transcript and the résumé have been properly authenticated. The trial will be held in a jurisdiction that has adopted all of the Federal Rules of Evidence.

1.   **What evidence, if any, proffered by the guard to impeach the inmate should be admitted? Explain.**

2.   **What evidence, if any, proffered by the inmate to impeach the guard should be admitted? Explain.**

MBE SUBJECTS - RELEASED ESSAY QUESTIONS

EVIDENCE
MEE Question - February 2016

A victim had just walked out of a jewelry store carrying a package containing a diamond bracelet when someone grabbed him from behind, put a gun to his back, and demanded the package. The victim handed the package over his shoulder to the robber. The robber said, "Close your eyes and count to 20. I'll be watching, and if you mess up, I'll shoot you." The victim did as he was told, and when he opened his eyes, the robber was gone. The victim immediately called 911 on his cell phone.

The victim did not see the robber. A witness on the other side of the street saw the entire encounter. While the victim was speaking to the 911 operator, the witness ran over to the victim and shouted, "Are you all right? I saw it all!"

A police officer arrived five minutes later and took a statement from the witness, who was wringing her hands and pacing. The police officer asked the witness, "What did you see?" The witness responded, "The robber is about six feet tall. He has brownish hair, almost buzzed to the scalp. He was wearing jeans and a blue jacket." The police officer called in the description to the police station.

The defendant, who is over six feet tall and has buzzed brown hair, was picked up 30 minutes later. When the police officer stopped him, he was six blocks from the scene of the robbery. The defendant was wearing jeans and a blue jacket but did not have a gun or the bracelet in his possession. He was brought to the police station for questioning and was placed in a lineup.

The police officer brought the witness to the police station to view the lineup. The witness viewed the lineup and identified the defendant as the robber. The defendant was arrested and charged with robbery.

One week after the robbery, the witness moved overseas. One year later, at the time of the defendant's trial, the witness could not be found.

The victim and the police officer both testified at trial for the prosecution. The police officer testified as follows:

> Question: When you arrived at the scene of the robbery, did you obtain a description of the robber?

> Answer: Yes. The witness said that the robber was about six feet tall, with very short, brownish hair, almost buzzed to the scalp, and that he was wearing jeans and a blue jacket.

> Question: Did you gather any other evidence indicating that the defendant committed this robbery?

Answer: Yes. When I was walking into the police station with the victim, we overheard the defendant in an adjoining room. As soon as the victim heard the defendant's voice, the victim said, "That's the voice of the guy who robbed me."

Question: What do you know about the defendant?

Answer: He's a known drug dealer who had been hanging around in the area where the jewelry store is located for six months before the robbery, constantly causing trouble.

The trial was held in a jurisdiction that has rules identical to the Federal Rules of Evidence. Defense counsel made timely objections to the admission of the following evidence:

(a) The police officer's testimony recounting the witness's statement at the scene.

(b) The police officer's testimony recounting the victim's statement while walking into the police station.

(c) The police officer's testimony that the defendant is a "known drug dealer who had been hanging around in the area where the jewelry store is located for six months before the robbery, constantly causing trouble."

The trial judge overruled all of defense counsel's objections.

Was this evidence properly admitted? Explain.

MBE SUBJECTS - RELEASED ESSAY QUESTIONS

EVIDENCE
MEE Question - July 2016

A defendant was tried before a jury for a robbery that had occurred at Jo-Jo's Bar on November 30. At trial, the prosecutor called the police officer who had investigated the crime. Over defense counsel's objection, the officer testified as follows:

> Officer: I arrived at the defendant's home on the morning of December 1, the day after the robbery. He invited me inside, and I asked him, "Did you rob Jo-Jo's Bar last night?" The defendant immediately started crying. I decided to take him to the station. Before we left for the station, I read him Miranda warnings, and he said, "Get me a lawyer," so I stopped talking to him.

> Prosecutor: Did the defendant say anything to you at the station?

> Officer: I think he did, but I don't remember exactly what he said.

Immediately after this testimony, the prosecutor showed the officer a handwritten document. The officer identified the document as notes she had made on December 2 concerning her interaction with the defendant on December 1. The prosecutor provided a copy of the document to defense counsel. The document, which was dated December 2, stated in its entirety:

> The defendant burst into tears when asked if he had committed the robbery. He then received and invoked Miranda rights. I stopped the interrogation and didn't ask him any more questions, but as soon as we arrived at the station the defendant said, "I want to make a deal; I think I can help you." I reread Miranda warnings, and this time the defendant waived his rights and said, "I have some information that can really help you with this case." When I asked him how he could help, the defendant said, "Forget it—I want my lawyer." When the defendant's lawyer arrived 30 minutes later, the defendant was released.

The officer then testified as follows:

> Prosecutor: After reviewing your notes, do you remember the events of December 1?

> Officer: No, but I do remember making these notes the day after I spoke with the defendant. At that time, I remembered the conversation clearly, and I was careful to write it down accurately.

Over defense counsel's objection, the officer was permitted to read the document to the jury. The prosecutor also asked that the notes be received as an exhibit, and the court granted that request, again over defense counsel's objection. The testimony then continued:

Prosecutor: Did you speak to the defendant any time after December 1?

Officer: Following my discovery of additional evidence implicating the defendant in the robbery, I arrested him on December 20. Again, I read the defendant his Miranda rights. The defendant said that he would waive his Miranda rights. I then asked him if he was involved in the robbery of Jo-Jo's Bar, and he said, "I was there on November 30 and saw the robbery, but I had nothing to do with it."

Defense counsel objected to the admission of this testimony as well. The court overruled the objection.

The defendant's trial for robbery was held in a jurisdiction that has adopted all of the Federal Rules of Evidence.

Were the following decisions by the trial court proper?

1.   **Admitting the officer's testimony that the defendant started crying. Explain.**

2.   **Permitting the officer to read her handwritten notes to the jury. Explain.**

3.   **Admitting the officer's handwritten notes into evidence as an exhibit. Explain.**

4.   **Admitting the officer's testimony recounting the defendant's statement, "I have some information that can really help you with this case." Explain.**

5.   **Admitting the officer's testimony recounting the defendant's statement, "I was there on November 30 and saw the robbery, but I had nothing to do with it." Explain.**

MBE SUBJECTS - PRACTICE ESSAY QUESTIONS

EVIDENCE
Question 1

Defendant (D) teaches group computer classes for children aged 6 to 12 in the basement of his home. Following an investigation by local police, D was charged with committing acts of child molestation on a 6-year-old boy (V) who was enrolled in the computer class. D claims none of the alleged acts occurred.

During its case-in-chief, the prosecution plans to call V, who will testify about the alleged molestation. In addition, the prosecution will call the following witnesses:

(1) Witness #1, a psychologist employed by the police department, will testify based on her review of the videotape of V's police interview and on discussions she had with V's parents. Witness #1 will testify that although initially V claimed that nothing inappropriate happened to him, she believes that V suffers from "Child Sexual Abuse Accommodation Syndrome" (CSAAS). Witness #1 will testify that CSAAS is a disorder first recognized in 1983 that explains the seemingly inconsistent behavior of abuse victims. She will testify that children suffering from CSAAS deny the abuse occurred as a way of coping with adult disbelief and a tendency on the part of adults to blame the children for anything that might have occurred. She will also testify that this, in turn, causes the children to blame themselves, feel self-hatred, and to become alienated from friends and family.

(2) Witness #2, an adult, will testify that within the past year she met D in a bar, and agreed to leave with D. When she refused to have sex with him, D raped her.

In his defense, D plans to call the following witnesses:

(1) Witness #3 will testify that Ms. X, V's mother, told Witness #3 that Ms. X initiated the police investigation of D by falsely claiming that D had molested V. Ms. X died before the trial. Witness #3 will also testify that Ms. X was a former business associate of D who had severed her ties with D following a bitter business dispute.

(2) Witness #4, will testify that she has lived in the same community as D for many years and that she is familiar with D's reputation for sexual and social propriety. She will testify that D is known as the type of person who is very trustworthy with children.
(3) Witness #5, a friend of Witness #1 (the psychologist) will testify that Witness #1 recently told her that Witness #1 always believes the child's story, and even if the story is sometimes inaccurate, it is "better to be safe than sorry."

Analyze the evidentiary issues that will arise from the testimony of these witnesses when the case goes to trial. Assume the Federal Rules of Evidence apply.

MBE SUBJECTS - PRACTICE ESSAY QUESTIONS

EVIDENCE
Question 2

A credible, reliable informant tells police that Ruth Rogers was involved in a burglary that had occurred a couple of days earlier, in which valuable jewelry was stolen.

Officer Stevens located and transported Rogers to the stationhouse and placed her in an interrogation room. Counsel for Rogers and the State's Attorney stipulate that Rogers was in custody from this point on.

Officer Stevens then gave Rogers *Miranda* warnings. Upon hearing the warnings, Rogers said: "I think I want a public defender. I probably shouldn't talk to you at all. I think you're trying to get me in big trouble."

Officer Stevens said, "Well, you're asking me whether it's in your best interests to talk to me, and it's only right that I tell you what's what. The fact is, once we get you a lawyer I won't be able to help you. My hands will be tied. This is your last chance to let me help you."

Rogers then asked, "What do you mean? How can you help me? What do I need to do to get help?"

Officer Stevens replied, "If you want my help, you have to tell me you don't want to exercise your *Miranda* rights, and then explain your role in the burglary."

Rogers then stated that she understood her rights and wanted to waive them and talk to Officer Stevens. She proceeded to confess to the burglary. No electronic recording was made of any part of the conversation.

As part of her confession, Rogers informed the police that she had hidden the stolen jewelry in a dresser drawer in her bedroom. This information gave police probable cause to obtain a warrant to search Rogers' bedroom. They obtained the warrant, conducted the search, and found the jewelry. Rogers was charged with burglary.

Prior to trial, her attorney filed a motion to suppress her confession, and also to suppress the jewelry. Rogers stipulates that she had no sixth amendment right to counsel at any relevant time, so this issue should not be addressed.

Analyze and discuss all other arguments for suppression of Rogers' confession and the jewelry. Offer your opinions as to the likelihood of the success of the suppression motions.

MBE SUBJECTS - PRACTICE ESSAY QUESTIONS

EVIDENCE
Question 3

Fred was engaged and planned to be married to Betty on Saturday, May 15. On May 12, Fred went to Acme Motors and ordered an expensive car -- a Jaguar sports coupe -- for delivery on May 15, his wedding day. On May 13, two days before the planned wedding, Fred died of an aneurysm. Fred's will left his entire estate to his brother Tony, who was also his executor. The Jaguar was delivered to Tony. Betty filed suit against the estate to recover the Jaguar. The case was tried to a jury and during trial, the following events took place.

1. Betty's attorney called Salesperson who sold the Jaguar to Fred. Salesperson stated that he spoke with Fred on May 12 in Acme Motors' office and that no other person was in the room at the time. When Betty's attorney asked Salesperson to tell the jury what Fred said to him, defense counsel objected. The objection was sustained. If permitted to answer, Salesperson would have stated that Fred told him he was buying the car as a wedding present for Betty.

Analyze and discuss what objection(s) defense counsel should have made and whether it was error to sustain the objection(s).

2. When Betty took the stand, her attorney asked if Fred had sent her any communication relative to the Jaguar. Betty produced a paper copy of an e-mail about the Jaguar that she had received from Fred on May 11. Defense counsel objected and the objection was sustained. Betty would have stated that she replied to Fred's e-mail using the e-mail address on the original message and that the paper was an accurate copy of the original e-mail which she had received, but that she had erased the e-mail message itself as soon as she had printed it out. The text of the e-mail reads as follows:

Subject: Re Our Wedding Day
Date: May 11, 2001 10:32:12 EDT
From: Fred@ISP.com
To: Betty@Net.com

"My darling, I am going to buy you a super wedding gift – a new Jag."

Analyze and discuss what objection(s) defense counsel should have made and whether it was error to sustain the objection(s).

3. Defense counsel cross-examined Betty. Over plaintiff counsel's objections, defense counsel asked Betty if she had been convicted on January 10, 1989, in the U.S. District Court for the District of Minnesota on a plea of *nolo contendere* to 10 counts of wire fraud for which she received a five-year suspended sentence on promise of restitution, and 200 hours of community service. Betty answered, "yes." The court made no specific findings of fact before allowing this cross-examination.

Analyze and discuss what objection(s) plaintiff's counsel should have made and whether the court erred in overruling the objection(s).

MBE SUBJECTS - PRACTICE ESSAY QUESTIONS

EVIDENCE
Question 4

United States Border Patrol Agent (Agent) came across a van on a deserted desert road. Inside the van were 10 men, all of whom were suffering from exhaustion and the effects of the heat. None of the men spoke English. At the scene, Agent interviewed the men using an interpreter (Interpreter). Agent would ask a question, Interpreter would translate for the men, and then Interpreter would translate the men's answers into English.

Interpreter told Agent that nine of the men gave the following account:

   o   they paid a women named Mary to smuggle them into the country;
   o   they were in a van and the van broke down in the location where Agent found it;
   o   Mary left them in the van, saying she was going to get help;
   o   Mary never returned.

The 10th man, Victor, appeared to be in a great deal of pain and had difficulty speaking. According to Interpreter, Victor gave the same account as the nine men except that Victor said the smuggler was a man named Douglas. That same day, Agent located Douglas in a makeshift tent two miles from the van. The government obtained an indictment against Douglas for alien smuggling for profit, a federal crime. Douglas denies the charge and claims the following:

   o   that he was among the men who had paid Mary to smuggle them into the country;
   o   that when Mary did not return after a day, he left the van to try to get help;
   o   that he became too weak to go on and camped out waiting for help.

The government deported the nine men found in the van before Douglas or his attorney were able to interview them. They can no longer be found. At trial, the government plans to call Agent to testify about his observations at the scene as well as his arrest of Douglas. Agent will also testify that Victor named Douglas as the smuggler.
Douglas plans to testify as follows:

   o   that Mary was the smuggler;
   o   that the van broke down and Mary left after saying she would get help;
   o   that when Mary did not return after a day, Douglas left to try to get help;
   o   that he became too weak after walking a couple of miles and made a crude camp, hoping to be rescued.

Douglas also plans to call Interpreter to recount the fact that nine of the 10 men named Mary as the smuggler. Finally, Douglas will offer into evidence the notes made by Agent concerning his interviews with the 10 men.

Fully analyze and discuss the evidentiary issues that will arise from these facts when the case goes to trial.

MBE SUBJECTS - PRACTICE ESSAY QUESTIONS

EVIDENCE
Question 5

Over a period of several days, five (5) people in River City reported to police that their wallets or purses had been stolen while they were walking along River City's busiest shopping street. Each of the victims described the incidents to the police as occurring like this: while walking along the busy sidewalk, a person in front of them suddenly stopped; then someone bumped them slightly from behind. Moments later each discovered that his/her wallet or purse was gone.

After a brief investigation, police arrested Defendant #1 (D1), a young male, and Defendant #2 (D2), a young female, and charged each with robbery in connection with all five (5) incidents.

During its case-in-chief, the prosecution plans to call all five (5) victims, who will testify to the facts stated above. In addition, the prosecution plans to call the following witnesses:

(1) Witness #1, the investigating police officer, will testify that when she asked the victims to describe the person who suddenly stopped in front of them, all of the victims identified the person as a young male.

(2) Witness #2, a police officer who has spent ten (10) years in River City's fraud unit, will be presented with a hypothetical question containing the basic facts testified to by the victims. After listening to the hypothetical question, Witness #2 will testify that in her opinion, the events were characteristic of a two-person scam called the "bump and go" often used by street thieves that involves distracting the victim so that the victim does not realize that his/her belongings are being stolen.

The prosecution also plans to present evidence that six (6) months earlier, D1 and D2 conducted several "bump and go" robberies on another shopping street in River City.

Defendants intend to call several witnesses, including the following:

(1) Witness #3 will testify that she was with D1 and D2 in Mountain View, another city, during the entire period in which the charged crimes occurred. On cross-examination, the prosecutor plans to ask Witness #3 the following question: "Is it not a fact that you, D1, and D2 are all members of the same church?" In addition, the prosecutor plans to ask Witness #3 if, shortly after D1 and D2 were arrested, she told the police that she had been in River City, along with D1 and D2, during the days on which the crimes were committed.

(2) Witness #4 will testify that she works in a restaurant in Mountain View, and that she saw D1 and D2 in the restaurant many times during the days on which the crimes were committed. On cross-examination, the prosecutor plans to introduce evidence that two (2) years prior to this trial, Witness #4 was convicted of a felony hit-and-run driving offense.

You are the law clerk to the judge before whom the trial is scheduled. The judge has asked you to prepare a memorandum of law detailing how all the evidentiary issues presented by these facts are likely to be raised at trial. Analyze how the court should resolve these issues. Assume that the Federal Rules of Evidence apply.

MBE SUBJECTS - PRACTICE ESSAY QUESTIONS

EVIDENCE
Question 6

Taxpayer Dobbs, a certified public accountant, is charged with federal tax evasion by failing to report $100,000 in income for 1999. The matter will go to trial soon. The prosecution will offer the following evidence:

1.) Dobbs' 1999 Federal Individual Income Tax Return (Exhibit 1) which shows that he reported $200,000 in income for 1999. All of this income appears on his W-2 as income from his position as an in-house accountant to a local company.

2.) Three witnesses will be called to prove the unreported income.

- Tom Tubman will testify that in March 1999, he spoke with Dobbs and asked if he (Dobbs) would help prepare Tubman's 1998 tax return which was due the following month. Tubman's regular accountant had insisted Tubman disclose earned gratuities (tips) and Tubman did not want to do so. Taxpayer Dobbs, according to Tubman, said he would complete the return, excluding the gratuities, but at extra cost. The total fee, he said, would be $10,000. Tubman agreed. Taxpayer Dobbs then prepared the return and Tubman filed it. Tubman then gave Taxpayer Dobbs a check for $10,000 drawn on Tubman's account, dated April 20, 1999, and payable to Taxpayer Dobbs (Exhibit 2).

- Kerri Kurner will testify that in April 1999, she paid Taxpayer Dobbs in cash for his assistance in preparing her tax return. Kurner does not remember the exact amount of the payment. But Kurner's diary (Exhibit 3) shows she wrote an entry every evening describing the events of the day, including an entry on April 10, 1999, stating that she paid Dobbs $8,500.

- Mr. Dobbs' wife, from whom he has been separated since January 1, 2001, is willing to testify for the prosecution. Mrs. Dobbs will testify that some time in the late fall of 1999, as they were planning a vacation, Dobbs told her that his side business netted about $100,000 in 1999.

Assume you are a law clerk for the federal judge before whom the matter will be tried. The judge has asked you to review the facts as described above and advise her of all possible evidentiary issues which may arise at trial. Advise how she should resolve these evidentiary issues and why.

MBE SUBJECTS - PRACTICE ESSAY QUESTIONS

EVIDENCE
Question 7

Defendant is charged with robbing a bank in River City. The robbery was committed by several persons. During the course of the robbery, one of the participants shot the bank Security Guard who died a few days later. Defendant claims to have had nothing to do with the robbery or the shooting.

During its case-in-chief, the prosecution plans to call several witnesses including Teller, who was present at the time of the robbery, who will testify that Defendant took part in the robbery.

In addition, the prosecution plans to call the following witnesses:

- Imogene, who was granted immunity in exchange for testifying, will testify that a week before the robbery, a man she knew named Xavier asked her for her advice in planning a bank robbery. Xavier told Imogene that a third person was needed to carry out the robbery and that Defendant had already agreed to take part.
- Police Officer will testify that the day after the robbery, he showed a series of photographs to Security Guard who had been shot in the robbery, and that the Security Guard identified a photo of Defendant as one of the robbers.

Defendant intends to call several witnesses, including the following:

- Bank Customer who will testify that she was in the bank making a withdrawal, that she looked at all the robbers, and that none of them looked like Defendant.

Assume the prosecution intends to ask Bank Customer on cross-examination, whether she was in fact making a deposit, not a withdrawal, when the robbery took place.

If Bank Customer does not admit to this fact, the prosecutor plans to show her the bank's original transaction record. The record shows a deposit, not a withdrawal.

The prosecution also plans to ask Bank Customer if it isn't true that she testified before the grand jury that one of the robbers "looked a little bit" like Defendant.

- Defendant will also call Bank Customer's Friend, who will testify that she has known Bank Customer for many years and that in her opinion, Bank Customer is an honest person.

Analyze the legal issues that will arise from the testimony of these witnesses at trial.

MEE RELEASED ESSAY QUESTIONS

FAMILY LAW
July 2002

Ann and Bert, a married couple, were unable to have biological children because Bert was infertile. They decided to try artificial insemination by an anonymous donor. Their doctor performed the procedure after obtaining written consent *from* both Ann and Bert. As a result of the artificial insemination, Ann became pregnant.

During the last months of Ann's pregnancy, she and Bert argued constantly, and Ann moved *out* of the family home into her *own* apartment. The baby, Daughter, was born while Ann and Bert were living apart. Bert visited Ann and Daughter in the hospital and paid their medical expenses. He tried to convince Ann to reconcile with him, but Ann refused, leaving the hospital with Daughter and returning to her apartment. Bert continued to visit them and contributed to Daughter's support.

Shortly after Daughter's birth, Ann began an affair with Walt. Walt also spent some time with Daughter and grew fond of her. When Daughter was *one* year old, Ann discovered she was pregnant by Walt. When Walt learned Ann was pregnant, he became very upset and began to abuse Ann verbally and physically. Ann immediately broke off the relationship with Walt. Shortly thereafter, she reconciled with Bert.

Ann, Bert, and Daughter were living together when Ann's baby, Sonny, was born. Walt, Sonny's biological father, contacted Ann, apologized *for* his past abusive behavior, and requested to see Sonny. He also offered to pay the expenses of Sonny's birth and to contribute to Sonny's support. Ann rejected both his request and his offer.

When Sonny was six months old and Daughter was two years old, Ann was killed in an automobile accident. She left a valid will stating that if she died while her children were minors, she wanted Bert to be named custodian and guardian of both of them.

Walt has sued Bert, seeking to establish himself as Sonny's legal father and requesting custody of both children. Bert claims that he is the legal father of both Daughter and Sonny and wants to maintain physical custody of both children. Under the law of the jurisdiction, both parties have standing to raise these issues.

How should the court rule on Walt's and Bert's claims? Explain.

MEE RELEASED ESSAY QUESTIONS

FAMILY LAW
February 2003

Husband and Wife married in State X in 1992 and resided there for the following 10 years. They have three children, ages 5, 7, and 9.

In early February 2002, Husband told Wife that he wanted a divorce and was moving to State Z for a new job. He asked Wife to let him take the children. Wife refused. The next day, Husband moved to State Z without the children.

In March 2002, six weeks after arriving in State Z (the minimum period of residence for divorce in State Z), Husband filed an action for divorce. In this action, he also sought primary custody of the three children, asserting that Wife had been violent and abusive toward him throughout their marriage.

Wife was served with the summons and complaint in Husband's action at the family home in State X. Wife, who has never been to State Z, did not answer or appear in Husband's divorce proceeding.

In July 2002, the State Z court granted Husband a default judgment granting Husband a divorce, dividing their property, awarding him primary custody of the three children, and giving Wife "reasonable visitation." Husband served Wife with the judgment.

In August 2002, Wife allowed the children to go to State Z for a two-week visit with Husband, whom they had not seen for nearly five months. This was the children's first time in State Z. At the end of the two-week period, Husband notified Wife that he would not return the children to Wife.

Wife immediately filed an action in State X for divorce, property division, and custody.

Husband appeared in Wife's State X action and contested her claims. He sought enforcement of the State Z judgment awarding him custody. He also argued that Wife's other claims were precluded by Husband's State Z judgment of divorce.

1. **Is the State X court required to enforce the State Z custody decree? Explain.**

2. **Are Wife's claims for divorce and property division precluded by Husband's State Z judgment? Explain.**

MEE RELEASED ESSAY QUESTIONS

FAMILY LAW
July 2003

On July 1, 1990, Ann and Burt got married in State X, where they have lived all their lives. At the time of their marriage, Ann and Burt were each 22 years old. Burt had graduated from high school and had been working for one year as a data entry technician, earning $30,000 annually. Ann had graduated from high school and had worked since graduation as a grocery store cashier, earning $27,000 annually. Ann had a trust fund that she acquired when she was 18 years old. The trust fund was worth $200,000, and Burt knew all about it. Neither had any other property or debts. Ann knew that Burt planned to become a lawyer, and Burt knew that Ann intended to be a homemaker.

Three months prior to the marriage, Burt told Ann that he would not marry her unless they signed a premarital agreement. Ann was surprised because Burt had never told her this was a precondition to their marriage. She reluctantly agreed, and they immediately went to the office of Burt's lawyer, Lawyer. Lawyer showed Ann and Burt a draft agreement under which both Ann and Burt would waive all rights to separate and marital property titled solely in the other's name if they divorced. They would also waive any right to claim child support if they divorced. Lawyer told Ann that by signing the agreement she would be waiving her rights to marital property and child support. Lawyer also told Ann that he represented only Burt, and not her, and that she should retain her own lawyer. Ann decided not to retain her own lawyer because she trusted Burt. Ann read the agreement the next day and expressed no reservations about signing it. Ann and Burt then both signed the agreement.

After the marriage, Burt became a very successful lawyer. Ann became a homemaker and had no out-of-home employment. The value of the property acquired from Burt's earnings during the marriage is $900,000. The value of Ann's trust fund, managed at all times by her father, is now over $800,000. Ann and Burt have two children, currently ages seven and ten. Ann now sues Burt for divorce in State X. Ann and Burt agree that Ann will have custody of the children. However, the parties cannot agree on the division of property.

Ann seeks property division and child support under the marital dissolution statute. Burt argues that (a) the court should enforce the premarital agreement, and (b) if the court invalidates the premarital agreement, that Ann's trust fund is marital property subject to distribution.
Ann concedes that the premarital agreement was and is substantively fair. Nonetheless, she argues that it is unenforceable (a) because she lacked legal counsel, and (b) because it addresses property distribution and child support upon divorce. She also argues that (c) regardless of the premarital agreement's validity, her trust fund is not subject to division.

1.   **How should the court rule on Ann's and Burt's arguments regarding the premarital agreement? Explain.**

2.   **How should the court rule on Ann's and Burt's arguments regarding the trust fund? Explain.**

MEE RELEASED ESSAY QUESTIONS

FAMILY LAW
February 2004

NOTE: Applicants answering this question in a community property state should use community property principles. For this purpose, the phrase "marital property" means community property.

Harold is the CEO and sole owner of a real estate business that he began about 25 years ago, shortly after he married Wendy. Wendy quit her job when they married and has ever since been a full-time homemaker. Last year, Harold became romantically involved with Carol, an employee of his real estate business. Wendy recently discovered this affair and also learned that Harold had bought expensive gifts for Carol, including a house purchased in Carol's name. Wendy sued Harold for divorce, based on his adultery with Carol.

Wendy would agree that she has never been a good housekeeper. The house was often dirty until the weekly visit by a cleaning company. Meals were often brought in from local restaurants. Wendy spent much of her time tending to the couple's two children, who are now adults, although a live-in nanny helped her until both children entered school. At Harold's request, Wendy occasionally entertained Harold's clients.

Harold has sole title to the real estate business and a private vested pension to which he has contributed since beginning his real estate business. Harold and Wendy have joint title to their family home and a bank account. These assets were acquired with funds Harold earned during the marriage. Wendy has sole title to 1,000 shares of stock she inherited shortly after she married Harold.

1. **Are the real estate business, Harold's pension, the jointly titled family home, the joint bank account, and the stock subject to division at divorce? Explain.**

2. **What effect, if any, would Harold's affair with Carol and his gifts to her have on any property division? Explain.**

3. **What arguments regarding property division are available to Harold and Wendy based on Wendy's role as a mother and homemaker? Explain.**

MEE RELEASED ESSAY QUESTIONS

FAMILY LAW
July 2004

Husband and Wife were married for 12 years. The couple had one child, Boy, age 7. Husband and Wife were both devoted parents.

Wife filed for divorce shortly after she learned that Husband and Secretary were having an affair. In the divorce action, Husband and Wife each sought sole custody of Boy.

The court appointed a child custody evaluator. Both parents told the evaluator they were not willing or able to share custody. Boy told the evaluator that he was very upset because his parents were getting a divorce and that he wanted to live with his father. Based upon the child custody evaluator's recommendation, the court awarded Husband sole custody of Boy and gave Wife liberal visitation rights. Neither party appealed this decree. Husband's and Wife's relationship has remained bitter and hostile.

Three months after the custody decree was filed, Secretary moved into Husband's house. Immediately thereafter, Wife filed a petition seeking to modify the custody decree and obtain sole custody of Boy.

At a hearing on Wife's petition, Boy testified, "I miss my mom and I am sad that my parents are divorced." Husband testified that there had been no change in Boy's behavior since Secretary moved into his home and that Boy got along well with Secretary. Wife testified that Boy should not be exposed to his father's nonmarital cohabitation. There was no other testimony. Neither Husband nor Wife sought joint custody.

The court modified the custody decree and awarded Husband and Wife joint custody. Under the modified decree, Boy will reside with each parent for alternating two-week periods and the parents will share decision-making responsibilities. The court held that "this arrangement will give Boy the best of both parents and allow each parent to counteract any negative influence on Boy by the other parent."

Husband appeals the court's determination.

1.   Did the court err in modifying the custody decree? Explain.

2.   Did the court err in awarding joint custody? Explain.

MEE RELEASED ESSAY QUESTIONS

FAMILY LAW
February 2005

Harold and Wendy were divorced in State A and awarded joint custody of their two children, John, age 5, and Amanda, age 3. Under the terms of the divorce decree, both parents were to share in decisions concerning the care, education, religion, medical treatment, and general welfare of the children, but Wendy was awarded primary physical custody, which, in this case, meant that the children would live with her except during alternate weekends and the month of July. Harold was also ordered to pay monthly child support in the amount of $500 per child until each child reached the age of 18.

Two years after the divorce, Wendy was offered a job in State B that would double her salary but necessitate a move to an area of State B located about 100 miles from Harold's home in State A. When Wendy told Harold of her desire to accept the job offer and move to State B, he objected that such a move would prevent him from exercising his visitation rights.

Harold petitioned the State A court to issue an order prohibiting Wendy from relocating with the children. The court found that Wendy's decision to move was motivated by a desire to improve her family's standard of living. It denied Harold's petition. Wendy then moved with the children to State B, where she began her new job, set up a new residence, and registered the child support order.

After Wendy and the children moved to State B, Harold stopped making child support payments. In response, Wendy sought enforcement of the State A support order in a State B court. Wendy also petitioned the State B court to extend Harold's obligation to pay child support until the children reach age 21, as authorized under the law of State B. Under the law of State A, there is no obligation to pay child support for children over the age of 18. She further petitioned the court to modify the State A custody order by eliminating the joint decision-making provision. Harold was personally served when he came to State B to take the children on vacation.

In response to Wendy's petition, Harold claimed that the State B court did not have jurisdiction to enforce or modify any of the State A orders.

1. **Was the State A court's decision to allow Wendy to relocate with the children to State B correct? Explain.**

2. **May the State B court enforce the State A child support order? Explain.**

3. **May the State B court modify the State A child support order by extending the support obligation to age 21? Explain.**

4. **May the State B court modify the State A custody decree by eliminating the joint decision-making provision? Explain.**

MEE RELEASED ESSAY QUESTIONS

FAMILY LAW
July 2005

Husband and Wife married and lived together in State X. While married to Husband, Wife had an affair with Fred and gave birth to Fred's child, Child. Both Husband and Fred knew that Fred was Child's biological father.

After Child's birth, Husband and Wife separated. Wife and Child immediately moved in with Fred and stayed with him for three months. During those three months, Fred supported Wife and Child and told friends and neighbors that Child was his son.

At the end of this three-month period, Wife reconciled with Husband. She and Child left Fred's home and resumed living with Husband. Husband held Child out as his son and supported Child. Although Fred no longer supported Child, he communicated with Child approximately twice a year.

When Child was four years old, Fred filed a petition claiming paternity of Child under the law of State X. State X law provides that "a proceeding brought by an individual, other than the child, to adjudicate the parentage of a child having a presumed father must be commenced not later than two years after the birth of the child." The court dismissed Fred's petition, holding that the two-year statute of limitations barred his action.

Shortly after Fred's paternity claim was dismissed, Husband, Wife, and Child moved to another city in State X, and Fred could not locate them.

Two years later, Wife sued Husband for divorce. In her divorce action, she sought custody of Child and child support. Husband objected to Wife's child support claim on the ground that Fred, Child's biological father, should be required to pay support instead of Husband. A State X court awarded Wife custody of Child and ordered Husband to pay child support.

Shortly after the divorce was final, Fred located Wife and Child. Fred filed a visitation petition under a State X statute permitting "any person to petition for visitation at any time" and authorizing a court to grant visitation whenever "visitation serves the best interests of the child." The trial court granted Fred's petition over Wife's objection, holding, as a matter of law, that "it is always in a child's best interests to know his or her biological parents, regardless of the custodial parent's views about the child's needs."

1. **Did the court violate Fred's substantive due process rights under the U.S. Constitution by dismissing his paternity petition? Explain.**

2. **Did the court properly order Husband to pay child support? Explain.**

3. **Did the court violate Wife's substantive due process rights under the U.S. Constitution by granting Fred visitation? Explain.**

MEE RELEASED ESSAY QUESTIONS

FAMILY LAW
February 2006

Herb petitioned for divorce from Ann after a 20-year marriage. One year later, the court entered a decree of divorce based on irreconcilable differences. The court also awarded Ann a share of the marital property and $1,000 per month in spousal maintenance until her death or remarriage.

After Herb's petition was filed but before the court issued a final decree, Herb married Betty. Betty believed that Herb's divorce was final. After the court issued a final decree, Ann married Charles. Herb then stopped paying spousal maintenance to Ann.

After her marriage to Charles, Ann learned that Charles had misrepresented the value of his stock. Charles said that he owned stock worth "millions." In fact, Charles's stock was worth only $300,000. Ann has filed for annulment of her marriage to Charles. In a separate action, she seeks reinstatement of the spousal maintenance she was awarded in her divorce from Herb.

Betty has petitioned for divorce from Herb. Herb has filed a motion to dismiss the divorce petition on the ground that he and Betty were not lawfully married.

1.   **If Ann is granted an annulment of her marriage to Charles, can she obtain reinstatement of the spousal maintenance she was awarded in her divorce from Herb? Explain.**

2.   **Can Ann obtain an annulment of her marriage to Charles based on Charles's misrepresentation of his assets? Explain.**

3.   **Can Herb obtain dismissal of Betty's divorce petition based on the claim that he and Betty were not lawfully married? Explain.**

MEE RELEASED ESSAY QUESTIONS

FAMILY LAW
July 2006

Ten years ago, Matt Smith, a musician, and Wendy Jones, a business executive, began living together in State A. One year later, they invited fifty friends and relatives to a "ceremony of commitment" at which they publicly vowed to "treat each other as an equal owner of all worldly goods acquired during our life together" and to "forsake all others" until "death do us part." Matt and Wendy did not obtain a marriage license. After the ceremony, Matt and Wendy consistently referred to each other as "my companion." They also opened a joint bank account and rented a house as "Wendy Jones and Matt Smith."

Five years ago, Matt and Wendy moved to State B, where Wendy gave birth to Child. Matt and Wendy thereafter shared child-care responsibilities and spent relatively equal amounts of time with Child.

One year ago, Wendy left Matt and married Steve in State B. After the wedding, Wendy and Child moved to Steve's home, and Wendy began to work part time.

Since her marriage to Steve, Wendy has allowed Matt to visit Child infrequently and only at her home. Matt has tried to give Wendy money for Child's support, but Wendy has refused to take it.

Matt has filed a petition in State B seeking to establish his paternity and obtain joint custody of Child. In a separate State B action, Matt seeks a share of Wendy's property acquired during the time they lived together. Wendy and Steve have filed an adoption petition seeking Child's adoption by Steve. Matt opposes this petition. All of these actions have been consolidated for trial.

Pretrial discovery has established that Matt is Child's biological parent, that Wendy has assets worth $300,000, all obtained from income earned while she lived with Matt, and that Matt has assets worth $1,500. Matt and Wendy each currently earn about $30,000 per year.

A common law marriage can be contracted in State A but not in State B.

1.   **May the State B court award Matt a share of Wendy's property? Explain.**

2.   **May the State B court grant Steve's adoption petition over Matt's opposition? Explain.**

MEE RELEASED ESSAY QUESTIONS

FAMILY LAW
February 2007

Twelve years ago, Husband and Wife married in State A. Their marriage appeared to be happy and stable. However, one year ago, without warning, Husband left Wife and moved to State B, 500 miles away. Husband obtained a new job in State B and rented an apartment there. He has told Wife that he never intends to return to State A.

Last week, Wife was personally served in State A with a copy of Husband's State B divorce petition. The petition requests the State B court to grant a divorce on grounds of a six-month separation and irreconcilable differences. The petition also requests the State B court to award Husband the following assets, all of which are titled solely in Husband's name:

1.   The marital home in State A, which Husband purchased five years before the marriage. During the marriage, Husband made mortgage payments on the home with his employment income.

2.   Stock, which Husband inherited from his grandmother during the marriage.

3.   Bonds, which Husband purchased with his employment income during the marriage.

All of these assets appreciated significantly in value during the marriage. Wife has no assets titled in her name alone or held jointly with Husband.

Wife is determined to fight this divorce. She has never visited State B, knows no one there, and does not believe she should have to defend a divorce action there. At the same time, she wishes to save her marriage. She has called Husband several times urging him to return to State A and enter marriage counseling, but he has refused. Wife is convinced that Husband is going through a "mid-life crisis" and would "return to his senses" with proper counseling and support. She believes she can get him that support and counseling if he returns to State A. Finally, if there must be a divorce, Wife believes that she should receive a share of the assets owned by Husband.

1.   **Does the State B court have jurisdiction to grant Husband a divorce and award Husband property acquired during the marriage? Explain.**

2.   **Can Wife prevent Husband from obtaining a divorce on the grounds that she does not consent to the divorce and that the marriage might yet be saved? Explain.**

3.   **Without regard to any jurisdictional issues, would Wife, in the event of a divorce, be entitled to a share of any of Husband's assets? Explain.**

MEE RELEASED ESSAY QUESTIONS

FAMILY LAW
July 2007

Husband and Wife married eleven years ago when both were age 19 and college students. Husband planned to go to medical school and Wife planned to become an accountant. They decided that Wife would defer her educational plans in order to provide support while Husband completed his medical studies. Accordingly, Wife dropped out of college, took a job as a file clerk, and did all of the household chores in order to allow Husband more time to study. This arrangement continued while Husband completed his remaining three years of college, four years of medical school, and a three-year medical residency. Wife expended all of her earnings to support Husband and herself. Husband made minimal financial contributions to the marriage. Throughout the marriage, Husband was verbally abusive to Wife and occasionally hit her. Husband was always contrite after these incidents and attributed his behavior to stress resulting from his studies. Three months before Husband completed his medical residency, he and Wife had an argument. During the argument, Husband assaulted Wife and broke her arm. Wife left Husband and filed a petition for divorce.

Husband suggested to Wife that they meet with a divorce mediator, Mediator. Wife agreed to this proposal. Husband and Wife both gave Mediator information about their assets and incomes. Husband indicated that his post-residency salary would be $150,000 per year, listed no assets, and listed school debts totaling $50,000. Wife indicated that her salary was $30,000 per year and listed no assets. Wife also indicated that she intended to return to college in the fall and that her income would then decline.

Last month, Husband and Wife met with Mediator. Mediator did not explain anything about the mediation process or divorce law, nor did she inform Husband and Wife that they could obtain independent legal advice about any agreement reached through mediation. Instead, Mediator asked Husband for a settlement proposal. Husband proposed that each spouse keep his or her personal property and that Husband bear responsibility for his educational loans. Mediator responded, "That sounds like a fair settlement. I'll prepare the paperwork unless Wife objects." Within the view of Mediator and Wife, Husband tightened his fist and gave Wife a menacing look. Wife said, "I have no objection."

After signing the agreement prepared by Mediator, Wife learned that Mediator was an attorney who had represented Husband's family for many years and that Husband had talked to Mediator about the settlement shortly before their meeting. No divorce judgment has yet been entered.

Wife has petitioned the trial court to set aside the settlement agreement she and Husband had signed and to award her spousal maintenance of $25,000 per year for three years.

1. **On what grounds, if any, could the court set aside the settlement agreement? Explain.**

2. **If the settlement agreement is set aside, is Wife entitled to spousal maintenance? Explain.**

MEE RELEASED ESSAY QUESTIONS

FAMILY LAW
February 2008

Husband and Wife married 10 years ago. Shortly thereafter, Husband adopted Wife's two children, Amy, age 6, and Bert, age 9. Neither Amy nor Bert has ever had a relationship with their biological father.

One year ago, Husband and Wife were divorced. The divorce decree provided that:

(1)   Husband shall pay Wife $1,000 per month in child support for Amy until Amy is 18 years old;

(2)   Husband shall pay child support in the form of college tuition up to $20,000 per year for both Amy and Bert.

Three months ago, Husband stopped making support payments for Amy and college tuition payments for Bert. Husband stopped paying for two reasons:

First, Husband was disinclined to continue supporting Amy and Bert, now ages 16 and 19, respectively. Since the divorce, Husband has quarreled frequently with both children. Bert also disobeyed Husband and joined a rock band that plays at a local bar four nights per week. Since joining the band, Bert's college grades slipped from A's to C's, and he was arrested for driving while intoxicated. Bert has refused Husband's requests that he leave the band and devote more time to study.

Second, Husband, who formerly worked 40 to 60 hours per week, is now working only 10 to 20 hours per week so that he can finish writing a novel. Husband has worked on the novel sporadically over the past few years, but has not had time to complete it. Husband's current income is only 25% of what it was when he was employed full time.

Wife, who works full time at the job she has held since her marriage to Husband, has neither reduced nor increased her income since the divorce. Since Husband stopped paying support, she has been borrowing money to meet the family's expenses.

Wife recently filed a petition to obtain a judgment against Husband for the child-support arrears and Bert's tuition. Husband responded with a petition seeking:

(1)   a dissolution of his adoption of Amy and Bert on the basis of irreconcilable differences;

(2)   downward modification of all of his support obligations, on account of his reduced income, retroactive to the date on which Husband stopped making support and tuition payments; and

(3)   a declaration that Husband need not pay Bert's college tuition so long as Bert continues to perform in a rock band.

The age of majority in the state is 18. The trial court entered judgment in favor of Wife and denied Husband's petition in all respects.

Did the trial court err? Explain.

MEE RELEASED ESSAY QUESTIONS

FAMILY LAW
July 2008

Six years ago, Hal and Wendy were married in State A. Both of them had been previously divorced. Hal, age 40, was a successful businessman earning $200,000 per year. Wendy, age 30, was a struggling songwriter earning $20,000 per year.

Two weeks before their wedding, Hal told Wendy that his lawyer (Lawyer) had advised him not to marry Wendy unless she signed a premarital agreement. Hal gave Wendy a copy of the agreement Lawyer had proposed and suggested that she review it with Lawyer or another attorney of her own choosing. The agreement specified that in the event of divorce:

1.   Each spouse waives all claims to property acquired by the other during the first five years of the marriage;

2.   The spouses will share joint physical and legal custody of any children born to them during the marriage.

When Hal gave Wendy the proposed agreement, she burst into tears. Wendy was very angry and hurt, but she did not want to call off the wedding at such a late date. Reluctantly, she agreed to discuss the matter with Lawyer.

Lawyer gave Wendy an accurate list of Hal's assets and a copy of Hal's tax returns for the past three years. Lawyer urged her to consult another attorney. After conferring with her family, but not an attorney, Wendy decided to sign the proposed agreement. The day before their wedding, she and Hal signed the agreement in Lawyer's office in State A.

Four years ago, Hal and Wendy had a child (Child).

Six months ago, Hal and Wendy moved to State B. Hal's business has continued to prosper. He currently earns $300,000 per year. Since the marriage, Hal has used his business income to acquire assets worth about $500,000. Wendy has continued to write songs. Her current income is $30,000 per year.

Three months ago, after Wendy discovered that Hal was having an affair, she took Child and moved back to State A, where she plans to remain. Since leaving Hal, Wendy has written and recorded several songs about her marriage. Wendy's agent believes that these songs "will hit the top of the charts."

State A has adopted the Uniform Premarital Agreement Act. State B has not. The premarital agreement contains no choice-of-law provision.

1.   **Which state's law governs the enforceability of the premarital agreement? Explain.**

2.   Is the waiver-of-property-rights provision in the premarital agreement enforceable? Explain.

3.   Is the child-custody provision in the premarital agreement enforceable? Explain.

4.   Are the profits to be derived from Wendy's songs written after she left Hal subject to division at divorce? Explain.

MEE RELEASED ESSAY QUESTIONS

FAMILY LAW
February 2009

Fourteen years ago, Mom and Dad had a brief romance while Dad was on vacation in State A, where Mom lived. Nine months after Dad returned to his home in State B, Mom telephoned Dad. Mom told Dad that she had just given birth to Child and that Dad was Child's father. Mom also told Dad that, if he would agree to waive his right to establish his paternity of Child, she would sign a release waiving all rights to seek child support from him. Dad agreed to Mom's proposal, and they signed a written contract containing the terms outlined by Mom.

Mom is a college graduate and had an excellent job when Child was born. However, she has developed a chronic disease and is no longer able to fully provide for herself and Child, now age 14.

Mom brought an action against Dad in State A seeking to establish his paternity of Child and obtain child support, claiming that the contract waiving her right to child support is unenforceable. She served Dad by registered mail in State B, where he has continued to live since Child's birth. Dad has not visited State A since his vacation there more than 14 years ago and has never met Child.

State A's long-arm statute provides that a court has personal jurisdiction over an alleged parent for purposes of determining paternity and support obligations if the alleged parent "engaged in sexual intercourse in this state and the child may have been conceived by that act of intercourse."

Dad moved to dismiss Mom's petition on the ground that the State A court's assertion of personal jurisdiction over him to determine paternity and child support would violate due process requirements. The trial court denied the motion, and Dad entered a special appearance, preserving his right to appeal on the jurisdictional claim.

On the merits, Dad argues that the contract he and Mom made shortly after Child's birth should be enforced. In the event that the court declines to enforce the contract, Dad argues that the equities of the case require that the value of any child support awarded to Mom be calculated based on state public-assistance benefit levels or, in the alternative, that he be awarded custody of Child. Dad also seeks liberal visitation with Child in the event that the court awards custody to Mom.

1. **Was the court's assertion of personal jurisdiction over Dad to determine Dad's paternity and support obligations consistent with due process requirements? Explain.**

2. **Assuming the court has personal jurisdiction over Dad, how should the court rule on the child support, custody, and visitation issues? Explain.**

MEE RELEASED ESSAY QUESTIONS

FAMILY LAW
July 2009

Two years ago, Husband and Wife divorced in State A. The divorce decree specified that

> (a) Husband and Wife shall have joint custody of their 10-year-old child, Son, who shall reside with Wife Sunday through Wednesday and with Husband Thursday through Saturday of each week; and
> (b) Husband shall pay Wife $1,000 per month in child support until Son turns 18.

Three months ago, Wife accepted a job in State B, about 600 miles from State A. Wife's new job raises her net income by $1,000 per month and offers excellent opportunities for promotion. Wife's parents also live near Wife's new job in State B, and Wife believes that Son will benefit from spending more time with his grandparents.

Two months ago, Wife moved to State B with Son. Given the distance between Wife's new home in State B and Husband's home in State A, Wife can no longer transport Son to Husband's home in compliance with the State A custody decree. Wife therefore telephoned Husband and said, "Son can visit you for six weeks during the summer," to make up the time that Husband will lose with Son each week.

Husband has never visited State B and owns no property there; he opposed Wife's move to State B. Husband also told Wife that, given her higher earnings from her new job, he would immediately stop paying child support. Husband has not paid child support since making this statement.

Ten days ago, Wife filed a petition in a State B court seeking modification of the State A custody decree so as to give her sole custody of Son and to substitute a six-week summer visitation period for Husband's weekly time with Son. Wife also registered and sought to enforce the State A child support order. Wife personally served this petition on Husband in State A.

Five days ago, Husband filed a petition in State A court seeking modification of the custody decree so as to give him sole custody of Son and to substitute an eight-week summer visitation period for Wife's weekly time with Son. Husband also requested elimination of his support obligation retroactive to the date of Wife's move. Husband personally served this petition on Wife in State B.

1.   **Should the State B court enforce the State A child support order? Explain.**

2.   **Should the State B court modify the State A custody order by awarding sole custody of Son to Wife and substituting a six-week summer visit for Husband's weekly time with Son? Explain.**

3.   **Should the State A court modify the State A custody order by awarding sole custody of Son to Husband and substituting an eight-week summer visit for Wife's weekly time with Son? Explain.**

4.   **Should the State A court modify the State A child support order either retroactively or prospectively? Explain.**

MEE RELEASED ESSAY QUESTIONS

FAMILY LAW
February 2010

Harry and Wendy married when they were both 23, shortly after Harry began his first year of law school. They decided that Wendy, who had completed two years of college, would temporarily quit college and get a full-time job until Harry started practicing law.

Wendy obtained a full-time job as a supermarket cashier. All of her earnings were used for Harry's and Wendy's support. Harry did not work during the school year but worked full-time during summers. All of Harry's earnings were used to pay his law school tuition.

Harry recently earned his law degree, passed the bar examination, and began working as a public defender. Last month, after three years of marriage, Harry told Wendy that he felt they had drifted apart and that he wanted a divorce. Although deeply hurt, Wendy decided to separate amicably. Harry and Wendy had no children.

Harry suggested that he draw up a settlement agreement in order to avoid the expense of hiring a lawyer. Harry proposed that each spouse keep his or her own personal property and that he bear full responsibility for his educational loans. Harry also told Wendy that a divorce court would "definitely not impose any further obligations" on him because there were no children of the marriage. Wendy agreed to the terms of the settlement agreement proposed and prepared by Harry, and both parties signed it. In the agreement, each spouse waived "any and all rights to the past or future income of the other party." Thereafter, following Harry's instructions, Wendy filed a petition for a no-fault divorce, requesting that the court incorporate their settlement agreement into the final divorce decree.

Prior to any hearing on the petition, Wendy learned that Harry had been involved in an adulterous relationship with another woman. Angry and mistrustful, Wendy contacted an attorney, who urged her to amend her divorce petition. The attorney suggested that Wendy petition the court to invalidate the settlement agreement, seek a divorce on grounds of adultery, and request alimony and a cash award representing her share of the value of Harry's law license, which he acquired during the marriage.

State law does not authorize reimbursement alimony.

1.   **Should the court invalidate the settlement agreement? Explain.**

2.   **What, if any, are the advantages to Wendy of obtaining a divorce based on Harry's adultery instead of on no-fault grounds? Explain.**

3.   **Assuming the court invalidates the settlement agreement, can Wendy obtain**

a) a cash award representing her share of the value of Harry's law license? Explain.

b) alimony? Explain.

MEE RELEASED ESSAY QUESTIONS

FAMILY LAW
July 2010

Fifteen years ago, Husband and Wife married in State A. At the time of the marriage, Husband and Wife were both 35 years old, and each had a high school education. Wife worked as an administrative assistant for a manufacturing company, where she had been employed for six years. Husband was unemployed.

Husband was a spendthrift with a history of selling his possessions to fund unsuccessful business ventures. Aware of his personal failings, Husband asked Wife to enter into a premarital agreement under which (a) Wife would become the sole owner of all assets owned by Husband before his marriage to Wife; (b) Wife would pay all of Husband's premarital debts; (c) if Husband and Wife divorced, Wife would have exclusive rights to all assets acquired by either Husband or Wife during their marriage; and (d) if Husband and Wife divorced, both would waive all claims to alimony. Wife agreed to Husband's proposal. Husband and Wife both disclosed their assets to each other.

Attorney thereafter prepared a premarital agreement based on Husband's and Wife's understanding. Husband and Wife signed the agreement one week after a meeting at which Attorney explained the consequences of signing the agreement. The agreement contained a provision stating that both Husband and Wife had chosen to forgo individual representation by a lawyer. After signing the agreement, Husband transferred title to his assets to Wife.

Throughout the marriage, Wife has performed virtually all household chores. Wife has also worked full time at the manufacturing company; at times, she has also held a part-time job to pay for household expenses. Wife paid Husband's premarital debts with her earnings and with some of the assets Husband had transferred to her. She sold the balance of the assets Husband had transferred to her to pay for flying lessons for Husband. Husband got a commercial pilot's license after taking these lessons but never tried to find work as a pilot. Instead, Husband worked at part-time odd jobs until five years ago, when he was injured in a car accident. Thereafter, Husband claimed he was disabled and ceased working altogether. Wife currently earns $35,000 per year.

Wife has sued Husband for divorce in State A, which terms spousal support "alimony." Husband claims that he is entitled to alimony and a share of the couple's assets. Wife claims that she is entitled to all assets titled in her name and in Husband's name. These assets are (a) the marital home, purchased by Wife during the marriage and titled in Wife's name; (b) Wife's employment pension; and (c) real estate inherited by Husband during the marriage and titled in Husband's name.

Wife has asked your law firm these questions:

1.   **Is the premarital agreement enforceable? Explain.**

2.   **If the premarital agreement is unenforceable, what assets are divisible at divorce? Explain.**

3.   **If the premarital agreement is unenforceable, is Husband entitled to alimony? Explain.**

MEE RELEASED ESSAY QUESTIONS

FAMILY LAW
February 2011

Husband and Wife married 12 years ago. Two years later, Wife gave birth to Child. Both Husband and Wife are employed, and each earns approximately $80,000 per year.

Four months ago, Husband and Wife decided to divorce and entered into a written separation agreement drafted by their respective attorneys. Under this agreement, Wife obtained sole title to assets worth $175,000 and Husband obtained sole title to assets worth $125,000. All assets were acquired during the marriage with employment income; there were no other assets. The separation agreement provided that Wife would have sole custody of Child. It required Husband to pay to Wife $500 per month in spousal support until her death or remarriage and $400 per month in child support until Child reaches the age of 18.

At the time he signed the separation agreement, Husband was living with Fiancee, a woman with two teenage children. Indeed, his planned marriage to Fiancee was the primary reason for Husband's willingness to sign the separation agreement.

Three months ago, Child was injured in an automobile accident. As a result of blood tests performed following the accident, Husband discovered that he is not Child's biological parent.

Two months ago, at a hearing in the Husband-Wife divorce action, Husband petitioned the trial court to invalidate the separation agreement based on unconscionability and fraud. The trial court refused and entered a divorce decree incorporating the terms of the separation agreement.

After entry of the divorce judgment, Husband and Fiancee got married. Husband then filed a motion to modify the divorce decree to

    (a) grant him an equal share of the marital assets,
    (b) award Wife no more than $200 per month in spousal support so that Husband could "meet the needs of [his] new family," and
    (c) eliminate his child-support obligation based on Husband's "nonpaternity of Child."

The trial court denied Husband's motion to modify the divorce decree.

1. **Did the trial court err in denying Husband's petition to invalidate the separation agreement on the basis of unconscionability and fraud? Explain.**

2. **Did the trial court err in denying Husband's motion to modify the divorce decree according to each of the terms set forth in his motion? Explain.**

MEE RELEASED ESSAY QUESTIONS

FAMILY LAW
July 2011

Dave and Meg lived in State A. Three years ago, they began dating. Two years ago, Meg became pregnant with their child. Shortly thereafter, Dave and Meg discussed marriage. Dave told Meg, "Perhaps we should get married if we're going to have a child." Meg told Dave, "I am committed to marrying you, but I want a real wedding, and we can't afford that now." Meg proposed that Dave move in with her so that "we can save money to get married." Dave agreed and began living in Meg's rented apartment. Meg did not tell her landlord about Dave. She did tell her family and friends that "Dave, my fiancé, has moved in."

Fifteen months ago, Meg gave birth to Child. Meg and Dave agreed that Child's birth certificate would identify Dave as Child's father. Meg and Dave sent birth announcements to friends and relatives noting the birth of "our son, Child." After Child's birth, Meg quit work. Dave took on a second job in order to support Meg and Child.

Five months ago, Meg took Child and abruptly left Dave. Dave hired a private investigator to find Meg and Child. The investigator recently discovered that they are living in State B with Husband, whom Meg married three months ago. The investigator also discovered that Meg and Husband have filed a petition to terminate Dave's parental rights and authorize Husband's adoption of Child.

State B permits a mother or a married father to veto the adoption of his or her child unless he or she "has willfully refused to support said child for a period of one or more years."

State B permits an unmarried father to veto the adoption of his child only if he (a) "has consistently supported such child" and (b) "has maintained a residential relationship with such child for at least 9 of the 12 months immediately preceding the filing of an adoption petition."

State B does not have a putative father registry.

State A recognizes common law marriage. State B does not. Both State A and State B have adopted the Uniform Child Custody Jurisdiction and Enforcement Act (UCCJEA).

1.   **Will State B recognize a common law marriage contracted in State A? Explain.**

2.   **Did Dave and Meg enter into a common law marriage in State A? Explain.**

3.   **Assuming that Dave is an unmarried father, can State B constitutionally grant Meg and Husband's adoption petition over Dave's opposition? Explain.**

4.   **Does the UCCJEA permit State B to terminate Dave's parental rights or issue an order awarding custody of Child to Meg? Explain.**

MEE RELEASED ESSAY QUESTIONS

FAMILY LAW
July 2012

Fifteen years ago, Mom and Dad were married in State A, where both were domiciled.

Fourteen years ago, Mom gave birth to Daughter in State A. Dad is Daughter's biological father.

Four years ago, Dad died in State A. After Dad's death, Mom relied heavily on Dad's parents, Grandparents. Mom and Daughter moved to an apartment near Grandparents in State A. Thereafter, Grandparents visited Mom's home at least once a week. Daughter was also a frequent visitor at Grandparents' home. Grandparents also helped Mom to support Daughter financially.

Four months ago, Mom married Stepdad and moved with Daughter to Stepdad's home in State B, 500 miles from Mom's former residence in State A. Stepdad believes that Grandparents discouraged Mom's marriage to him, and he asked Mom not to invite Grandparents to visit. Mom agreed to Stepdad's request. However, she allowed Daughter to visit Grandparents in State A during a school vacation.

One week ago, Grandparents sent Daughter a bus ticket. Without revealing her plans to Mom, Daughter used the ticket to go to Grandparents' home in State A. When she arrived at Grandparents' home, Daughter telephoned Mom and said, "I hate State B, I dislike Stepdad, and I want to live with Grandparents in State A until you leave Stepdad and return to State A, too."

On the same day that Mom received this telephone call, she was served with a summons to appear in a State A court proceeding, brought by Grandparents, in which Grandparents seek custody of Daughter. Grandparents' petition was brought pursuant to a State A statute that authorizes the award of child custody to a grandparent when the court finds that (1) the "child has been abandoned or one of the child's parents has died" and (2) an award of custody to the petitioner grandparent "serves the child's best interests."

Both State A and State B have enacted the Uniform Child Custody Jurisdiction and Enforcement Act (UCCJEA).

Mom has sought advice from your law firm. She asks the following questions:

1.   **Does State A have jurisdiction to award custody of Daughter to Grandparents? Explain.**

2.   **On the merits, may a court deny Grandparents' custody petition if Daughter testifies that she wants to live with Grandparents? Explain.**

3.   **Is the State A statute authorizing the award of custody to grandparents constitutional? Explain.**

MEE RELEASED ESSAY QUESTIONS

FAMILY LAW
July 2013

Seven years ago, a married couple had a daughter.

Recently, the mother joined a small religious group. The group's members are required to contribute at least half their earnings to the group, to forgo all conventional medical treatments, and to refrain from all "frivolous" activities, including athletic competitions and sports. The mother has decided to adhere to all of the group's rules.

Accordingly, the mother has told the father that she has given half of her last two paychecks to the group and that she plans to continue this practice. The father objects to this plan and has accurately told the mother that "we can't pay all the bills without your salary."

The mother has also said that she wants to stop giving their daughter her prescribed asthma medications. The father opposes this because the daughter has severe asthma, and the daughter's physician has said that regular medication use is the only way to prevent asthma attacks, which can be life-threatening. The mother also wants to stop the daughter's figure-skating lessons. The father opposes this plan, too, because their daughter loves skating. Because the father works about 60 hours per week outside the home and the mother works only 20 hours, the father is afraid that the mother will do what she wants despite his opposition.

The mother, father, and daughter continue to live together. They do not live in a community property jurisdiction.

1. **Can the father or the state child welfare agency obtain an order**

    (a)   **enjoining the mother from making contributions from her future paychecks to the religious group? Explain.**

    (b)   **requiring the mother to take the daughter to skating lessons? Explain.**

    (c)   **requiring the mother to cooperate in giving the daughter her prescribed asthma medications? Explain.**

2. **If the father were to file a divorce action against the mother, could a court award custody of the daughter to him based on the mother's decision to follow the religious group's rules? Explain.**

MEE RELEASED ESSAY QUESTIONS

FAMILY LAW
July 2014

In 1994, a man and a woman were married in State A.

In 1998, their daughter was born in State A.

In 2010, the family moved to State B.

In 2012, the husband and wife divorced in State B. Under the terms of the divorce decree:

(a) the husband and wife share legal and physical custody of their daughter;
(b) the husband must pay the wife $1,000 per month in child support until their daughter reaches age 18;
(c) the marital residence was awarded to the wife, with the proviso that if it is sold before the daughter reaches age 18, the husband will receive 25% of the net sale proceeds remaining after satisfaction of the mortgage on the residence; and
(d) the remaining marital assets were divided between the husband and the wife equally.

Six months ago, the husband was offered a job in State A that pays significantly less than his job in State B but provides him with more responsibilities and much better promotion opportunities. The husband accepted the job in State A and moved from State B back to State A.

Since returning to State A, the husband has not paid child support because, due to his lower salary, he has had insufficient funds to meet all his obligations.

One month ago, the wife sold the marital home, netting $10,000 after paying off the mortgage. She then moved to a smaller residence. The husband believes that he should receive more than 25% of the net sale proceeds given his financial difficulties.

Last week, when the wife brought the daughter to the husband's State A home for a weekend visit, the husband served the wife with a summons in a State A action to modify the support and marital-residence-sale-proceeds provisions of the State B divorce decree. The husband brought the action in the State A court that adjudicates all domestic relations issues.

1.   **Does the State A court have jurisdiction to modify**
      (a)   the child support provision of the State B divorce decree? Explain.
      (b)   the marital-residence-sale-proceeds provision of the State B divorce decree? Explain.

2.   **On the merits, could the husband obtain**
      (a)   retroactive modification of his child support obligation to the daughter? Explain.
      (b)   prospective modification of his child support obligation to the daughter? Explain.

    (c)   **modification of the marital-residence-sale-proceeds provision of the State B divorce decree? Explain.**

MEE RELEASED ESSAY QUESTIONS

FAMILY LAW
February 2016

Eight years ago, a woman and a man began living together. The woman worked as an investment banker, and the man worked part-time as a bartender while he struggled to write his first novel. The couple lived in a condominium that the woman had purchased shortly before the man moved in. The woman had purchased the condominium for $300,000 using her own money and had taken title in her own name.

Four years ago, the woman and the man were married at City Hall. One week before the wedding, the woman presented the man with a proposed premarital agreement and an asset list. The asset list correctly stated that the woman owned the condominium, then worth $350,000, and a brokerage account, then worth $500,000. The agreement specified that, in the event of divorce, each spouse would be entitled to retain "all assets which he or she then owns, whether or not those assets are acquired during the marriage." The man was surprised when the woman gave him the agreement to sign, and he contacted a lawyer friend for advice. The lawyer urged the man not to sign the agreement. Nonetheless, the man signed the agreement, telling the woman, "I'm a little hurt, but I guess I understand that you want to keep what you earn." The woman signed the agreement as well.

After their wedding, the woman and the man continued to live in the woman's condominium and to work at the jobs each held before the marriage. The man also continued to work on his novel.
Six months ago, the man's novel was accepted by a publisher. The novel will be released next spring. The publisher has estimated that the royalties may total as much as $200,000 over the next five years.

Two months ago, the woman and the man separated. The woman remained in the condominium, now worth $400,000 as a result of market appreciation. The woman's brokerage account, worth $500,000 when she and the man married, is now worth $1,000,000 as a result of market appreciation and additional investments that the woman made with employment bonuses she received during the marriage. The woman has made no withdrawals from this account.

One month ago, the woman won, but has not yet received, a $5 million lottery jackpot.

One week ago, the man filed for divorce. In the man's divorce petition, he asks the court to invalidate the premarital agreement and seeks half of all assets owned by the woman, i.e., the woman's brokerage account, her condominium, and her right to the lottery payment. The man owns no assets except for personal effects and the book contract under which he will receive future royalties based on sales of his novel.

This jurisdiction has adopted the Uniform Premarital Agreement Act, which in relevant part provides that "the party against whom enforcement [of the premarital agreement] is sought must prove (1) involuntariness or (2) *both* that 'the agreement was unconscionable when it was executed' *and* that he or she did not receive or waive a 'fair and reasonable' disclosure and 'did not have or reasonably could not have had . . . an adequate knowledge' of the other's assets and obligations.

The jurisdiction's divorce law requires "equitable distribution" of all marital (community) assets and prohibits the division of separate assets.

Is the premarital agreement enforceable? Explain.

Assuming that the agreement is unenforceable, what assets are subject to division in the divorce action, and what factors should a court consider in distributing those assets? Explain

MEE RELEASED ESSAY QUESTIONS

FEDERAL CIVIL PROCEDURE
July 2002

Seller manufactures vending machines at a facility located in State A, where Seller is incorporated and has its principal place of business. Buyer, a German company with its principal place of business in Munich, Germany, contracted to purchase 1,000 vending machines from Seller for a total price of $500,000.

The contract was carefully negotiated during lengthy discussions held in Germany. Early in the negotiations, each side insisted that the contract should be governed by its own law and that disputes should be resolved in its own courts. In the end, however, the parties agreed on contract clauses that provided: (1) "the substantive rights and remedies of the parties to this contract shall be governed by the Commercial Code of State N"; (2) "any and all litigation brought concerning this contract shall be brought in the state or federal courts of State N"; and (3) "Seller and Buyer hereby consent to venue, jurisdiction, and service of process by courts in State N." Apart from these clauses, there is no connection between State N and the parties or the transaction. State N is located on the eastern seaboard of the United States. The parties chose State N because it has convenient air links to Germany and a widely respected judiciary that is regarded as expert in commercial law matters.

Seller shipped the vending machines to Germany, but Buyer refused the shipment after discovering that the goods had been seriously damaged during the ocean voyage and arrived in Germany in a worthless condition. Seller then sued Buyer in federal district court in State A, properly invoking the court's subject matter jurisdiction and seeking recovery of the $500,000 contract price on the ground that the risk of damage to the goods during transport was on Buyer throughout the ocean voyage.

In responding to Seller's complaint, Buyer moved to transfer the case to the federal district court in State N, pursuant to 28 U.S.C. § 1404(a) and the forum-selection clause in the contract. Seller resisted Buyer's transfer request on the grounds that (a) State A was a more convenient forum for Seller, and (b) the forum-selection clause was unenforceable under State A law, which declares such clauses to be "void as a matter of public policy."

While the transfer motion was pending, Seller delivered a notice of deposition to Buyer, demanding that Buyer's chief executive officer appear for a deposition. Buyer responded by asking the court for a protective order on the ground that its "officers, directors, and managing agents" are all in Germany and are therefore beyond the subpoena power or other authority of the court.

Assume that there are no applicable international law principles or treaties.

1.   **Should the federal district court in State A transfer the action to State N? Explain.**

2.   **Irrespective of how the court rules on the transfer motion, should Buyer's request for a protective order be granted? Explain.**

MEE RELEASED ESSAY QUESTIONS

FEDERAL CIVIL PROCEDURE
February 2003

Acme Corporation, a citizen of State X, manufactures widgets. Acme widgets are distributed to retailers throughout the United States by Widgets, Inc., a citizen of State Y. Plaintiff, a citizen of State Y, purchased an Acme widget from a retailer in her hometown. Shortly after purchasing the widget, Plaintiff was seriously injured when the widget overheated and exploded.

Plaintiff sued Acme in the federal district court located in State Y, properly invoking the court's diversity jurisdiction. Plaintiff sought $100,000 in damages on two state-law tort theories: (1) failure to warn, and (2) sale of a dangerously defective product.

Under the applicable state law, a manufacturer's duty to warn is fully discharged if a proper warning is affixed to the product *at the point of delivery to its distributor*. A distributor's duty is fully discharged if the warning is affixed a*t the point of delivery to the retailer*. State law further provides that both manufacturers and distributors may be held separately and strictly liable for selling a "dangerously defective" product, even if they have given adequate warning of the risks. Plaintiff's complaint alleged both that Acme had failed to affix a warning label to the product and that Acme's widgets had a dangerous propensity to overheat.

After extensive discovery, Acme filed a motion for summary judgment on the failure to warn claim. It attached to its motion the supporting affidavits of employees of both Acme and Widgets attesting that a proper warning label had been affixed to the widget both at the time of delivery to Widgets and at the time of distribution to the retailer who sold the widget to Plaintiff. While conceding that the warning label usually provided with the product did give adequate notice of the danger of overheating and explosion under certain circumstances, Plaintiff nevertheless contested the motion for summary judgment with her own affidavit, in which she stated that there had been no warning label affixed to her widget when she purchased it from her local retailer.

The federal court granted Acme's motion for summary judgment on the failure to warn claim and entered judgment on that claim against Plaintiff. No appeal was taken. Soon afterward, Acme and Plaintiff settled the dangerous defect claim for an undisclosed amount.

Shortly after the conclusion of the federal litigation, Plaintiff filed suit in the state court of State Y, asserting against Widgets, Inc., the same two claims she had asserted against Acme in federal court: failure to warn and sale of a dangerously defective product. Widgets answered and then moved to dismiss on grounds of claim and issue preclusion.

1. **In Plaintiff's suit against Acme, did the federal court properly grant Acme's motion for summary judgment on the failure to warn claim? Explain.**

2. **Should the State Y state court give preclusive effect to the federal court judgment and dismiss Plaintiff's claims against Widgets? Explain.**

MEE RELEASED ESSAY QUESTIONS

FEDERAL CIVIL PROCEDURE
July 2003

Farmer brought a class action lawsuit in federal district court in State A, alleging that the defendant, Truckco, marketed a line of pickup trucks with defective shock absorbers. Farmer's complaint identified the members of the class as 100,000 individuals nationwide who had bought the trucks from 1995-2000 and suffered losses as a result of the defective shock absorbers. The alleged losses ranged from the $250 cost of replacing the shock absorbers to serious personal injuries suffered in accidents alleged to have been caused by the defective shock absorbers. The only claim personal to Farmer was the $250 replacement cost claim. Farmer properly asserted that federal jurisdiction was based on a breach of warranty claim under a recently enacted federal automobile safety statute.

Farmer moved to certify the class. Opposing this motion, Truckco submitted court papers from lawsuits brought by individual owners who claimed to have suffered a wide variety of personal injuries as a result of accidents said to have resulted from the failure of the defective shock absorbers during the years in question. Truckco also noted that Farmer had previously filed (and still has pending) a class action against Truckco in a state court in State Z. In the State Z case, which was premised on state-law warranty claims, Farmer sought relief similar to the relief sought in the federal action and asked to represent the same class of plaintiffs. Finally, Truckco pointed out that Farmer's lawyer in both actions was a recent bar admittee who had not previously handled class action litigation.

In addition to arguing against certification of the class, Truckco asked the federal district court to abstain from adjudicating the class action in light of the pendency of the state court class action.

The federal district court first denied Truckco's motion for abstention. The court then denied Farmer's motion for class certification, finding that class certification was "inappropriate under the circumstances."

1.   **Was the court's ruling on Truckco's motion for abstention correct? Explain.**

2.   **Was the court's ruling on Farmer's motion for class certification appropriate? Explain.**

MEE RELEASED ESSAY QUESTIONS

FEDERAL CIVIL PROCEDURE
February 2004

Motorist was driving his automobile in the northbound lane on a highway in State X. Exceeding the posted maximum speed limit by 10 miles per hour, Motorist was gaining on a slow-moving U.S. Army truck convoy traveling in the same lane. At the same time, a motorcycle, driven by Husband with Wife as a passenger, was approaching the convoy from the opposite direction. Husband was operating the motorcycle at the posted speed limit and was traveling in the proper (southbound) lane.

The soldier driving the last truck in the convoy was feeling drowsy because he had not slept the night before. Suddenly, realizing that he had driven his truck far too close to the Army truck just ahead of him, he slammed on his brakes. Motorist, who had nearly overtaken the convoy, reacted to the sight of the truck's brake lights by frantically swerving his automobile into the southbound lane, where he sideswiped Husband's motorcycle. Husband was thrown to the pavement and seriously injured. Wife, however, miraculously avoided physical injury.

At the time of the accident, Husband and Wife were citizens of State Y, but a few months later they moved permanently to State X. Motorist was at all times a citizen of State X.

Shortly after moving to State X, Husband and Wife filed an action in the United States District Court for the District of State X seeking to recover for the injuries they suffered as a result of the accident. In the action, Husband claimed $50,000 in damages for his injuries, and Wife claimed $5,000 for her loss of Husband's consortium. They named as defendants both the United States of America and Motorist. Their claims against the United States are based on the Federal Tort Claims Act, which provides that federal district courts have exclusive jurisdiction over tort claims against the United States government. Their claims against Motorist are based on the tort law of State X, where the accident occurred.

1.   Can Husband and Wife, as plaintiffs, join their respective personal injury and loss-of-consortium claims in a single action in the U.S. district court? Explain.

2.   Can Husband and Wife join their respective claims against the United States and Motorist, as defendants, in a single action in the U.S. district court? Explain.

3.   Does the U.S. district court have subject matter jurisdiction over the state law claims of Husband and Wife against Motorist? Explain.

MEE RELEASED ESSAY QUESTIONS

FEDERAL CIVIL PROCEDURE
July 2004

Plaintiff, a domiciliary of State X, was severely injured in a car accident in State X. Tortfeasor, the uninsured owner and driver of the other vehicle involved in the accident, was also a citizen of State X. Before any litigation regarding the accident began, Tortfeasor died of a heart attack.

Following Tortfeasor's death, Plaintiff commenced an action against Executor, the legal representative of Tortfeasor's estate. Executor is a citizen of State Y. Plaintiff sued Executor in the federal district court of State Y. The complaint, which alleged that Tortfeasor's negligence caused the accident and Plaintiff's injuries, sought damages in excess of $500,000.

Executor answered the complaint, denying the allegations of negligence but admitting the court's subject matter jurisdiction. A year later, however, after extensive discovery, Executor moved to dismiss the complaint for lack of subject matter jurisdiction. After the submission of briefs and oral argument on the jurisdictional issue, the federal court denied Executor's motion to dismiss, ruling that "jurisdiction exists and, in any event, the motion was untimely." A trial was held and the jury rendered a verdict in Plaintiff's favor for $80,000.

The federal court entered judgment on the verdict. No appeal was taken.

When Executor declined to pay the judgment, Plaintiff commenced suit in a state court in State X to enforce the federal judgment. In the state suit, Executor challenged the validity of the judgment, claiming that the federal district court of State Y lacked subject matter jurisdiction.

1.   **Did the federal district court of State Y err in denying Executor's motion to dismiss for lack of subject matter jurisdiction? Explain.**

2.   **Should the state court in State X enforce the federal judgment? Explain.**

MEE RELEASED ESSAY QUESTIONS

FEDERAL CIVIL PROCEDURE
February 2005

Buyer and Seller were both citizens of State X, where they attended State University. Just before they graduated, Buyer purchased Seller's car for $2,500. At the time, Seller told Buyer that the car was "in good working order" and that it was a "safe, reliable little car." Seller knew, however, that a local mechanic's inspection of the car had revealed that its brakes were so worn that they presented a significant safety hazard and required immediate replacement. Instead of informing Buyer of the danger, Seller showed Buyer the mechanic's bill and told him that the car "has just been checked out."

After graduation, Buyer decided to move permanently to Big City in State Y. Buyer decided to use the car he bought from Seller for the move. He believed that in a few round-trips he could transport all of his belongings to his new apartment in Big City. On his way back to his State X apartment after his first trip to his new apartment in Big City, Buyer was seriously injured in a one-car accident on a highway in State X. Friend, a citizen of State X and a passenger in Buyer's car, was the only witness to the accident. He and Buyer will testify that the accident happened when the brakes failed as Buyer attempted to negotiate a curve in the highway.

After weeks of hospitalization in State X, Buyer settled permanently in his apartment in Big City in State Y. Having discovered Seller's deceit, Buyer sued Seller in the U.S. District Court for the District of State X, seeking to recover $500,000 under State X tort law for his injuries and lost wages. In addition, Buyer claimed Seller's misrepresentations constituted a breach of warranty under State X contract law and sought recovery of the $2,500 paid for the car.

One week after the suit was filed, Seller also decided to relocate from State X to Big City, taking a job there and assuming State Y citizenship.

Seller has filed a motion to dismiss Buyer's two claims for lack of subject matter jurisdiction. Seller has also moved for a change of venue to the U.S. District Court for the District of State Y.

1. **Should the court dismiss Buyer's tort claim, Buyer's contract claim, or both for lack of subject matter jurisdiction? Explain.**

2. **How should the court rule on Seller's motion for a change of venue? Explain.**

MEE RELEASED ESSAY QUESTIONS

FEDERAL CIVIL PROCEDURE
July 2005

Drugco, a State B corporation with its principal place of business in State B, employs sales representatives and assigns them to work in exclusive geographical areas. The Drugco sales representatives provide pharmacists in their areas with product literature, pricing information, and highly confidential sheets (known as "chem sheets") listing the chemical composition of each drug. The chem sheets ensure that the pharmacists understand how each Drugco drug interacts with other commonly prescribed drugs.

Drugco hired Claire, a resident of State A, under an employment agreement that contained a "non-compete" clause barring her, for one year following the termination of her employment with Drugco, from soliciting any pharmacists in her territory (defined as Elm, Maple, and Cherry counties of State A) or from engaging in any other activity competitive with Drugco's business within her territory. The agreement also included a trade-secrets clause, which required Claire to return to Drugco all pricing information and chem sheets in her possession upon termination of her employment.

The laws of State A and State B provide that: (1) chemical formulas and drug pricing information are trade secrets and (2) non-compete clauses in employment agreements are valid so long as they are reasonable in duration and geographical scope.

Claire was an excellent sales representative for Drugco, and she quickly developed strong working relationships with the pharmacists in her territory. Eighteen months after she began working for Drugco, Claire tendered her resignation to Drugco and the next day began working for Medico, a competing pharmaceuticals firm. Claire, who had retained a number of Drugco chem sheets, was contacting the same pharmacists in the same geographical area that she had covered for Drugco. Moreover, she was selling Medico products that were in direct competition with Drugco products.

Drugco has properly invoked diversity jurisdiction and has sued Claire in federal district court in State A for breach of contract.

Drugco seeks to enforce the non-compete clause in Claire's employment contract and to bar her from soliciting the pharmacists with whom she developed relationships while working for Drugco. Drugco fears that it may take more than a year to litigate the case to final judgment and wants to bar Claire from soliciting these pharmacists *now*. Drugco also wants to compel Claire to return immediately all Drugco chem sheets and pricing information within her possession.

What provisional remedies might Drugco seek to enforce the non-compete and trade-secrets clauses immediately and during the pendency of the lawsuit, and what is the likelihood that the court will grant each such remedy? Explain.

MEE RELEASED ESSAY QUESTIONS

FEDERAL CIVIL PROCEDURE
February 2006

Defendant is a political commentator and free-lance journalist who moved from his home state of State A to State B approximately three years ago. Defendant has told his family and friends that he still considers State A "home" and intends to return "someday," but that "I'm happy in State B for now." Defendant votes, pays taxes, and owns property only in State B.

Defendant publishes an online newsletter called "Nothing But the Truth" that is accessible over the Internet from his website, www.NBT.com. Viewers can access www.NBT.com and download articles, but they cannot post their messages through the site. The central computer that people access when they view the website is located in State B.

The political commentary and journalism posted on the www.NBT.com website focus almost exclusively on people and events in State A—Defendant's old stomping grounds and the region where he is best known as a political reporter. Indeed, Defendant's website receives so many hits from people in State A that most of the advertisers on the website are State A firms seeking to attract customers who live in State A.

Plaintiff is a resident and domiciliary of State A who previously worked as a high-level State A government employee. In a recent story posted on his website, Defendant reported on rumors he had heard concerning Plaintiff's alleged acceptance of kickbacks for the award of State A contracts.

Shortly after Defendant published this story on his website, Plaintiff was dismissed from employment with State A. Plaintiff maintains that the allegations contained in Defendant's article about Plaintiff are patently false. Plaintiff contacted Defendant shortly after the initial publication, asking Defendant to retract the story. Defendant refused and insisted that he was protected by the First Amendment of the United States Constitution, even if the story was false, so long as he had not acted maliciously.

Plaintiff has filed a lawsuit against Defendant in the United States District Court for the District of State A. Her complaint alleges that the story published on Defendant's website defamed Plaintiff under applicable state law. In addition, the complaint asserts that the First Amendment does not shield Defendant from the defamation claim under these circumstances. The complaint alleges facts establishing damages for Plaintiff in the amount of $200,000. Convinced that Defendant acted maliciously, Plaintiff also seeks punitive damages in the amount of $1,000,000. The complaint alleges that jurisdiction is proper on both federal question and diversity grounds.

The State A long-arm statute provides that the courts of State A may exercise jurisdiction over absent defendants to the "full extent permitted by the due process clause of the United States Constitution."

In lieu of an answer to the complaint, Defendant has filed a motion to dismiss for lack of subject matter and personal jurisdiction.

1.   **On what basis, if any, would a federal district court have subject matter jurisdiction over the lawsuit by Plaintiff against Defendant? Explain.**

2.   **Would the United States District Court for the District of State A have personal jurisdiction over Defendant? Explain.**

MEE RELEASED ESSAY QUESTIONS

FEDERAL CIVIL PROCEDURE
July 2006

Pat, a State A resident, was driving in State B when her car was struck by a truck driven by Driver. A sign on the truck's door read "Smith Brothers Transport Co." The police accident report correctly listed Driver's name and license number, but mistakenly identified the truck's owner as Smith Brothers Trucking Company, Inc., instead of the correct owner, Smith Brothers Transport Company, Inc. Smith Brothers Trucking and Smith Brothers Transport are both owned and operated by Robert and William Smith. The two companies share office space. The Smith brothers are careful, however, to maintain the two corporations as separate and distinct legal entities, following all legal requirements to avoid any alter ego problems. Both companies are incorporated in and have their principal places of business in State B. Both companies identify Robert Smith as agent for service of process.

Two days before the deadline for filing suit under the applicable statute of limitations, Pat filed a proper diversity action in federal court in State B, alleging damages exceeding $75,000 against both Driver and Smith Brothers Trucking (the incorrect defendant). The summons and complaint were promptly served on Robert Smith, as agent for Smith Brothers Trucking.

Five days after filing her complaint and before any responsive pleading had been served, Pat's attorney realized that she had incorrectly named Smith Brothers Trucking as defendant. She promptly amended her complaint to name Smith Brothers Transport as defendant and served that amended complaint and an amended summons on Robert Smith, as agent for Smith Brothers Transport.

Two days later, Smith Brothers Transport moved to dismiss the amended complaint on the ground that the applicable statute of limitations had run before the amended complaint was filed. The court denied this motion and refused Smith Brothers Transport's request for certification of the matter as appropriate for an immediate appeal.

Following the filing of responsive pleadings, the judge directed the attorneys for all parties to appear before her for a pretrial conference to discuss the possibility of settlement. The attorneys for Pat and Smith Brothers Transport appeared, but the attorney for defendant Driver did not appear. Instead, Driver's attorney left a message for the judge, stating that he would not appear because Driver was not prepared to engage in settlement discussions.

The judge noted Driver's attorney's nonappearance and conducted the pretrial conference between the attorneys representing Pat and Smith Brothers Transport. The judge also ordered Driver's attorney to appear before her to explain why she should not impose sanctions on Driver for his attorney's non-attendance at the pretrial conference. Driver's attorney appeared and argued that he did not attend the pretrial conference because his client had no intention of negotiating a settlement and had directed him (the attorney) not to "waste my money" by attending. The judge, angry at this apparent disregard of her authority, ordered that Driver's answer be stricken and that a post-answer default judgment be entered against Driver.

1.   Did the trial court err in refusing to dismiss the amended complaint against Smith Brothers Transport? Explain.

2.   May Smith Brothers Transport immediately appeal the denial of its motion to dismiss? Explain.

3.   Did the trial court err in striking Driver's answer and ordering the entry of a default judgment as a sanction for the failure of Driver's attorney to participate in a pretrial conference? Explain.

MEE RELEASED ESSAY QUESTIONS

FEDERAL CIVIL PROCEDURE
February 2007

Transit Authority, Inc. (Transit Authority) operates a bus system in Big City. Last month, a Transit Authority bus collided with a passenger car driven by Tourist. The accident occurred when Tourist suddenly veered into the bus operator's lane at a major intersection. The bus operator was unable to stop the bus in time to avoid the collision, and Tourist was injured. Immediately after the accident occurred, the bus operator telephoned his supervisor to report the accident. Then, following Transit Authority's standard procedures, the bus operator completed an "Operator's Report of Accident" form. The completed form included the date, time, and place of the accident, the road conditions, the names of witnesses, a brief description of how the accident occurred, and a description of the personal injuries and property damage caused by the accident.

When a Transit Authority supervisor arrived twenty minutes after the accident occurred, she took a statement from the bus operator and recorded that statement on a "Supervisor's Investigative Report" form. Then she interviewed Tourist and recorded Tourist's statement on the "Supervisor's Investigative Report" form. The supervisor noted all witnesses' names, addresses, and telephone numbers in her report. She took photographs of the accident scene, including the position of each vehicle. Finally, she drew a diagram of the scene on the last page of the "Supervisor's Investigative Report" form.

Tourist has filed a personal injury action against Transit Authority in federal court, properly invoking the court's diversity jurisdiction. Tourist alleges that the bus operator, Transit Authority's employee, was driving negligently. She further alleges personal injury and property damage in a total amount exceeding $200,000. Transit Authority has filed an answer denying the claim of negligence and asserting contributory negligence.

Tourist served two requests for production of documents on Transit Authority. One request was for "any and all accident reports, diagrams, photographs, and any other documents which relate in any way to the collision between the bus and the car." A second request was for the bus operator's "entire personnel file that is maintained by Transit Authority, including disciplinary actions, safety records, and driving records." Transit Authority has refused to produce the accident reports that the operator and the supervisor created on the grounds that the reports were "prepared in anticipation of litigation." In addition, Transit Authority refuses to produce the bus operator's personnel file because the information that it contains "is not relevant."

Tourist has made a motion to compel production of the accident reports and the bus operator's "entire personnel file."

Should Tourist's motion be granted in whole or in part? Explain.

MEE RELEASED ESSAY QUESTIONS

FEDERAL CIVIL PROCEDURE
July 2007

Al is a citizen and domiciliary of State A. While Al was visiting his parents in State B, he was involved in an automobile accident. Al's sports car was demolished in the accident, but he was miraculously unhurt. He returned to his home in State A shortly after the accident. Bert, a citizen and domiciliary of State B who was the driver of the other automobile involved in the accident, was not so lucky. Bert was seriously injured in the accident and was hospitalized for several weeks.

Shortly after Bert's release from the hospital, Al sued him in the federal district court for State B. Al's complaint properly invoked the court's diversity jurisdiction, alleged that the collision had been caused by Bert's negligence, and sought $90,000 in damages (the value of Al's demolished sports car).

Bert, who was uninsured and unemployed, failed to answer Al's complaint and did not defend the action, despite having been properly served and having received notice of the action. The court entered a default judgment against Bert for $90,000. The judgment was not paid, and Al took no steps to enforce it.

One year after the accident, Al died at his home in State A. His estate is being administered by Executor, who is a citizen of State B.

Bert recently filed a timely lawsuit against Executor, as administrator of Al's estate. The lawsuit, filed in state court in State B, alleges that Al's reckless driving was the cause of the accident and that Bert is permanently disabled by the injuries he suffered in the accident. Bert is seeking $3 million in damages from Al's estate.

Executor filed a timely notice of removal of the state action with the federal district court in State B. She then served the notice on Bert and filed a copy with the State B state court. She also arranged for copies of all records and proceedings in the state court action to be filed with the clerk of the federal district court in State B. Executor then filed a timely motion with the federal district court to dismiss Bert's case with prejudice on the grounds that it was barred by the prior default judgment awarded to Al in his earlier suit against Bert.

Bert has filed a timely motion with the federal court asking it to remand the action to state court on the ground that the requirements for removal are not met on these facts. Alternatively, in the event the federal court retains the action, Bert has asked it to deny Executor's motion to dismiss.

1.   **Was removal of Bert's claim to federal district court appropriate? Explain.**

2.   **If the federal court retains the action, should it grant Executor's motion to dismiss Bert's suit? Explain.**

MEE RELEASED ESSAY QUESTIONS

FEDERAL CIVIL PROCEDURE
February 2008

Plaintiff worked for Corporation. In her fifth year of employment, Plaintiff complained that she had been passed over for promotion to a management position in favor of a less experienced male colleague. Shortly after voicing her discontent, Plaintiff was fired. Plaintiff sued Corporation in federal district court alleging that she was fired because of sex discrimination in violation of federal law. Corporation filed an answer denying the material allegations of the complaint and alleging that Plaintiff was fired for inadequate work performance.

During voir dire, the court asked each prospective juror whether he or she had ever been a party to an employment discrimination lawsuit. None of the prospective jurors answered in the affirmative.

At trial, Plaintiff offered evidence to support her claim that she had been fired for discriminatory reasons. Her evidence included testimony by a former co-worker relating a conversation the co-worker had had with Plaintiff's supervisor. In the conversation, the supervisor reportedly said that women were ill-suited for managerial positions and that men didn't like taking orders from women.

At the close of Plaintiff's evidence, Corporation moved for judgment as a matter of law (JMOL). The court denied the motion. Corporation then submitted its own evidence. The evidence consisted primarily of Plaintiff's employment records and testimony by Plaintiff's supervisor, who testified that Plaintiff's work had been rated unsatisfactory several times in the past.

At the close of all the evidence, neither party made further motions. After instructions from the court, the case was submitted to the jury. The jury deliberated for several hours and then returned a verdict for Plaintiff. The jury specifically found that Plaintiff had been passed over for promotion and fired as the result of sex discrimination and that she was entitled to backpay and reinstatement.

Two days after the entry of judgment, Corporation learned for the first time that the jury foreperson had previously filed and lost two employment discrimination lawsuits and that, upon learning she was part of the jury pool in this case, had said to a friend, "I'm going to get on that jury and stick it to Corporation. Somebody needs to teach these companies not to discriminate."

Eight days after the entry of judgment, Corporation moved for a post-judgment JMOL or, in the alternative, for a new trial. Corporation made two arguments. First, Corporation claimed that the evidence it presented at trial regarding the reasons for Plaintiff's termination was more persuasive and more credible than Plaintiff's evidence. Second, Corporation claimed that a new trial is required because of the jury foreperson's failure to disclose during voir dire her prior involvement in employment discrimination lawsuits.

The trial judge believes that Corporation's evidence at trial was more credible and persuasive than Plaintiff's. The trial judge also believes that Corporation's information about the jury foreperson's prior experiences and her statements to her friend is credible and suggestive of possible juror bias.

1.   Was Corporation's motion for a post-judgment JMOL procedurally proper? Explain.

2.   Without regard to its procedural propriety, should the trial court grant Corporation's motion for a post-judgment JMOL? Explain.

3.   Should the trial court grant Corporation's motion for a new trial on the ground that Corporation's evidence was more persuasive and credible than Plaintiff's evidence? Explain.

4.   Should the trial court grant Corporation's motion for a new trial because of the jury foreperson's conduct? Explain.

MEE RELEASED ESSAY QUESTIONS

FEDERAL CIVIL PROCEDURE
July 2008

Guest, a citizen of State A, ate oysters at Ron's Restaurant in State B. Guest paid for the meal with a $50 check. Ron's Restaurant is owned and operated by Ron, a citizen of State B.

After eating the oysters at Ron's Restaurant, Guest ate an ice cream sundae at the ice cream shop next door, which is owned and operated by CreamCorp, a State B corporation with its principal place of business in State B.

An hour later, Guest became ill and went to a hospital emergency room. Guest had to be admitted to the hospital for several days of tests, treatment, and observation. Ultimately, the doctors concluded that Guest was suffering from a severe case of food poisoning. Guest's hospital bills exceeded $75,000.

Guest stopped payment on the $50 check to Ron's Restaurant before the check cleared and has not otherwise paid for the meal.

Guest sued Ron (doing business as Ron's Restaurant) in the federal district court for the District of State B. Guest's complaint alleged that the oysters she ate at Ron's Restaurant caused her food poisoning. Guest further alleged that her damages exceed $75,000, exclusive of costs and interest.

Ron doubts that the oysters were contaminated because no other patrons suffered an adverse reaction to the oysters served that day. Ron believes that Guest became ill because the ice cream served at CreamCorp's shop was made with unpasteurized milk. Thus, Ron has moved to compel the joinder of CreamCorp as an additional defendant in the lawsuit so that, if the jury concludes Guest became sick from the ice cream, it can render a verdict against CreamCorp and not Ron. Ron has also added to his answer a claim against Guest for the unpaid $50.

Guest objects to the joinder of CreamCorp. Guest has also moved to strike Ron's claim for the unpaid $50 from Ron's answer.

1. **Should the court order the joinder of CreamCorp as an additional defendant? Explain.**

2. **Do the Federal Rules of Civil Procedure permit Ron to join his claim against Guest for the unpaid $50 to Guest's lawsuit against Ron? Explain.**

3. **If the Federal Rules of Civil Procedure permit Ron to join his claim against Guest for the unpaid $50, will the court have subject matter jurisdiction to hear that claim? Explain.**

MEE RELEASED ESSAY QUESTIONS

FEDERAL CIVIL PROCEDURE
February 2009

Bearco is a corporation incorporated under the laws of State A. Bearco maintains its corporate and administrative offices in State A; its factories are located in State B. Bearco's popular stuffed toy bear, "Griz," is sold throughout the United States. Bearco has registered the trademark "Griz" with the United States Patent and Trademark Office.

Copyco is a corporation incorporated under the laws of Country X, a foreign country, where Copyco has its manufacturing facilities and corporate offices. Copyco sells a line of toy bears called "Griz," which look remarkably similar to the Bearco "Griz" bears. Copyco sells its bears to consumers throughout the United States. However, it sells only on the Internet, using a parcel delivery service to deliver the bears to consumers. The Copyco website does not list a telephone number, street address, or post office box for the company. It lists only an e-mail address and an Internet address.

Bearco has filed an action against Copyco in the United States District Court for State A, properly invoking the court's federal question and diversity jurisdiction. Bearco alleges both trademark infringement (a federal law claim) and unfair competition (a tort claim that, in the United States, is based on state law).

State A and State B have materially different unfair-competition laws. Unfair competition is not actionable under the law of Country X.

To address choice-of-law problems, State A follows the "most significant relationship" approach of the Restatement (Second) of Conflict of Laws. State B applies the "vested rights" approach of the Restatement (First) of Conflict of Laws. Country X's choice-of-law methodology is unknown.

Bearco has been unable to determine Copyco's street address or post office box address either in the United States or in Country X and has filed a motion requesting that the district court authorize service of the summons and complaint by e-mail. There are no international agreements that affect the court's resolution of the issues in this case.

1.   **If the United States District Court for State A permits service of process on Copyco by e-mail, would such e-mail service be consistent with the Federal Rules of Civil Procedure and the United States Constitution? Explain.**

2.   **Which jurisdiction's law should the United States District Court for State A apply to resolve Bearco's unfair-competition claim? Explain.**

MEE RELEASED ESSAY QUESTIONS

FEDERAL CIVIL PROCEDURE
July 2009

Ann and Bill, both citizens of State X, were walking by a construction site in State X when an overhead crane dropped a load of plate glass windows on the sidewalk near them. The windows shattered when they hit the pavement, and both Ann and Bill were struck by flying glass. Ann's injuries were severe; she incurred more than $450,000 in medical expenses. Bill suffered only minor injuries and had medical bills of $500.

At the time of the accident, the glass windows were being installed in a new skyscraper by GlassCo, Inc., a State Y corporation with its principal place of business in State Y. The crane operator was a GlassCo employee, and the crane was owned by GlassCo. A subsequent investigation by GlassCo's insurance company concluded that the accident was due to crane operator error and improper crane maintenance.

Ann and Bill have joined as plaintiffs and filed a suit against GlassCo in a state trial court in State X. Ann is seeking more than $1,000,000 in damages, and Bill is seeking $5,000. They have both refused GlassCo's request to enter into settlement negotiations.

You are an associate in the law firm that has been retained by GlassCo. The partner in charge of the case wants to remove the lawsuit from state to federal court. She has asked:

1.   **What must GlassCo do to remove the case from state to federal court? Explain.**

2.   **If the case is removed to federal court, do the Federal Rules of Civil Procedure permit the separate claims of Ann and Bill to remain joined in a single lawsuit? Explain.**

3.   **If Ann's and Bill's claims remain joined, will the federal court have jurisdiction over the case? Explain.**

MEE RELEASED ESSAY QUESTIONS

FEDERAL CIVIL PROCEDURE
February 2010

Husband is an American citizen domiciled in State A. Wife is a citizen of a foreign country who was admitted to permanent residency in the United States five years ago and has been domiciled in State A since then.

After struggling with infertility, Husband and Wife consulted with Doctor, who created embryos in a laboratory using Husband's sperm and Wife's ova. Husband and Wife then entered into a surrogacy contract with Surrogate, a domiciliary of State B. Pursuant to the contract, Surrogate agreed to carry the couple's embryo, to relinquish to them any child born as a result of the implantation, and to waive any and all parental and/or custodial rights to the child. Husband and Wife also agreed, jointly and severally, to pay all of Surrogate's expenses and to assume custody and full financial and legal responsibility for any child born as a result of the implantation.

Doctor implanted one of the embryos in Surrogate. Surrogate gave birth to a baby in State A and listed Husband and Wife as the parents on the baby's birth certificate. Husband and Wife obtained a judgment from a State A court declaring that they were the legal parents of the baby and were entitled to sole custody.

The baby had serious medical problems at birth and remained in the State A hospital for three months. When the baby left the hospital, she went home with Husband and Wife. Surrogate returned to her home in State B.

The hospital sent the bill for the baby's medical care, which exceeded $500,000, to Surrogate. Surrogate has medical insurance with Insureco, an insurance company incorporated under the laws of State A with its principal place of business in State C. Surrogate's insurance policy covers all reasonable and necessary medical expenses incurred by Surrogate and her dependent(s), including "any natural child of Surrogate born after the policy is in force." However, Surrogate's policy expressly provides that Insureco will not cover expenses if a third party is liable for those expenses.

Insureco has refused to pay the baby's medical bill on the grounds that she is not a "natural child" of Surrogate within the meaning of the insurance policy and that the baby's expenses are Husband and Wife's responsibility.

Husband and Wife have also refused to pay the bill, claiming that they cannot afford to pay it and that the surrogacy contract is unenforceable under the applicable state law.

Surrogate has filed suit in the federal district court of State A against Insureco, Husband, and Wife. Surrogate alleges that Husband and Wife breached the surrogacy contract and that Insureco breached the terms of the insurance policy. Surrogate seeks to compel any or all of the defendants to pay the $500,000 hospital bill.

The defendants have moved to dismiss the action on the grounds that (i) the federal court lacks jurisdiction over the case, (ii) the case involves state-law domestic-relations issues (i.e., the biological parentage of the child and the enforceability of a surrogacy contract) that are inappropriate for resolution by a federal court, and (iii) Surrogate improperly joined her separate claims against Insureco, on the one hand, and Husband and Wife, on the other, in a single action.

1.   **Does the federal district court of State A have subject-matter jurisdiction over Surrogate's claims? Explain.**

2.   **Should the federal district court of State A dismiss the action because it involves domestic-relations issues? Explain.**

3.   **Did Surrogate properly join Insureco, Husband, and Wife as defendants in a single action? Explain.**

MEE RELEASED ESSAY QUESTIONS

FEDERAL CIVIL PROCEDURE
July 2010

Until recently, Paul had always lived in State A. Last year, he decided he would move to State B for at least one year and, after a year, decide whether to remain in State B or return to State A. Six months ago, Paul moved to State B, rented an apartment, and took a job as a temporary employee. Paul has enjoyed living in State B so much that he recently left his temporary job and accepted a position as a permanent employee at a law firm in State B.

Shortly after he moved to State B, Paul bought a vacation home in State A, which he visits about once a month for two or three days. To pay for the vacation home, Paul obtained a loan from Credit Union in State A. Credit Union is incorporated in and chartered by State A. Its only office, located in State A, is both its corporate headquarters and the place where it transacts business with its customers. Ninety-five percent of Credit Union's customers are State A residents who do business with Credit Union in person at its State A office.

Paul's loan agreement with Credit Union provides that he will repay the loan in monthly installments over a 30-year period. Credit Union has a mortgage on Paul's vacation home to secure the debt. The loan paperwork lists Paul's State B address as his mailing and home address. The loan agreement also contains a privacy provision whereby Credit Union agrees not to disclose Paul's personal information to any third party without Paul's written permission. Credit Union sends a loan statement and payment coupon to Paul's State B address each month, and Paul returns the payment coupon with a check for the payment amount.

After the loan closed, a Credit Union employee mailed copies of all the loan paperwork to Paul. Unfortunately, the employee misread Paul's address in State B and sent the paperwork to an incorrect address. Several months later, Paul discovered that someone had gotten his loan paperwork and had used the information (including Paul's Social Security number and credit card numbers) to steal his identity. The identity thief had quickly accumulated $150,000 in unpaid bills in Paul's name. Paul's credit rating was ruined, and no one would extend him new credit.

Paul has sued Credit Union in the United States District Court for the District of State B for breach of the privacy provisions of the loan contract. The parties have stipulated that Paul's actual loss was $80,000. Paul's suit seeks $240,000 in damages, plus attorney's fees, pursuant to a State A statute that entitles victims of identity theft to recover treble damages and attorney's fees from anyone who wrongfully discloses their personal information. Paul's complaint also asserts that a federal statute restricting damages in state-law identity-theft cases to actual damages is unconstitutional and therefore does not preempt the treble damages provisions of the State A statute. The complaint asserts that the State B federal court has both diversity and federal-question jurisdiction over the case.

The long-arm statute of State B extends personal jurisdiction as far as the Constitution allows.

1.   May the United States District Court for the District of State B exercise personal jurisdiction over Credit Union? Explain.

2.   Does the United States District Court for the District of State B have diversity jurisdiction over the case? Explain.

3.   Does the United States District Court for the District of State B have federal-question jurisdiction over the case? Explain.

MEE RELEASED ESSAY QUESTIONS

FEDERAL CIVIL PROCEDURE
February 2011

Plaintiff, a citizen of State B, was vacationing in State A, where he visited the O.K. Bar. While he was at the bar, Plaintiff was attacked and seriously beaten by Dave, a regular bar patron and a citizen of State A. Bartender, a citizen of State A, attempted to stop the attack and was also injured by Dave.

Plaintiff sued Dave and Bartender in the United States District Court for the District of State A, properly invoking the court's diversity jurisdiction. Plaintiff's complaint states a state law battery claim against Dave, seeking damages from Dave in excess of $75,000. Plaintiff's complaint also states a claim against Bartender based on Bartender's alleged negligence in serving alcohol to Dave after Dave became visibly intoxicated and belligerent. Plaintiff's complaint seeks damages from Bartender in excess of $75,000. Plaintiff's damages claims are reasonable in light of the injuries Plaintiff suffered in the attack.

Dave was personally served with the summons and complaint. However, the process server could not find Bartender. He therefore taped the summons and complaint to the front door of the O.K. Bar, where Bartender found them the next day.

Bartender made a timely motion to dismiss Plaintiff's complaint for failure to state a cause of action. When that motion was denied by the district court judge, Bartender filed a second motion to dismiss for insufficiency of service of process. The judge also denied that motion.

Bartender then filed an answer to the complaint, denying liability. The answer also stated a state law claim for battery against Dave, seeking $20,000 damages for the injuries Bartender suffered when he tried to stop Dave's attack on Plaintiff.

Dave has moved to dismiss Bartender's cross-claim on the grounds of improper joinder and lack of subject-matter jurisdiction.

1. **Did the United States District Court for the District of State A properly deny Bartender's motion to dismiss for insufficiency of service of process? Explain.**

2. **Do the Federal Rules of Civil Procedure permit Bartender to join a claim for battery against Dave in Bartender's answer to Plaintiff's complaint? Explain.**

3. **Assuming that the Federal Rules of Civil Procedure permit Bartender to join his state law claim against Dave, does the United States District Court for the District of State A have subject-matter jurisdiction over that claim? Explain.**

MEE RELEASED ESSAY QUESTIONS

FEDERAL CIVIL PROCEDURE
July 2011

OfficeEquip is a U.S. distributor of office machines. It is incorporated in State A, where it has its principal place of business. BritCo is a manufacturer of copiers. It is incorporated in Scotland and has its principal place of business in London, England. OfficeEquip sued BritCo, alleging that BritCo had breached a long-term contract to supply copiers to OfficeEquip.

The suit was filed in the United States District Court for State A, and OfficeEquip properly invoked the court's diversity (alienage) jurisdiction.

BritCo made a timely motion to dismiss the complaint on the ground that it was filed in violation of a forum-selection clause in the supply contract that required all contract disputes to be adjudicated in London. While its motion to dismiss was pending, BritCo filed an answer to the complaint.

In its answer, BritCo denied breaching the supply contract. BritCo also made a counterclaim seeking damages for OfficeEquip's alleged breach of a contractual covenant not to compete with BritCo.

OfficeEquip filed a motion for judgment on the pleadings on BritCo's counterclaim, arguing that the covenant not to compete was unenforceable as a matter of law.

After a short period of discovery, the district judge issued the following two orders:

> OfficeEquip's motion for judgment on the pleadings is granted. The contractual covenant not to compete is void as a matter of public policy and is therefore unenforceable. Given that this is strictly a legal issue and entirely severable from OfficeEquip's breach of contract claim, there is no just reason for delay, and I accordingly direct that judgment should be entered in favor of OfficeEquip on BritCo's counterclaim.

> BritCo's motion to dismiss is denied. Enforcement of the forum-selection clause would be unreasonable in this case. OfficeEquip has never done business in London, and it would be extremely inconvenient for it to litigate there.

Trial on the breach of contract claim is scheduled in three months.

1. **Can BritCo immediately appeal the district court's order granting OfficeEquip's motion for judgment on the pleadings with respect to BritCo's counterclaim? Explain.**

2. **Can BritCo immediately appeal the district court's order denying its motion to dismiss? Explain.**

MEE RELEASED ESSAY QUESTIONS

FEDERAL CIVIL PROCEDURE
February 2012

The owner of a rare antique tapestry worth more than $1 million is a citizen of State A. The owner contacted a restorer, a citizen of State B, to restore the tapestry for $100,000. The owner and the restorer met in State A and negotiated a contract, but the final documents, prepared by the parties' respective attorneys, were drafted and signed in State B. The contract has a forum-selection clause that specifies that any litigation arising out of or relating to the contract must be commenced in State B.

The restorer repaired the tapestry in State B and then informed the owner that the restoration was complete. The owner picked up the tapestry and paid the restorer $100,000. Subsequently, the owner discovered that the restorer had done hardly any work on the tapestry.

Despite the forum-selection clause in the contract, the owner filed suit against the restorer in a state court in State A, claiming breach of contract. The owner's suit sought rescission of the contract and a return of the full contract price—$100,000.

The laws of State A and State B are different on two relevant points. First, State A courts do not enforce forum-selection clauses that would oust the jurisdiction of State A courts, regarding such clauses as against public policy; State B courts always enforce forum-selection clauses. Second, State A would allow contract rescission on these facts; State B would not allow rescission but would allow recovery of damages.

Under the conflict-of-laws rules of both State A and State B, a state court would apply its own law to resolve both the forum-selection clause issue and the rescission issue.

After the owner filed suit in State A court, the restorer removed the case to the United States District Court for the District of State A and then moved for a change of venue to the United States District Court for the District of State B, citing the contractual forum-selection clause in support of the motion. (There is only one United States District Court in each state.) The owner moved for remand on the ground that the federal court did not have removal jurisdiction over the action. Alternatively, the owner argued against the motion to transfer on the basis that the forum-selection clause was invalid under State A law.

1. **Does the federal court in State A have removal jurisdiction over the case? Explain.**

2. **Should the change-of-venue motion, seeking transfer of the case to the federal court in State B, be granted? Explain.**

3. **Would a change of venue affect the law to be applied in resolving the rescission issue? Explain.**

MEE RELEASED ESSAY QUESTIONS

FEDERAL CIVIL PROCEDURE
July 2012

Plaintiff, a female employee of Defendant, a large manufacturing firm, sued Defendant in federal district court for violating a federal statute that creates a right to be free of sex discrimination in the workplace. Plaintiff alleged the following: (1) Plaintiff worked for Defendant in a position for which females had seldom been hired in the past. (2) Shortly after Plaintiff was hired, male coworkers began to make sexually charged remarks to Plaintiff. (3) Plaintiff's male supervisor asked her out on dates and became angry each time she refused. (4) There were occasional incidents in which the supervisor or another male worker "accidentally" made contact with various parts of Plaintiff's body. (5) No one from company management ever took steps to monitor or limit behavior of this sort. (6) As a result of this behavior, Plaintiff began to suffer from various physical ailments that were related to stress. (7) Plaintiff made no complaint to management about the situation because the job paid very well and there were, to her knowledge, no comparable opportunities that would be available to her if she lost this particular job.

Defendant's answer to the complaint admitted that Plaintiff was an employee and that the individual named as her supervisor was her supervisor. Defendant denied all allegations relating to the alleged sex discrimination.

A well-established affirmative defense is available in cases of this sort if the defendant employer proves that (a) the plaintiff employee was not subject to any adverse job action (firing, demotion, loss of promotion opportunity, etc.), (b) the employer exercised reasonable care to prevent and promptly correct any sexually harassing behavior, and (c) the plaintiff employee unreasonably failed to take advantage of any preventive or corrective opportunities provided by the employer.

In a pretrial deposition, Plaintiff admitted that she had suffered no loss of pay or promotion opportunity. Plaintiff also admitted that she was aware of company policies forbidding sex discrimination and sexual harassment, as well as the procedures that employees could use to complain about perceived discrimination. Plaintiff stated that although she was aware of those policies and procedures, she had not seen any effort on the part of Defendant to enforce the policies and was afraid that she would suffer retaliation if she made use of the procedures available to complain of sex discrimination.

After the close of discovery, Defendant moved to amend its answer to add the affirmative defense set forth above. It also moved for summary judgment, claiming that Plaintiff's deposition testimony sufficiently established the elements of the affirmative defense to warrant a judgment in Defendant's favor.

Plaintiff opposed both motions. The trial judge ruled in Defendant's favor, allowing the amendment and granting summary judgment.

Did the judge err? Explain.

MEE RELEASED ESSAY QUESTIONS

FEDERAL CIVIL PROCEDURE
February 2013

Mother and Son, who are both adults, are citizens and residents of State A. Mother owned an expensive luxury car valued in excess of $100,000. Son borrowed Mother's car to drive to a store in State A. As Son approached a traffic light that had just turned yellow, he carefully braked and brought the car to a complete stop. Driver, who was following immediately behind him, failed to stop and rear-ended Mother's car, which was damaged beyond repair. Son was seriously injured. Driver is a citizen of State B.

Son sued Driver in the United States District Court for the District of State A, alleging that she was negligent in the operation of her vehicle. Son sought damages in excess of $75,000 for his personal injuries, exclusive of costs and interest. In her answer, Driver alleged that Son was contributorily negligent in the operation of Mother's car. She further alleged that the brake lights on Mother's car were burned out and that Mother's negligent failure to properly maintain the car was a contributing cause of the accident.

Following a trial on the merits in Son's case against Driver, the jury answered the following special interrogatories:

> Do you find that Driver was negligent in the operation of her vehicle? <u>Yes.</u>

> Do you find that Son was negligent in the operation of Mother's car? <u>No.</u>

> Do you find that Mother negligently failed to ensure that the brake lights on her car were in proper working order? <u>Yes.</u>

The judge then entered a judgment in favor of Son against Driver. Driver did not appeal.

Two months later, Mother sued Driver in the United States District Court for the District of State A, alleging that Driver's negligence in the operation of her vehicle destroyed Mother's luxury car. Mother sought damages in excess of $75,000, exclusive of costs and interest.

State A follows the same preclusion principles that federal courts follow in federal-question cases.

1.   **Is Mother's claim against Driver barred by the judgment in *Son v. Driver*? Explain.**

2.   **Does the jury's conclusion in *Son v. Driver* that Mother had negligently failed to maintain the brake lights on her car preclude Mother from litigating that issue in her subsequent suit against Driver? Explain.**

3.   **Does the jury's conclusion in *Son v. Driver* that Driver was negligent preclude Driver from litigating that issue in the *Mother v. Driver* lawsuit? Explain.**

MEE RELEASED ESSAY QUESTIONS

FEDERAL CIVIL PROCEDURE
July 2013

A woman was born and raised in the largest city ("the city") of State A, where she also attended college.

Three years ago, the woman purchased a 300-acre farm and a farmhouse in neighboring State B, 50 miles from the city. She moved many of her personal belongings to the State B farmhouse, registered her car in State B, and acquired a State B driver's license. She now spends seven months of the year in State B, working her farm and living in the farmhouse. She pays income taxes in State B, but not in State A, and lists State B as her residence on her federal income tax returns.

However, the woman has not completely cut her ties with State A. She still lives in the city for five months each year in a condominium that she owns. She still refers to the city as "home" and maintains an active social life there. When she is living on the farm, she receives frequent weekend visits from her city friends and occasionally spends the weekend in the city at her condominium. She is a member of a health club and a church in the city and obtains all her medical and dental care there. She is also registered to vote and votes in State A.

A food product distributor sells food items to grocery stores throughout a five-state region that includes States A and B. The distributor is a State C corporation. Its corporate headquarters are in State B, where its top corporate officers, including its chief executive officer (CEO), have their offices and staff. The distributor's food processing, warehousing, and distribution facilities are all located in State A.

Three years ago, the woman and the distributor entered into a 10-year written contract providing that the woman would sell all the produce grown on her farm each year to the distributor. The contract was negotiated and signed by the parties at the distributor's corporate headquarters in State B.

The woman and the distributor performed the contract for two years, earning her $80,000 per year. Recently, the distributor decided that the woman's prices were too high. At a meeting at its corporate headquarters, the distributor's CEO asked the woman to drop her prices. When she refused, the CEO informed her that the distributor would no longer buy produce from her and that it was terminating the contract.

The woman has sued the distributor for anticipatory breach of contract. She seeks $400,000 in damages. She has filed suit in the United States District Court for the District of State A, invoking the court's diversity jurisdiction.

State A's long-arm statute provides that "a court of this State may exercise personal jurisdiction over parties to the fullest extent permitted by the due process clause of the Fourteenth Amendment to the United States Constitution."

The distributor has moved to dismiss the woman's action for lack of subject-matter jurisdiction and for improper venue.

1.   **Should the court grant the motion to dismiss for lack of subject-matter jurisdiction? Explain.**

2.   **Should the court grant the motion to dismiss for improper venue? Explain.**

MEE RELEASED ESSAY QUESTIONS

FEDERAL CIVIL PROCEDURE
February 2014

A builder constructed a vacation house for an out-of-state customer on the customer's land. The house was completed on June 1, at which point the customer still owed $200,000 of the $800,000 contract price, which was payable in full five days later.

On June 14, the basement of the house was flooded with two inches of water during a heavy rainfall. When the customer complained, the builder told the customer, "The flooding was caused by poorly designed landscaping. Our work is fine and fully up to code. Have an engineer look at the foundation. If there's a problem, we'll fix it."

The customer, pleased by the builder's cooperative attitude, immediately hired a structural engineer to examine the foundation of the house. On June 30, the engineer provided the customer with a written report on the condition of the foundation, which stated that the foundation was properly constructed.

Unhappy with the conclusions in the engineer's report, the customer then hired a home inspector to evaluate the house. The home inspector's report concluded that the foundation of the house had been poorly constructed and was inadequately waterproofed.

On July 10, the customer sent the builder the home inspector's report with a note that said, "Until you fix this problem, you won't get another penny from me." The builder immediately contacted an attorney and directed the attorney to prepare a draft complaint against the customer for nonpayment. Hoping to avoid litigation, the builder sent several more requests for payment to the customer. The customer ignored all these requests.

On September 10, the builder filed suit in federal district court, properly invoking the court's diversity jurisdiction and seeking $200,000 in damages for breach of contract. The customer's answer denied liability on the basis of alleged defective construction of the house's foundation.

Several months later, the case is nearly ready for trial. However, two discovery disputes have not yet been resolved.

First, despite a request from the builder, the customer has refused to provide a copy of the report prepared by the structural engineer who examined the foundation of the house. The customer claims that the report is "work product" and not discoverable because the customer does not intend to ask the engineer to testify at trial. The builder has asked the court to order the customer to turn over the engineer's report.

Second, the customer has asked the court to impose sanctions for the builder's failure to comply with the customer's demand for copies of all emails concerning construction of the foundation of the house. The builder has truthfully informed the customer that all such emails were destroyed on August 2. This destruction was pursuant to the builder's standard practice of permanently deleting all project-related emails from company records 60 days after construction of a project is complete. There is no relevant state records-retention law.

1.   **Should the court order the customer to turn over the engineer's report? Explain.**

2.   **Should the court sanction the builder for the destruction of emails related to the case, and if so, what factors should the court consider in determining those sanctions? Explain.**

MEE RELEASED ESSAY QUESTIONS

FEDERAL CIVIL PROCEDURE
July 2014

The United States Forest Service (USFS) manages public lands in national forests, including the Scenic National Forest. Without conducting an environmental evaluation or preparing an environmental impact statement, the USFS approved a development project in the Scenic National Forest that required the clearing of 5,000 acres of old-growth forest. The trees in the forest are hundreds of years old, and the forest is home to a higher concentration of wildlife than can be found anywhere else in the western United States.

The USFS solicited bids from logging companies to harvest the trees on the 5,000 acres of forest targeted for clearing, and it ultimately awarded the logging contract to the company that had submitted the highest bid for the trees. However, the USFS has not yet issued the company a logging permit. Once it does so, the company intends to begin cutting down trees immediately.

A nonprofit organization whose mission is the preservation of natural resources has filed suit in federal district court against the USFS. The nonprofit alleges that the USFS violated the National Environmental Policy Act (NEPA) by failing to prepare an environmental impact statement for the proposed logging project. Among other remedies, the nonprofit seeks a permanent injunction barring the USFS from issuing a logging permit to the logging company until an adequate environmental impact statement is completed. The nonprofit believes that the logging project would destroy important wildlife habitat and thereby cause serious harm to wildlife in the Scenic National Forest, including some endangered species.

Assume that federal subject-matter jurisdiction is available, that the nonprofit has standing to bring this action, and that venue is proper.

1.   If the logging company seeks to join the litigation as a party, must the federal district court allow it to do so as a matter of right? Explain.

2.   What types of relief could the nonprofit seek to stop the USFS from issuing a logging permit during the pendency of the action, what must the nonprofit demonstrate to obtain
that relief, and is the federal district court likely to grant that relief? Explain.

MEE RELEASED ESSAY QUESTIONS

FEDERAL CIVIL PROCEDURE
February 2015

MedForms Inc. processes claims for medical insurers. Last year, MedForms contracted with a data entry company ("the company") to enter information from claims into MedForms's database. MedForms hired a woman to manage the contract with the company.

A few months after entering into the contract with the company, MedForms began receiving complaints from insurers regarding data-entry errors. On behalf of MedForms, the woman conducted a limited audit of the company's work and discovered that its employees had been making errors in transferring data from insurance claims forms to the MedForms database.

The woman immediately reported her findings to her MedForms supervisor and told him that fixing the problems caused by the company's errors would require a review of millions of forms and would cost millions of dollars. In response to her report, the supervisor said, "I knew we never should have hired a woman to oversee this contract," and he fired her on the spot.

The woman properly initiated suit against MedForms in the United States District Court for the District of State A. Her complaint alleged that she had been subjected to repeated sexual harassment by her supervisor throughout her employment at MedForms and that he had fired her because of his bias against women. Her complaint sought $100,000 in damages from MedForms for sexual harassment and sex discrimination in violation of federal civil rights law.

After receiving the summons and complaint in the action, MedForms filed a third-party complaint against the company, seeking to join it as a third-party defendant in the action. MedForms alleged that the company's data-entry errors constituted a breach of contract. MedForms sought $500,000 in damages from the company. MedForms served the company with process by hiring a process server who personally delivered a copy of the summons and complaint to the company's chief executive officer at its headquarters.

MedForms is incorporated in State A, where it also has its headquarters and document processing facilities. The woman is a citizen of State A. The company's only document processing facility is located in State A, but its headquarters are located in State B, where it is incorporated and where its chief executive officer was served with process.

State A and State B each authorize service of process on corporations only by personal delivery of a summons and complaint to the corporation's secretary.

The company has moved to dismiss MedForms's third-party complaint for (a) insufficient service of process, (b) lack of subject-matter jurisdiction, and (c) improper joinder.

How should the District Court rule on each of the grounds asserted in the company's motion to dismiss? Explain.

MEE RELEASED ESSAY QUESTIONS

FEDERAL CIVIL PROCEDURE
July 2015

A woman attended a corporation's sales presentation in State A. At this presentation, the corporation's salespeople spoke to prospective buyers about purchasing so-called "super solar panels," rooftop solar panels that the corporation's salespeople said were 100 times as efficient as traditional solar panels. The salespeople distributed brochures that purported to show that the solar panels had performed successfully in multiple rigorous tests. The brochures had been prepared by an independent engineer pursuant to a consulting contract with the corporation.

Based on what she was told at this presentation and the brochure she received, the woman decided to purchase solar panels from the corporation for $20,000. The corporation shipped the panels to the woman from its manufacturing facility in State B. The woman had the panels installed on the roof of her house in State A. The panels failed to work as promised, even though they were properly installed.

A federal statute prohibits "material misstatements or omissions of fact in connection with the sale or purchase of solar panels" and provides an exclusive civil remedy for individuals harmed by such statements. This remedy preempts all state-law claims that would otherwise apply to this purchase.

Relying on this federal statute, the woman has sued the corporation and the independent engineer in the U.S. District Court for the district of State A. She alleges that the statements made by the engineer in the brochure and the statements made by the corporation's salespeople at the presentation were false and misleading with respect to the solar panels' performance and value. She seeks damages of $30,000 (the cost of the solar panels plus the expense of installing them).

The woman is a State A resident. The corporation is incorporated in State B and has its principal place of business in State B. The engineer, who has never been in State A, is a State B resident with his principal place of business in State B. He prepared the brochures in State B and delivered them to the corporation there. He knew that the brochures would be distributed to prospective buyers at sales presentations around the country.

The federal statute has no provision on personal jurisdiction. State A's long-arm statute has been interpreted to extend personal jurisdiction as far as the U.S. Constitution allows.

The engineer has timely moved to dismiss the complaint against him for lack of subject-matter and personal jurisdiction. The engineer has also filed an answer (subject to his motion to dismiss) denying the claims against him and asserting a cross-claim against the corporation.

The engineer's cross-claim alleges that the corporation must indemnify the engineer for any damages he may have to pay the woman. The indemnity claim is based on the terms of the consulting contract between the corporation and the engineer.

The corporation has filed timely motions to dismiss the woman's complaint for lack of subject- matter and personal jurisdiction and to dismiss the engineer's cross-claim for lack of subject- matter jurisdiction.

1.   **Does the State A federal district court have personal jurisdiction over**
       (a) the corporation? Explain.
       (b) the engineer? Explain.

2.   **Assuming that there is personal jurisdiction over both defendants, does the State A federal district court have subject-matter jurisdiction over**
       (a) the woman's claim against the corporation and the engineer? Explain.
       (b) the engineer's cross-claim against the corporation? Explain.

MEE RELEASED ESSAY QUESTIONS

FEDERAL CIVIL PROCEDURE
July 2016

A woman and a man have both lived their entire lives in State A. The man once went to a gun show in State B where he bought a gun. Otherwise, neither the woman nor the man had ever left State A until the following events occurred.

The woman and the man went hunting for wild turkey at a State A game preserve. The man was carrying the gun he had purchased in State B. The man had permanently disabled the gun's safety features to be able to react more quickly to a turkey sighting. The man dropped the gun and it accidentally fired, inflicting a serious chest wound on the woman. The woman was immediately flown to a hospital in neighboring State C, where she underwent surgery.

One week after the shooting accident, the man traveled to State C for business and took the opportunity to visit the woman in the hospital. During the visit, the woman's attorney handed the man the summons and complaint in a suit the woman had initiated against the man in the United States District Court for the District of State C. Two days later, the woman was released from the hospital and returned home to State A where she spent weeks recovering.

The woman's complaint alleges separate claims against the man: 1) a state-law negligence claim and 2) a federal claim under the Federal Gun Safety Act (Safety Act). The Safety Act provides a cause of action for individuals harmed by gun owners who alter the safety features of a gun that has traveled in interstate commerce. The Safety Act caps damages at $100,000 per incident, but does not preempt state causes of action. The woman's complaint seeks damages of $100,000 on the Safety Act claim and $120,000 on the state-law negligence claim. Both sets of damages are sought as compensation for the physical suffering the woman experienced and the medical costs the woman incurred as a result of the shooting.

The man has moved to dismiss the complaint, asserting (a) lack of personal jurisdiction, (b) lack of subject-matter jurisdiction, and (c) improper venue. State C's jurisdictional statutes provide that state courts may exercise personal jurisdiction "to the limits allowed by the United States Constitution."

With respect to each asserted basis for dismissal, should the man's motion to dismiss be granted? Explain.

MBE SUBJECTS – RELEASED QUESTIONS

REAL PROPERTY
MEE Question - February 2009

Several years ago, Parent, the record owner of a farm in fee simple absolute, conveyed the farm as a gift "jointly in fee to my beloved daughters, Jessie and Karen, equally, to share and share alike." Parent delivered the deed to Jessie and Karen. The deed was never recorded.

Two years ago, Jessie borrowed $60,000 from Credit Union, securing the loan by granting Credit Union a mortgage on her interest in the farm. Credit Union properly and promptly recorded the mortgage.

Six months ago, Jessie validly contracted to sell her one-half interest in the farm for $90,000 to Buyer, who was very anxious to acquire Jessie's interest. Buyer paid Jessie $40,000 as earnest money and agreed in the contract to accept a deed with no warranties of any kind and to accept the title regardless of whether title was marketable. Buyer had no actual notice of the mortgage Jessie had granted to Credit Union.

Two months ago, before closing the sale with Buyer, Jessie died, survived by Karen. At the time of Jessie's death, the loan secured by Credit Union's mortgage was still outstanding. Jessie's will provided: "I give all of my real property to Devisee and all of my personal property to Legatee." Both Devisee and Legatee survived Jessie.

Last month, the executor of Jessie's estate executed a deed purporting to convey a one-half interest in the farm to Buyer in exchange for the balance of the purchase price.

The jurisdiction has a notice-type recording statute and a grantor-grantee index system.

1.   **Did Parent convey the farm to Jessie and Karen as "tenants in common" or as "joint tenants with right of survivorship"? Explain.**

2.   **Assuming Jessie and Karen acquired a joint tenancy with right of survivorship in the farm, what are the rights, if any, of Karen, Credit Union, and Buyer in the farm? Explain.**

3.   **Assuming Jessie and Karen acquired a joint tenancy with right of survivorship in the farm, who is entitled to the balance of the purchase price Buyer paid the executor of Jessie's estate? Explain.**

MBE SUBJECTS – RELEASED QUESTIONS

REAL PROPERTY
MEE Question - February 2010

In 1960, Owen, the owner of vacant land, granted a power-line easement over the land to an electric company by a properly executed written instrument. This easement was never recorded. Consistent with the easement, the electric company erected power lines over the land. The power lines and supporting poles remain on the land.

In 1961, Owen granted an underground gas-line easement on the land to a gas company by a properly executed written instrument. This easement was never recorded. Consistent with the easement, the gas company dug trenches, laid pipes, and restored the surface of the land to its pre-installation condition.

In 1970, Owen conveyed the land to Abe by a full covenant and warranty deed that made no mention of the easements. The Owen-to-Abe deed was promptly and properly recorded. Abe paid full value for the land and had no actual knowledge of the two easements Owen had previously granted.

In 1995, Abe conveyed the land to Bob by a full covenant and warranty deed that made no mention of the easements. The Abe-to-Bob deed was promptly and properly recorded. Bob, who paid full value for the land, knew of the underground gas line because he had helped dig the trenches on the land. Bob had not visited the portion of the land crossed by the power lines and had no actual knowledge of the power-line easement.

In 2009, Bob decided to build a house on the land and hired an engineer to evaluate the proposed building site. Following an inspection of the proposed site, the engineer told Bob that each easement precluded building on the site.

Relevant state statutes provide

> (1) "A conveyance of real property is not valid against any subsequent purchaser who, without notice, purchases said real property in good faith and for valuable consideration," and
> (2) "Easements by prescription are abolished."

1.   **Did Bob take the land subject to the power-line easement? Explain.**

2.   **Did Bob take the land subject to the gas-line easement? Explain.**

3.   **Assuming Bob took the land subject to either easement, may Bob obtain damages from Owen based upon a breach of the covenant against encumbrances? Explain.**

REAL PROPERTY
MEE Question - July 2010

Eighty years ago, Owner, the owner of vacant land known as Blackacre, conveyed Blackacre to a local school district (School) "if School uses Blackacre only to teach children aged 5 to 13." Shortly after acquiring title to Blackacre, School erected a classroom building on Blackacre and began teaching children aged 5 to 13 in that building.

Seventy years ago, Owner died and left his entire estate to Daughter.

School used the classroom building to teach its students aged 5 to 13 until three years ago when, due to increasing enrollments, School built a new classroom building three miles from Blackacre and converted the classroom building on Blackacre into administrative offices.

The building on Blackacre is now exclusively occupied by administrative offices, and all School students aged 5 to 13 are taught in the new classroom building.

Two years ago, Daughter died. Daughter did not object to School's altered use of Blackacre before her death. She devised her entire estate to her Husband for life, with the remainder to "my surviving children." Daughter was survived by Husband and two children, Ann and Bill.

One year ago, Bill died. Bill's entire estate passed to his wife, Mary.

One month ago, Husband, the life tenant under Daughter's will, died. Husband was survived by Ann and by Bill's widow, Mary.

State law provides:

    I.   "Actions to recover the possession of real property shall be brought within 10 years after the cause of action accrues."

    II.   "All future interests are alienable, devisable, and descendible to the extent they do not expire as a result of the holder's death."

    III.   "Conditions and limitations in a deed shall not be construed as covenants."

There are no other relevant statutes.

What interests, if any, do School, Ann, and Mary have in Blackacre? Explain.

MBE SUBJECTS – RELEASED QUESTIONS

REAL PROPERTY
MEE Question - July 2011

In 1980, Oscar sold undeveloped land that he owned in fee simple to Sam, but Sam failed to record the deed.

In 1985, Sam granted Railroad an easement to operate a rail line across a portion of the land to serve a grain storage facility located on a neighboring tract of land. Railroad recorded this easement, laid railroad tracks on the land, and operated trains weekly until the grain storage facility went out of business in 2000. The tracks are still in place and clearly visible, but no trains have operated over them since 2000.

In 1990, Sam conveyed the land to Daughter as a graduation gift. Daughter promptly recorded the deed given to her by Sam. Except for the railroad tracks, the land has remained undeveloped.

Oscar died six months ago. Unaware of the prior transactions, the executor of Oscar's estate sold the land to Purchaser for its fair market value. Purchaser was also unaware of these prior transactions. The executor gave Purchaser a quitclaim deed to the land. Purchaser promptly recorded this deed.

The state in which the land is located maintains its records under a grantor-grantee indexing system, and the state's recording act provides: "No conveyance or mortgage of real property shall be good against subsequent purchasers for value and without notice unless the same be recorded according to law."

just Notice statute

What are the rights, if any, of Purchaser, Daughter, and Railroad in the land? Explain.

MBE SUBJECTS – RELEASED QUESTIONS

REAL PROPERTY
MEE Question - February 2012

Blackacre, which is immediately to the west of Whiteacre, is bounded on its west by a state highway. Whiteacre is bounded on the east by a county road. Both roads connect to a four-lane highway.

Twenty years ago, Tom, who then owned Blackacre, sold to Sue, who then owned Whiteacre, an easement over a private gravel road that crossed Blackacre. This easement allowed Sue significantly better access to the four-lane highway from Whiteacre than she had had using only the county road adjacent to Whiteacre. The easement was promptly and properly recorded.

After acquiring this easement, Sue discontinued using the county road to the east of Whiteacre and used the private gravel road crossing Blackacre to travel between Whiteacre and the four-lane highway. Sue used the private gravel road across Blackacre for that purpose almost every day for the next 18 years.

Fifteen years ago, Sue purchased Blackacre from Tom. The deed from Tom to Sue was promptly and properly recorded.

Two years ago, Sue sold Whiteacre to Dan. The deed from Sue to Dan, which was promptly and properly recorded, did not mention the private gravel road crossing Blackacre, although Dan was aware that Sue had used the road to more easily access the four-lane highway.

Following the purchase of Whiteacre, Dan obtained a construction loan from Bank secured by a mortgage on Whiteacre. This mortgage was promptly and properly recorded. The loan commitment, in the amount of $1,500,000, which was reflected in the mortgage, obligated Bank to loan Dan $300,000 immediately. It further obligated Bank to loan Dan an additional $500,000 in 180 days and $700,000 in 280 days.

After obtaining the second loan installment from Bank, Dan realized that he would need additional funds and borrowed $400,000 from Finance Company. This loan was also secured by a mortgage on Whiteacre. Upon Dan's signing the note and mortgage, Finance Company immediately remitted the $400,000 to Dan and promptly and properly recorded its mortgage.

Thereafter, Bank advanced the final $700,000 loan installment to Dan.

Recently, Dan defaulted on the loans from both Bank and Finance Company. At the time of these defaults, Dan owed $1,500,000 to Bank and $400,000 to Finance Company.

At a proper foreclosure sale by Bank, Whiteacre was sold for $1,500,000 net of sale expenses.

1. **Immediately before Sue sold Whiteacre to Dan, did Sue have an easement over Blackacre? Explain.** *Yes. - express grant easement in writing → deed*

easement by grant is a deed allowing the grantee use of the property.

2. **Immediately after Sue sold Whiteacre to Dan, did Dan have an easement over Blackacre? Explain.** *Yes - Dan took the easement so it passes automatically.*

3. **How should the proceeds from the sale of Whiteacre be distributed between Bank and Finance Company? Explain.**

easement by implication go through the steps

only plausible easement. Highway

20 yrs ago

T → Sue easement (R) 20 yrs
Use = 18 yrs.

T → Sue B/A (R) 15 yrs

Sue → Dan W/A Ø easmnt (R) 2 yrs

Dan + Bank = mortgage (R)
1.5 M
   300k - imm
   500k - 180d
   700k - 280d

Dan + finance = 400k mortgage (R)

MBE SUBJECTS – RELEASED QUESTIONS

REAL PROPERTY
MEE Question - February 2013

In 2008, a landlord and a tenant entered into a 10-year written lease, commencing September 1, 2008, for the exclusive use of a commercial building at a monthly rent of $2,500. The lease contained a covenant of quiet enjoyment but no other covenants or promises on the part of the landlord.

When the landlord and tenant negotiated the lease, the tenant asked the landlord if the building had an air-conditioning system. The landlord answered, "Yes, it does." The tenant responded, "Great! I will be using the building to manufacture a product that will be irreparably damaged if the temperature during manufacture exceeds 81 degrees for more than six consecutive hours."

On April 15, 2012, the building's air-conditioning system malfunctioned, causing the building temperature to rise above 81 degrees for three hours. The tenant immediately telephoned the landlord about this malfunction. The tenant left a message in which he explained what had happened and asked the landlord, "What are you going to do about it?" The landlord did not respond to the tenant's message.

On May 15, 2012, the air-conditioning system again malfunctioned. This time, the malfunction caused the building temperature to rise above 81 degrees for six hours. The tenant telephoned the landlord and left a message describing the malfunction. As before, the landlord did not respond.

On August 24, 2012, the air-conditioning system malfunctioned again, causing the temperature to rise above 81 degrees for 10 hours. Again, the tenant promptly telephoned the landlord. The landlord answered the phone, and the tenant begged her to fix the system. The landlord refused. The tenant then attempted to fix the system himself, but he failed. As a result of the air-conditioning malfunction, products worth $150,000 were destroyed.

The next day, the tenant wrote the following letter to the landlord:

> I've had enough. I told you about the air-conditioning problem twice before yesterday's disaster, and you failed to correct it. I will vacate the building by the end of the month and will bring you the keys when I leave.

The tenant vacated the building on August 31, 2012, and returned the keys to the landlord that day. At that time, there were six years remaining on the lease.

On September 1, 2012, the landlord returned the keys to the tenant with a note that said, "I repeat, the air-conditioning is not my problem. You have leased the building, and you should fix it." The tenant promptly sent the keys back to the landlord with a letter that said, "I have terminated the lease, and I will not be returning to the building or making further rent payments." After receiving the keys and letter, the landlord put the keys into her desk. To date, she has neither responded to the tenant's letter nor taken steps to lease the building to another tenant.

On November 1, 2012, two months after the tenant vacated the property, the landlord sued the tenant, claiming that she is entitled to the remaining unpaid rent ($100,000) from September 1 for the balance of the lease term (reduced to present value) or, if not that, then damages for the tenant's wrongful termination.

Is the landlord correct? Explain.

MBE SUBJECTS – RELEASED QUESTIONS

REAL PROPERTY
MEE Question - February 2013

Two years ago, a builder constructed a house for a woman and conveyed that house to her for $300,000 at the closing by a warranty deed, which was promptly recorded. The sale contract contained no express warranties relating to the condition of the house. To finance the purchase, the woman borrowed $200,000 from a local bank secured by a mortgage on her new house. The mortgage note provided that in the event of the woman's failure to make two consecutive monthly mortgage payments, the balance would become immediately due and payable. The mortgage was promptly recorded.

One year ago, the woman accepted a new job and moved. At that time, her house was worth $360,000 and there was a balance on the mortgage of $195,000. She sold the house to a man and delivered a quitclaim deed to him in exchange for $160,000. The quitclaim deed was promptly recorded and made no reference to the woman's mortgage obligation. The mortgage obligation was not discharged at the closing. However, the man immediately began to make the woman's monthly mortgage payments to the bank after the closing.

Nine months ago, water seeped into the basement of the house during a major storm, causing substantial damage. It is undisputed that the seepage was due to defective concrete used by the builder and not to any negligence on the builder's part. The man called the builder, told him about the seepage, and demanded that the builder fix the concrete. The builder responded: "That's your problem." The man then repaired the concrete at a cost of $80,000.

Thereafter, the man sued the builder to recover the $80,000 he had spent to repair the concrete. While the case was pending, the man stopped making mortgage payments. The bank sued the man to foreclose on the mortgage and, if necessary, obtain a deficiency judgment against him on the note if the sale proceeds were insufficient to discharge the mortgage debt. The man has joined the woman as a third-party defendant in the lawsuit.

1. **Is the man likely to prevail against the builder to recover the $80,000 he spent to repair the concrete? Explain.**

2. **Is the man personally liable for the outstanding balance on the mortgage note between the woman and the bank? Explain.**

3. **If the bank is successful in its foreclosure action, will the man be able to recover damages from the woman? Explain.**

MBE SUBJECTS - RELEASED ESSAY QUESTIONS

REAL PROPERTY
MEE Question - July 2013

Two years ago, a builder constructed a house for a woman and conveyed that house to her for $300,000 at the closing by a warranty deed, which was promptly recorded. The sale contract contained no express warranties relating to the condition of the house. To finance the purchase, the woman borrowed $200,000 from a local bank secured by a mortgage on her new house. The mortgage note provided that in the event of the woman's failure to make two consecutive monthly mortgage payments, the balance would become immediately due and payable. The mortgage was promptly recorded.

One year ago, the woman accepted a new job and moved. At that time, her house was worth $360,000 and there was a balance on the mortgage of $195,000. She sold the house to a man and delivered a quitclaim deed to him in exchange for $160,000. The quitclaim deed was promptly recorded and made no reference to the woman's mortgage obligation. The mortgage obligation was not discharged at the closing. However, the man immediately began to make the woman's monthly mortgage payments to the bank after the closing.

Nine months ago, water seeped into the basement of the house during a major storm, causing substantial damage. It is undisputed that the seepage was due to defective concrete used by the builder and not to any negligence on the builder's part. The man called the builder, told him about the seepage, and demanded that the builder fix the concrete. The builder responded: "That's your problem." The man then repaired the concrete at a cost of $80,000.

Thereafter, the man sued the builder to recover the $80,000 he had spent to repair the concrete. While the case was pending, the man stopped making mortgage payments. The bank sued the man to foreclose on the mortgage and, if necessary, obtain a deficiency judgment against him on the note if the sale proceeds were insufficient to discharge the mortgage debt. The man has joined the woman as a third-party defendant in the lawsuit.

1.   **Is the man likely to prevail against the builder to recover the $80,000 he spent to repair the concrete? Explain.**

2.   **Is the man personally liable for the outstanding balance on the mortgage note between the woman and the bank? Explain.**

3.   **If the bank is successful in its foreclosure action, will the man be able to recover damages from the woman? Explain.**

MBE SUBJECTS - RELEASED ESSAY QUESTIONS

REAL PROPERTY
MEE Question - February 2015

Seventeen years ago, a property owner granted a sewer-line easement to a private sewer company. The easement allowed the company to build, maintain, and use an underground sewer line in a designated sector of the owner's three-acre tract. The easement was properly recorded with the local registrar of deeds.

Fifteen years ago, a man having no title or other interest in the owner's three-acre tract wrongfully entered the tract, built a cabin, and planted a vegetable garden. The garden was directly over the sewer line constructed pursuant to the easement the owner had granted to the sewer company. The cabin and garden occupied half an acre of the three-acre tract. The man moved into the cabin immediately after its completion and remained in continuous and exclusive possession of the cabin and garden until his death. However, he did not use the remaining two and one- half acres of the three-acre tract in any way.

Eight years ago, the man died. Under the man's duly probated will, he bequeathed to his sister "all real property in which I have or may have an interest at the time of my death." The man's sister took possession of the cabin and garden immediately after the man's death and remained in exclusive and continuous possession of them for one year, but she, too, did not use the remaining two and one-half acres of the tract.

Seven years ago, the man's sister executed and delivered to a buyer a general warranty deed stating that it conveyed the entire three-acre tract to the buyer. The deed contained all six title covenants. Since this transaction, the buyer has continuously occupied the cabin and garden but has not used the remaining two and one-half acres.

A state statute provides that "any action to recover the possession of real property must be brought within 10 years after the cause of action accrues."

Last month, the property owner sued the buyer to recover possession of the three-acre tract.

1.   **Did the buyer acquire title to the three-acre tract or any portion of it? Explain.**

2.   **Assuming that the buyer did not acquire title to the entire three-acre tract, can the buyer recover damages from the sister who sold him the three-acre tract? Explain.**

3.   **Assuming that the buyer acquired title to the entire three-acre tract or the portion above the sewer-line easement, can the buyer compel the sewer company to remove the sewer line under the garden? Explain.**

MBE SUBJECTS - PRACTICE ESSAY QUESTIONS

REAL PROPERTY
Question 1

Owner validly purchased three adjacent wooded parcels of land in the countryside years ago as an investment. When purchased, each parcel was undeveloped and no one lived on any of them. Each parcel is 10 acres across and 10 acres deep.

Owner decides that when she dies, she wants Daughter to have all three parcels. Owner has heard that it is best to avoid probate, so Owner properly executes a deed which purports to convey all three parcels to Daughter. Owner puts the deed in a joint safe deposit box to which only she and Daughter have access. Owner tells Daughter about the deed and the joint safe deposit box, and Owner instructs Daughter not to touch the deed until after Owner dies. Despite Owner's instructions, a few months later Daughter takes the deed out of the safe deposit box and records it.

Thereafter, Owner's financial situation deteriorates and Owner decides to sell the land. In exchange for valuable consideration, Owner properly executes and delivers a quitclaim deed to Friend. The quitclaim deed purports to convey all three parcels to Friend.

Friend clears the brush on parcel 1, then builds a house, moves into it, and farms parcel 1. Because Owner and Friend are such good friends, Friend never checked the state of the title in the recorder's office. Friend records the deed.

Thereafter, in exchange for valuable consideration, Daughter properly executes and delivers a quitclaim deed which purports to convey parcel 3 to Speculator, an out-of–state property speculator. Speculator never visited the area nor checked the state of the title in the recorder's office before purchasing the property. Speculator records the "Daughter to Speculator" deed.

Thereafter, Owner dies.

Assume the jurisdiction has adopted the following statute:

Every conveyance of real estate shall be recorded in the office of the county recorder of the county where such real estate is situated; and every such conveyance not so recorded shall be void as against any subsequent purchaser in good faith and for a valuable consideration of the same real estate, or any part thereof, whose conveyance is first duly recorded.

Who owns parcels 1, 2 and 3? Fully discuss the real property issues raised by the fact pattern.

MBE SUBJECTS - PRACTICE ESSAY QUESTIONS

REAL PROPERTY
Question 2

Olivia owns two parcels of land, lot 1 and lot 2. Both lots front to a street and back to a lake, as shown in the diagram below:

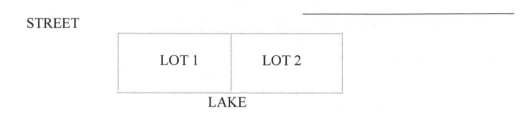

Neighbor lives just across the street and is a fishing buddy of Olivia's. Olivia orally grants "Neighbor and her heirs the right to walk across lot 1 to get to the lake." Neighbor walks across lot 1 several times a month to access the lake. Thereafter, Olivia properly executes and delivers a deed which transfers lot 1 "to Andy and Betty together." Andy and Betty, who are siblings, take possession of lot 1 and tell Neighbor she no longer has the right to walk across lot 1 to get to the lake.

Thereafter, Olivia leases lot 2 to Tenant, in writing, "for a term of ten years, at a rent of $24,000 per year payable $2,000 a month." The lease has no right of re-entry clause or approval clause in it. Three years into the lease, Tenant's employer transfers her to the company's European office for two years. Tenant enters into a written agreement with Tom that "subleases, transfers and assigns all of Tenant's interest in lot 2 to Tom for a term of two years." Tom pays rent to Tenant, and Tenant continues to pay rent to Olivia.

A year later, Tenant defaults on her rent payments to Olivia. When Olivia goes down to lot 2 to see what the problem is, she is shocked and surprised to find Tom in possession. Olivia gives Tom a 30 day notice to vacate, but Tom refuses to leave, claiming he is entitled to stay. Olivia sues to eject Tom on the grounds that Tenant had no right to transfer the right to possession in lot 2 to Tom. In addition, Olivia sues Tenant and Tom for the rent due.

Thereafter, Betty dies with a will that gives all of her property to Carol. When Carol shows up to take possession of lot 1, Andy asserts that Carol has no interest in lot 1 and refuses to let her in. In analyzing the issues, assume the jurisdiction has the following statute: "All grants and devises of land made to two or more persons shall be construed to create estates in common and not in joint tenancy, unless expressly declared to be in joint tenancy."

Fully analyze and discuss the issues raised by the fact pattern.

MBE SUBJECTS - PRACTICE ESSAY QUESTIONS

REAL PROPERTY
Question 3

Mother deeded to her adult children, Bob and Sue, a parcel of property by stating: "to Bob and Sue as joint owners in common."

A short time later, Bob sold his share of the property to Connie. After the sale, Bob suddenly died. Bob's sole heir is Junior.

Connie then seeks to partition the property.

Sue objects to the partition and argues that upon Bob's death, his share became hers as a right of survivorship. Sue now claims she owns the entire property. Sue argues in the alternative that even if she owns only a half share in the property, there should be no partition because she has been using the property as her family home. She also states that she has been laid off from work, and is very ill, and thus it would be a great hardship for her to move.

Junior also files an objection to partition and claims that he has inherited Bob's share of the property.

Who owns the property? Can Connie succeed with the partition? Please explain your answers fully.

MBE SUBJECTS - PRACTICE ESSAY QUESTIONS

REAL PROPERTY
Question 4

Greenacres is a piece of property owned by Owner. On January 1, 2000, Owner leased Greenacres to Tenant. The properly executed written lease provided that it is "for a term of five years, at a rent of $12,000 per year, payable monthly on the last day of the month." The lease was silent as to its transferability. On January 1, 2000, Tenant took possession of Greenacres, but failed to record the lease.

In November of 2000, Tenant received an offer to work overseas in Paris. A friend of his, Sally, expressed an interest in taking over the lease on Greenacres. Tenant properly executed a written instrument that provided that Tenant "transfers, assigns and subleases" all his interest in Greenacres to Sally. Sally took possession of Greenacres, but failed to record the instrument she received from Tenant.

Due to health problems, Owner had to sell Greenacres. On January 1, 2002, Owner agreed to sell Greenacres to an out of town purchaser, called Purchaser. Owner wrote Tenant a letter informing Tenant of Owner's plans to sell to Purchaser. Owner told Tenant that Owner is conveying Greenacres to Purchaser on March 31, 2002, that Owner is terminating the lease on that date, and that Tenant needs to vacate Greenacres on or before that date.

Tenant wrote back stating that he had transferred the lease to Sally. On February 15, 2002, Owner wrote Sally telling her that since Tenant transferred the lease without Owner's permission, Owner considers the transfer null and void. Moreover, Owner told Sally of the impending sale of Greenacres to Purchaser, and that Owner is terminating the lease effective March 31, 2002.

On March 31, 2002, in exchange for valuable consideration, Owner delivered a properly executed quitclaim deed that purported to convey Greenacres to Purchaser. Purchaser recorded the deed.

On June 1, 2002, Purchaser visited Greenacres for the first time. Purchaser was shocked to find Sally in possession. Purchaser informed Sally that he purchased Greenacres from Owner and that Sally must leave. Sally refused, claiming the right to stay pursuant to Tenant's lease that was transferred to her. Purchaser countered that when he checked the chain of title for Greenacres, he did not find any recorded lease. Sally refuses to leave.

Assume the jurisdiction has a race-notice recording act. Discuss the following issues only:

(1)   **Characterize Tenant's transfer of his interest to Sally.**

(2)   **Did Tenant violate his lease with Owner by transferring his interest to Sally without getting Owner's consent?**

(3) Did Owner properly terminate the lease?

(4) Is Purchaser entitled to protection from Sally's claim under the jurisdiction's recording act?

(5) Does Sally's continued possession of Greenacres constitute a breach of any of the covenants in the deed from Owner to Purchaser?

MBE SUBJECTS - PRACTICE ESSAY QUESTIONS

REAL PROPERTY
Question 5

Orla owns a 40-acre parcel of land, bordered on the north by wetlands owned by the state government and on the south by mountains that can be crossed only on horseback. The parcel is bordered on the east by Highway 99. On the west, the parcel is bordered by a navigable river. The cost of building a bridge over the river would be very high. Beyond the western shore of the navigable river is Water Road. Several years ago, Orla subdivided the land into two 20-acre tracts: Tract East and Tract West. Orla sold Tract West to Dan.

The deed to Dan did not mention any easements. However, since buying the property, Dan has reached the Tract West property from Highway 99 by a road that runs across Tract East close to its southern border.

Dan has now subdivided Tract West into 4 lots and has filed plans to build 4 individual fishing camps, one on each lot. He then plans to sell the camps to private individuals who will use the lots as recreational sites for families and friends who want to fish in the river. Dan says he has an easement across Tract East and plans to continue using it.

Orla says that if Dan goes ahead with his plans to sell the lots, she will take legal action. Orla denies that there ever was an easement.

What legal arguments should Dan raise in favor of an easement? What type of easement should he argue for? What significant counter-arguments is Orla likely to make? Who do you expect would prevail if the matter were litigated? Please explain fully.

MBE SUBJECTS - PRACTICE ESSAY QUESTIONS

REAL PROPERTY
Question 6

In 1995, O executed the following conveyance of Greenacre:

> "To my children B and C for life, and upon the death of the last of them, remainder to my grandchildren."

At the time of the conveyance, O was age 65, son B was age 40 and daughter C was age 35. O had one granddaughter at the time of the conveyance, D, who was age 12.

Greenacre is a 100 acre undeveloped parcel suitable for farming. Shortly after the conveyance by O in 1995, B entered into a 10-year lease with Tenant Farmer to farm the front 40 acres.

In 1996, Syl entered the back 60 acres and began farming it without anyone's permission. Syl planted and harvested crops on the 60 acres every year thereafter and continues to do so.

In 2002, B died. O is still alive.

You are asked to draft a memo analyzing the state of the title to Greenacre, and describing the interests, if any, held by each of the parties referred to above.

MBE SUBJECTS - PRACTICE ESSAY QUESTIONS

REAL PROPERTY
Question 7

Farmer subdivided Happy Valley Farm in 1982. The subdivision map contained the following restriction:

(1) No lot in this subdivision shall be used for any purpose other than single family residences. Lot #9 fronted on Pumpkin Place. Lot #10, located northeast of Lot #9, had no direct access to any street in the subdivision. A gravel drive extended from Lot #10 across Lot #9 to Pumpkin Place.

Farmer owned Lot #10 until 1988. Between 1982 and 1988, Farmer used the driveway across Lot #9 two (2) or three (3) times a year to get his truck to and from Lot #10.

In 1985, Farmer sold Lot #9 to Ashley, "subject to all easements and restrictions of record."

In 1988, Farmer sold Lot #10 to Barbara. Barbara took fee simple title to Lot #10 by warranty deed from Farmer. Her deed contained the following language: "Together with an easement for egress and ingress over and across Lot #9 to Pumpkin Place."

From 1988 to 1994, Barbara used the gravel driveway four (4) to six (6) times every day.

Later, Barbara noticed that the owner of Lot #8, Chuck, had put in an asphalt driveway that would also give her access to Pumpkin Place. She asked for and received oral permission from Chuck, to use Chuck's asphalt driveway to get access to Pumpkin Place. She stopped using the gravel driveway across Lot #9 when she received Chuck's permission to use his driveway. In 1999, Barbara obtained a special use permit from the County Plan Commission to start a group home for mentally retarded young adults on Lot #10. Her group home would house six (6) unrelated residents living together as a "family."

Ashley, who still owned Lot #9, objected to the group home. Ashley blocked the gravel drive, which still extended across her Lot #9 to Barbara's Lot #10, by placing a gate across the driveway and putting up "no trespassing" signs. Ashley then sued Barbara to enjoin the proposed group home as a violation of the restrictive covenant set out above. Barbara counter-claimed for an injunction to prevent the closure of the gravel driveway. Barbara wanted access through the gravel driveway. The gravel driveway was a shorter walk for group home residents than the asphalt driveway.

Assume that all relevant documents affecting title have been properly executed and recorded. Assume also that the state has a statute which requires that an action for recovery of real estate must be brought within 15 years of the invasion of the owner's rights.

Fully analyze and discuss all real property claims, counterclaims and potential defenses. How is the court likely to rule and why?

MEE RELEASED ESSAY QUESTIONS

SECURED TRANSACTIONS
July 2002

Debtor bought a motor home from Uptown RV Sales on credit. Debtor signed a security agreement granting Uptown a security interest in the motor home. Two years later, Debtor lost her job and then defaulted on her loan by failing to make several monthly payments. Without sending any notice of default to Debtor, Uptown dispatched Ernest, one of its employees, to take possession of the motor home.

Ernest located the motor home parked on a public street. When he opened the door with a duplicate key, he found Debtor inside and told her that he was there to repossess the motor home. Debtor began yelling at him, "Get out of my home or I'll throw you out! This is the only place I have to live, and, anyway, you don't have any right to take my clothes and other stuff." Ernest departed without the motor home.

Two weeks later, the owner of Uptown sent Ernest back, this time to post a coupon on the windshield of the motor home fictitiously advertising a free steak dinner at the grand opening of a local restaurant on Friday evening. Debtor fell for the ploy. She went to the restaurant on Friday evening, parked the motor home in the lot at the rear of the restaurant, and went inside to see about her free dinner. She had left the door to the motor home unlocked.

Ernest, who had followed Debtor, waited for Debtor to get inside the restaurant, entered the motor home through the unlocked door, "hot-wired" the engine, and drove the motor home back to Uptown's garage. Debtor came out of the restaurant to find her motor home was gone.

Uptown's owner had arranged with a uniformed deputy sheriff to stand by in case it became necessary to keep the peace. The deputy sheriff observed the events from her patrol car parked some distance away but did not otherwise assist in the repossession.

1. **Did Uptown have the right to repossess the motor home without sending notice of default to Debtor and without judicial process? Explain.**

2. **What arguments might Debtor reasonably make, based on the facts, that Uptown failed to carry out the repossession in a lawful manner? Explain.**

MEE RELEASED ESSAY QUESTIONS

SECURED TRANSACTIONS
July 2003

Debtor, the sole proprietor of a small restaurant, borrowed $20,000 from Bank. The loan was used to purchase kitchen equipment for Debtor's business, including a stove unit, a large refrigerator, two freezers, and a commercial microwave oven. Debtor signed a promissory note and a security agreement granting Bank a security interest in the items purchased. The security agreement contained clauses (1) waiving Debtor's right of redemption should default occur, and (2) providing that, if Debtor failed to make any regular installment payment, "the entire unpaid obligation due from Debtor to Bank shall, without further notice, immediately become due and payable." Bank properly perfected its security interest in the collateral.

Debtor missed four monthly installment payments. When Debtor was approximately $1,600 in arrears, Bank's representative drove a large truck to the alley behind the restaurant. Bank's representative was accompanied by two movers. The time was 11:10 p.m., shortly after the restaurant's closing time. Bank's representative pounded loudly on the locked back door, which was opened by one of the restaurant's employees. "We're here to repossess the kitchen equipment," stated Bank's representative. "Well, my boss isn't here, and I don't think I should let you in," replied the employee. Without further discussion, Bank's representative and the two movers walked right past the employee and began moving the kitchen equipment out to the truck. At first, the employee objected loudly, but soon he shrugged and watched quietly as they removed the equipment.

The next day, Debtor went to Bank and offered to pay the $1,600 arrearage in monthly payments. Bank refused the tender, reminding Debtor the entire balance was now due. When Debtor then offered to pay the entire balance due including Bank's repossession expenses, Bank told Debtor that it would not allow him to redeem because he had waived his right of redemption. Thereafter, Bank sent Debtor a notice of public sale and then duly held the sale, the terms of which were commercially reasonable. Bank now has threatened to sue Debtor for a deficiency judgment of $4,000, the difference between Debtor's unpaid loan obligation and what Bank recovered in the sale.

Debtor has had to close the restaurant because the kitchen equipment was repossessed.

What are Debtor's rights, remedies, and liabilities under the Uniform Commercial Code? Explain.

MEE RELEASED ESSAY QUESTIONS

SECURED TRANSACTIONS
February 2004

PC is a professional law corporation formed by Ted and Teresa. In 2002, PC obtained a $100,000 line of credit from First Bank, and PC authenticated a security agreement that granted First Bank a security interest in "all of PC's equipment, now owned or hereafter acquired."

Although PC did not specifically authorize it, First Bank promptly filed a financing statement in the appropriate state offices. The financing statement, which PC had not signed, recited erroneously that First Bank had a security interest in "all of PC's equipment, inventory, and accounts receivable." PC knew that First Bank had filed a financing statement but was unaware that the financing statement covered collateral not mentioned in the security agreement.

In 2003, PC entered into contracts to provide legal services to a number of municipalities, one of which was the City of Eden. To perform these contracts, PC decided to expand its operation by hiring an additional attorney, adding office staff, and increasing its office space. When First Bank refused to increase PC's line of credit to finance the expansion, PC approached Second Bank about obtaining a separate business expansion loan.

Second Bank agreed to loan PC $100,000, provided the loan was secured by a first security interest in PC's accounts receivable. However, the arrangement fell through when Second Bank discovered that First Bank had already filed a financing statement covering PC's accounts receivable. First Bank ignored repeated requests from PC to terminate or amend the financing statement, and Second Bank was unwilling to make a loan until First Bank's filing was changed. As a result, PC was not able to secure financing from Second Bank. Because of its inability to secure this financing, PC was unable to hire additional staff and could not adequately perform the contracts. After PC's attorneys failed to attend two important city council meetings because they were occupied with other duties, the City of Eden terminated its contract with PC, a contract that PC had expected to generate $250,000 in revenue over two years.

Also in 2003, Luke, a former employee of PC's, sued PC and won a judgment for $50,000. Luke immediately obtained a judicial lien against all of PC's assets, including its equipment and accounts receivable.

1. **As between Luke and First Bank, who has the superior claim to PC's equipment? Explain.**

2. **As between Luke and First Bank, who has the superior claim to PC's accounts receivable? Explain.**

3. **What claims, if any, does PC have against First Bank under the Uniform Commercial Code? Explain.**

MEE RELEASED ESSAY QUESTIONS

SECURED TRANSACTIONS
July 2004

Seller is in the business of selling new and used road construction equipment. On January 15, Buyer, a road builder, entered into a written purchase agreement with Seller for the sale of a used excavator for $100,000. The purchase agreement provided that Seller would add certain attachments to the excavator. The cost of the attachments was included in the purchase price. Buyer and Seller agreed that the specially equipped excavator would be ready for Buyer by April 5, in time for the start of the road construction season.

When Buyer signed the contract, Buyer gave Seller a $25,000 down payment. The remaining $75,000 was to be paid as follows: $25,000 on March 1; $25,000 on April 1; and $25,000 on May 1.

On January 20, Seller borrowed $1 million from Finance Co. to finance Seller's business operations. Finance Co. obtained a properly perfected security interest specifically assigning to Finance Co. all payments from Seller's accounts receivable and chattel paper.

On February 20, Seller failed to make a payment due on its loan from Finance Co. Finance Co. declared Seller in default. However, it informed Seller that it would not require immediate repayment of the full amount of the loan, but would instead begin collecting payments on all of Seller's outstanding accounts and chattel paper directly from the account debtors.

Finance Co. properly notified Buyer that Seller had assigned to Finance Co. the right to receive payment under the purchase agreement and that Buyer should make all future payments on the purchase agreement directly to Finance Co. However, Seller told Buyer to disregard Finance Co.'s notification and to continue to make payments directly to Seller. Buyer then sent its March and April payments directly to Seller.

On April 5, Buyer went to pick up the excavator from Seller. Buyer discovered that Seller had not equipped the excavator with any of the attachments required by their purchase agreement. Buyer informed Seller that it would take the excavator, despite its non-conformity with the contract, but that it would find and add the necessary attachments itself and would withhold from its final payment the cost of making the goods conform to the contract. Seller stated that it expected full payment but allowed Buyer to take the excavator.

On May 5, Finance Co. demanded that Buyer immediately pay Finance Co. $75,000, the full amount of the March, April, and May payments under the purchase agreement. Buyer refused, asserting that it made the March and April payments to Seller and that no remaining payment was due because the cost of bringing the excavator up to contract specifications exceeded $30,000, substantially more than the amount of the May payment.

How much, if anything, does Buyer owe Finance Co.? Explain.

MEE RELEASED ESSAY QUESTIONS

SECURED TRANSACTIONS
February 2005

Bill operated a restaurant in a building he owned. On March 1, he purchased a large oven on credit for $8,000 from Sal's Appliance Barn. On that same day, the oven was set aside in Sal's warehouse and marked with a tag reading, "Sold to Bill." Also on March 1, Bill signed a security agreement that gave Sal's a security interest in the oven to secure the unpaid purchase price of the oven.

On March 14, the oven was delivered and bolted permanently into a specially built niche in the kitchen in Bill's restaurant, thus becoming a fixture under local real estate law.

On March 26, the local sheriff came to the restaurant and announced that he was there to execute a levy to satisfy a $3,000 judgment against Bill in favor of Local Bank. The sheriff saw the new oven in the restaurant's kitchen and announced he was levying on the oven. He then physically disabled the oven by handcuffing it shut and placed a notice-of-levy sticker on it, which qualified as a valid levy under state law.

On March 28, after learning from Bill about what happened with the sheriff and the oven, Sal's filed its financing statement in the Secretary of State's office but not in the local real estate records office. Sal's financing statement properly described the oven.

On March 29, Bill obtained a $10,000 loan from Finance Company and gave Finance Company a mortgage on his building to secure repayment of the loan. On the same day, Finance Company properly perfected a valid lien against the restaurant building and accompanying fixtures by filing in the local real estate records office designated by state law.

1.   **As between Sal's and Local Bank, who has priority as to the oven? Explain.**

2.   **As between Sal's and Finance Company, who has priority as to the oven? Explain.**

MEE RELEASED ESSAY QUESTIONS

SECURED TRANSACTIONS
July 2005

On August 1, 2003, Builder, a construction company, borrowed $2 million from Lender to finance the purchase of a heavy-duty construction crane. Shareholder, a very wealthy shareholder of Builder, personally guaranteed the loan. Builder signed an agreement granting Lender a security interest in the new crane to secure the loan. However, Lender neglected to file a financing statement reflecting its security interest.

Due to severe cash flow problems, Builder stopped making scheduled loan payments four months ago, leaving a balance of $1.5 million on the loan.

In response to Builder's failure to make the scheduled loan payments, Lender hired a repossession service to recover the crane. Employees of the repossession service visited Builder's unprotected job site and, without notice to Builder, took the crane away. This occurred on Sunday, June 5, 2005, when no one from Builder was present and thus no dispute erupted.

On June 7, 2005, Lender mailed a notice to Builder announcing that Lender was going to sell the crane at an auction on June 21, 2005. Lender did not send separate notice of the auction to Shareholder. On the announced auction date, Lender sold the crane to Dealer, the highest bidder at the auction, for $1 million. Shareholder knew about the auction but did not bid at it. It can be proved that if Shareholder had bid, the bid would have been $1.2 million.

Builder asserts that: (a) Lender's actions amounted to a conversion of the crane because Lender's security interest was not perfected, and (b) Lender handled the repossession and sale improperly. Builder sues Lender for $1.7 million, which Builder says is the fair market value of the crane.

Lender counterclaims for the $500,000 deficiency, which it says is still owed by Builder on the loan after taking into account the proceeds received by Lender from the sale of the crane.

1.   **Did Lender have the right to repossess and sell the crane? Explain.**

2.   **Did Lender's handling of the repossession, foreclosure, and sale comply with all legal requirements, and is Lender entitled to recover the $500,000 deficiency from Builder? Explain.**

MEE RELEASED ESSAY QUESTIONS

SECURED TRANSACTIONS
February 2006

Specialty Audio, Inc. (Specialty) manufactures high-quality stereo speakers worth about $2,000 each. Because its business is fairly small, Specialty has no showroom or sales staff of its own.

Specialty entered into a consignment arrangement with Giant Electronics Store (Giant). Pursuant to the written consignment agreement, Specialty delivers speakers to Giant, and Giant displays those speakers on its showroom floor and sells them on behalf of Specialty. When a customer buys a pair of speakers, Giant keeps a commission as compensation for Giant's effort and pays the rest of the customer's purchase price to Specialty. At any given time, Giant has about two dozen pairs of Specialty's speakers on hand.

Specialty holds title to the speakers until they are sold. However, as far as any third party can discern, the speakers are part of Giant's own inventory. There is no indication that Specialty is the owner of the speakers. Moreover, Giant does not generally engage in the sale of goods for others and is not known by its creditors to do so.

After establishing the consignment relationship with Specialty, Giant borrowed $1 million from Bank to open new stores. As security for its obligation to repay the money, Giant granted Bank a security interest in "all inventory, whether now owned or hereafter acquired." Bank properly perfected its security interest by filing a financing statement in the appropriate state office.

Giant defaulted on its loan from Bank. Bank peaceably repossessed all of Giant's goods, including all the Specialty speakers Giant had on display and, after providing proper notice, sold everything at a commercially reasonable sale.

1. **Did Bank have the right to repossess and sell the Specialty speakers even though, under the consignment agreement, they belonged to Specialty and not to Giant? Explain.**

2. **What rights, if any, does Specialty have against Bank to recover the proceeds from the sale of the speakers? Explain.**

3. **What action might Specialty have taken to protect its interest in the speakers more completely? Explain.**

MEE RELEASED ESSAY QUESTIONS

SECURED TRANSACTIONS
July 2006

Joe purchased a boat for use by his family from Dealer. Dealer extended credit for the purchase and retained a security interest in the boat as collateral for payment of the balance due. Joe failed to make a number of the payments, and, on May 1, Dealer peacefully repossessed the boat as Dealer was entitled to do under the UCC.

On May 3, Dealer mailed Joe a letter that stated the following: the balance due on the boat was $10,000; Dealer had credited Joe with $7,500, Dealer's good faith estimate of the boat's value, leaving a deficiency balance due of $2,500; Dealer had disposed of the boat by purchasing it for use as a rental boat in Dealer's marina; and Dealer had saved Joe money by disposing of the boat in this way because, if Dealer had publicized the availability of the boat for sale to third parties, Joe would have had to pay the additional cost of the publicity. The letter also demanded that Joe pay the $2,500 deficiency.

This letter was the only communication between Dealer and Joe after the peaceful repossession of the boat.

Used boats are typically sold through privately negotiated sales or in occasional dealer auctions. There is no recognized market on which they are customarily sold. Moreover, used boats are not subject to standardized price quotations. Quoted pricing is widely variable, with used boats of the same age and model being subject to different prices depending on their condition and features. Sale prices are also heavily influenced by the negotiating skills of the parties to the transaction. Nonetheless, the $7,500 value that Dealer placed on Joe's boat was in the middle of the range of prices for which used boats of that age and model have sold in the area over the past year.

1.   **Did Dealer properly dispose of the collateral under the UCC? Explain.**

2.   **On these facts, what are Joe's rights, remedies, and obligations under the UCC? Explain.**

MEE RELEASED ESSAY QUESTIONS

SECURED TRANSACTIONS
February 2007

Nine months ago, Feagle Construction Company, Inc. (Feagle), which does business under the trade name of On Top Roofing, obtained a $150,000 loan from National Bank. To secure the loan, Feagle assigned to National Bank "all rights to payment owed to Feagle Construction Company, Inc. by Hotel Corporation for the roofing construction project on its Broadway Street Hotel." The Broadway Street Hotel roofing project was by far the largest of Feagle's fifteen roofing projects and represented its largest account receivable.

National Bank promptly filed a financing statement with this same collateral description, using the trade name of On Top Roofing for the debtor. The financing statement was filed in the appropriate location, and indexed only in the name of On Top Roofing.

Three months after these events, Feagle needed additional monies. It approached State Bank for a loan of $100,000. State Bank conducted a search of the filing office's records for financing statements relating to "Feagle Construction Company, Inc.," but its search did not retrieve National Bank's financing statement. Accordingly, State Bank granted the $100,000 loan and obtained a written agreement from Feagle granting State Bank a security interest in "all Feagle Construction Company, Inc.'s accounts, whether now owned or hereafter acquired." State Bank filed a financing statement in the appropriate location in the name of "Feagle Construction Company, Inc." as debtor.

Another six months later, mounting financial stress forced Feagle to default on its loans to both National Bank and State Bank. Feagle has about $75,000 worth of outstanding accounts receivable. In particular, Hotel Corporation still owes Feagle $50,000 for the hotel roofing project. In addition, Feagle is owed about $25,000 on a total of ten other roofing projects it has recently completed. Both National Bank and State Bank are seeking to recover some of what Feagle owes them by collecting from Hotel Corporation the amount it still owes Feagle.

Does National Bank or State Bank have first priority in the money owed to Feagle by Hotel Corporation? Explain.

MEE RELEASED ESSAY QUESTIONS

SECURED TRANSACTIONS
February 2008

On October 1, Dart Corporation (DC), a State A corporation, borrowed $300,000 from State Bank, a State A bank. On behalf of DC, DC's president signed a written security agreement giving State Bank a security interest in DC's State Bank checking account (a demand account) to secure its obligation to repay the loan. State Bank did not file a financing statement reflecting that interest.

On December 1, First Bank, another State A bank, agreed to loan $60,000 to DC. DC's president, on behalf of DC, signed a written security agreement granting First Bank a security interest in all of DC's "office equipment and deposit accounts." First Bank immediately advanced $60,000 to DC and filed a financing statement reflecting its interest.

First Bank's financing statement was filed in the correct filing office in State A and listed the collateral as "office equipment and deposit accounts." It correctly identified First Bank as the secured party, and it correctly gave the address of the debtor as "123 Smith Street, City, State A." However, First Bank's financing statement incorrectly listed the name of the debtor as "Dart Incorporated," rather than "Dart Corporation," the correct name of the company as reflected on its certificate of incorporation and other public records. Despite this error, a search under the name "Dart Corporation" using the State A filing office's standard search logic would turn up the financing statement listing "Dart Incorporated" as the debtor.

Shortly after receiving the loan from First Bank, DC defaulted on the obligations it owed to State Bank and First Bank.

On December 23, State Bank obtained a judgment against DC in connection with its unpaid $300,000 loan.

On January 3 of the following year, a State A sheriff levied on DC's office equipment on behalf of State Bank.

1. **As between First Bank and State Bank, which has a superior claim to DC's checking account at State Bank? Explain.**

2. **As between First Bank and State Bank, which has a superior claim to DC's office equipment? Explain.**

MEE RELEASED ESSAY QUESTIONS

SECURED TRANSACTIONS
July 2008

Debtor sells and delivers medical supplies to hospitals. It owns a fleet of 40 trucks that it uses to make deliveries. Debtor has a state-issued certificate of title for each truck. The state has a statute that provides: "All security interests in a motor vehicle must be noted on the vehicle's certificate of title as a condition for perfection."

On June 1, Bank made a $100,000 loan to Debtor. In order to secure the loan, Debtor signed a valid security agreement granting Bank a security interest in "all Debtor's inventory and equipment, whether now owned or hereafter acquired." Bank did not note its security interest on the certificates of title issued for the trucks. However, Bank immediately filed an appropriate financing statement in the proper state office that listed its collateral as "all Debtor's inventory and equipment, whether now owned or hereafter acquired."

On July 1, Finance Company loaned $75,000 to Debtor. On that same day, Debtor signed a valid security agreement granting Finance Company a security interest in 25 of Debtor's "delivery trucks" and "any accessories now or hereafter installed." Each truck was identified individually and by its vehicle identification number. Although Finance Company never filed a financing statement, its security interest was noted on the certificate of title for each truck.

On August 1, Debtor entered into a contract with Global Inc. to buy 40 global positioning system units (GPS units) to be installed on all 40 delivery trucks (including the 25 trucks covered by Finance Company's security agreement). GPS units are bolted on the dashboard of a vehicle and hooked up directly to the battery for power, but they otherwise operate independently of the vehicle.

The GPS units cost $50,000. Debtor made a down payment of $10,000 and signed an agreement to pay the remaining $40,000, plus interest, in equal monthly installments over a two-year period. To secure the amount owed on the contract, Debtor signed a security agreement giving Global a security interest in "the GPS units to be installed on Debtor's delivery trucks."

On August 2, Global properly filed a financing statement covering the GPS units. The GPS units were delivered to Debtor on August 10, and Debtor installed them on its delivery trucks shortly thereafter.

On October 1, Debtor defaulted on its obligations to Bank, Finance Company, and Global. Bank has repossessed all 40 of Debtor's trucks, and it is now negotiating with Finance Company and Global about their respective claims to the trucks and the 40 GPS units installed in them.

1.   **Which of Bank or Finance Company has the superior claim to the 25 delivery trucks claimed by Finance Company? Explain.**

2.   **Which of Global or Finance Company has the superior claim to the GPS units**

installed in the 25 delivery trucks claimed by Finance Company? Explain.

3. **Which of Bank or Global has the superior claim to the remaining 15 GPS units? Explain.**

MEE RELEASED ESSAY QUESTIONS

SECURED TRANSACTIONS
July 2009

Three years ago, Printco, a printing company, borrowed $250,000 from Bank and entered into an enforceable agreement giving Bank a security interest in "all Printco's equipment, whether now owned or hereafter acquired." Bank promptly filed a proper financing statement in the appropriate state office, listing itself as the secured party, listing Printco as the debtor, and indicating "all debtor's equipment, whether now owned or hereafter acquired" as collateral.

Two years after signing the security agreement with Bank, Printco entered into a signed agreement with Leaseco, a leasing company, pursuant to which Leaseco agreed to purchase a $100,000 printing press and to immediately lease the press to Printco. The agreement provided that Leaseco retained title to the printing press and required Printco to pay Leaseco $2,500 per month for five years for the use of the press. The agreement also provided that it could not be terminated by Printco for any reason. At the conclusion of the five-year lease, Printco was required to return the press to Leaseco or to purchase the press for $10.

Printco's full compliance with the agreement would allow Leaseco to recover rental payments equal to the full cost of the press plus an annual return of about 10%.

Leaseco delivered the printing press to Printco.

Bank was unaware of Printco's agreement with Leaseco, and Leaseco never filed a financing statement covering the printing press.

Recently, Printco defaulted on its obligations to Bank. At the time of the default, Printco owed $150,000 to Bank. Bank promptly and peacefully took possession of all of the equipment on Printco's premises, including the printing press. After giving proper notice of the sale to Printco, Bank sold all of Printco's equipment at a public auction for a total of $75,000. Purchaser, acting in good faith, bought the printing press for $50,000. All aspects of the auction and sale were commercially reasonable. One week after the sale, Leaseco contacted Bank and informed Bank that the printing press was Leaseco's property, not Printco's, and that Bank had no right to sell it. Leaseco demanded that Bank pay Leaseco $50,000, the amount that Bank received for the press. Leaseco also contacted Purchaser and demanded that Purchaser return the press to Leaseco.

1.   **What is the nature of Leaseco's interest in the printing press? Explain.**

2.   **Did Bank have a right to repossess and sell the printing press? Explain.**

3.   **As between Bank and Leaseco, which has a superior interest in the proceeds of the sale of the printing press? Explain.**

4.   **Does Leaseco have the right to recover the printing press from Purchaser? Explain.**

MEE RELEASED ESSAY QUESTIONS

SECURED TRANSACTIONS
February 2010

Six months ago, Kitchenware, a manufacturer of copper cookware, borrowed $200,000 from Bank and signed a security agreement granting Bank a security interest in "all inventory that Kitchenware now owns or that it manufactures or acquires in the future." Bank filed a properly completed financing statement reflecting this security interest in the appropriate state office.

Copperco is a company that produces high-quality copper sheet that is suitable for fabrication into cookware. Two months ago, Kitchenware entered into a contract with Copperco to buy two tons of copper sheet to be used by Kitchenware to produce cookware. The contract, which was signed by both parties, required Copperco to deliver the copper sheet to Kitchenware's factory in two installments, one ton in the first installment and the second ton 30 days later. Kitchenware was to pay for each of the installments separately, with one-half of the contract price due 25 days after the first delivery and the balance due 25 days after the second delivery. Copperco's obligation to ship the second installment was expressly made conditional on full payment for the first installment. The parties further agreed that Kitchenware would have no rights in an installment of the copper sheet until it received delivery of that installment and that Copperco would retain title to all the copper sheet until Kitchenware paid the full contract price.

Copperco promptly delivered the first ton of copper sheet to Kitchenware's factory. Twenty-three days after the delivery, Copperco loaded its truck with a second ton of copper sheet for delivery to Kitchenware's factory and planned to send the truck to Kitchenware in time to meet its delivery deadline. However, by 25 days after the first delivery, Kitchenware had not paid for the first installment of copper sheet. As a result, Copperco exercised its right under the contract to withhold shipment of the second installment and, accordingly, the truck with the second ton of copper sheet never left Copperco's plant.

Kitchenware has defaulted on its loan from Bank, and Bank would like to exercise its rights with respect to its collateral. The first ton of copper sheet delivered to Kitchenware is still at Kitchenware's factory, and the second ton of copper sheet that was not delivered to Kitchenware is still at Copperco's plant. Bank believes it has a security interest in both tons of copper sheet, while Copperco asserts that it has title to both tons of copper sheet and that its rights are superior to any rights of Bank.

1.   **As between Copperco and Bank, which has the superior claim to the first ton of copper sheet that was delivered to Kitchenware? Explain.**

2.   **As between Copperco and Bank, which has the superior claim to the second ton of copper sheet, which is still at Copperco's plant? Explain.**

MEE RELEASED ESSAY QUESTIONS

SECURED TRANSACTIONS
February 2011

Astronomy Corporation (Astronomy) sells expensive telescopes to home stargazers. Astronomy has a long-term financing arrangement pursuant to which it borrows money from Bank. In a signed writing, Astronomy granted Bank a security interest in all its present and future inventory to secure its obligations to Bank under the financing arrangement. Bank filed a properly completed financing statement reflecting this transaction. The financing statement lists Astronomy as the debtor and Bank as the secured party. The financing statement indicates that the collateral is inventory.

Astronomy sells telescopes to some of its customers on credit. For a credit sale, Astronomy requires the customer to sign an agreement granting Astronomy a security interest in the purchased item to secure the customer's obligation to pay the balance of the purchase price.

Six months ago, Johnson, an amateur stargazer, went to Astronomy's showroom, saw a $3,000 telescope that he liked, and bought it on credit from Astronomy. Johnson paid $500 in cash and agreed to pay the $2,500 balance in installment payments of $100 per month for the next 25 months, interest free. Consistent with Astronomy's policy for credit sales, Johnson signed an agreement granting Astronomy a security interest in the telescope to secure Johnson's obligation to pay the balance of the purchase price. Astronomy did not file a financing statement with respect to this transaction. At the time of the sale of the telescope to Johnson, Johnson was unaware of the financial arrangement between Astronomy and Bank.

One month ago, Johnson sold the telescope for $2,700 in cash to his neighbor, Smith, another amateur stargazer. Smith had no knowledge of any interest of Bank or Astronomy in the telescope. Johnson then left the country without paying the remaining $2,000 owed to Astronomy and cannot be located.

One week ago, Astronomy defaulted on its obligations to Bank.

Both Bank and Astronomy have discovered that Johnson sold the telescope to Smith. Bank and Astronomy each have demanded that Smith surrender the telescope on the grounds that it is collateral for obligations owed to them.

1.   **Does Bank have a security interest in the telescope that is enforceable against Smith? Explain.**

2.   **Does Astronomy have a security interest in the telescope that is enforceable against Smith? Explain.**

MEE RELEASED ESSAY QUESTIONS

SECURED TRANSACTIONS
July 2011

Decorator operates a business that sells decorative items for the office. Eight months ago, Decorator borrowed $10,000 from Lender and, pursuant to a properly completed and signed security agreement, granted Lender a security interest in all of Decorator's present and future inventory and equipment to secure that indebtedness. Lender filed a properly completed financing statement on the same day that the loan was made and the security agreement was signed.

Seven months ago, Clockwork and Decorator entered into a signed agreement pursuant to which Decorator bought and received delivery of 25 decorative clocks from Clockwork for resale to Decorator's customers. Under the terms of the agreement, Decorator agreed to pay the $2,500 purchase price in six months. The agreement also provides that, until the payment of the purchase price to Clockwork by Decorator, title to the clocks will be retained by Clockwork. No financing statement was filed in conjunction with this transaction.

Three months ago, Decorator leased an industrial vacuum cleaner from Vac for use in Decorator's business. The lease, which was signed by both parties, provides that, at the end of the four-year lease term (which cannot be terminated early), Decorator will automatically become the owner of the vacuum cleaner so long as all monthly payments have been made. No financing statement was filed in conjunction with this transaction.

Decorator has defaulted on all obligations to Lender, Clockwork, and Vac. Your law firm represents Lender, who has asked the following questions:

1.   **Who has a superior interest in the clocks? Explain.**

2.   **Who has a superior interest in the vacuum cleaner? Explain.**

MEE RELEASED ESSAY QUESTIONS

SECURED TRANSACTIONS
July 2012

On March 1, Recycled, a business that sells new and used bicycles and bicycle equipment, borrowed $100,000 from Bank. To secure its obligation to repay the loan, Recycled signed an agreement granting Bank a security interest in "all the inventory of Recycled, whether now owned or hereafter acquired."

On March 5, Bank filed a financing statement in the appropriate state office. The financing statement listed Recycled as debtor and "inventory" as collateral.

Over the next month, Recycled entered into the following transactions:

(a) On March 10, Recycled sold a new bicycle to Consumer for $1,500. The sale was made in accordance with the usual business practices of Recycled. Both parties acted honestly and in accordance with reasonable commercial standards of fair dealing, and Consumer was unaware of the financial relationship between Recycled and Bank.

(b) On March 15, Recycled traded a used bicycle to Student for a used computer that Student no longer needed. Recycled immediately began using the computer in its business.

(c) On March 31, Recycled bought 100 new bicycle helmets from Manufacturer. The sale was on credit, with payment due in 15 days. The written sales agreement, signed by Recycled, states that Manufacturer retains title to the helmets until Recycled pays their purchase price to Manufacturer. No financing statement was filed. None of the helmets has been sold by Recycled.

Recycled has not paid its utility bills for several months. On April 29, Utility obtained a judgment in the amount of $2,500 against Recycled and, pursuant to state law, obtained a judgment lien against all the personal property of Recycled.

Recycled is in default on its repayment obligation to Bank, and it has not paid the amount it owes to Manufacturer.

Bank claims a security interest in all the bicycles and bicycle helmets owned by Recycled, the bicycle bought by Consumer, and the computer obtained by Recycled in the transaction with Student. Manufacturer claims an interest in the bicycle helmets, and Utility seeks to enforce its lien against all the personal property of Recycled.

1. **As between Bank and Consumer, which has a superior claim to the bicycle sold to Consumer? Explain.**

2. **As between Bank and Utility, which has a superior claim to the used computer? Explain.**

3.   As among Bank, Manufacturer, and Utility, which has a superior claim to the 100 bicycle helmets? Explain.

MEE RELEASED ESSAY QUESTIONS

SECURED TRANSACTIONS
February 2013

On June 1, a bicycle retailer sold two bicycles to a man for a total purchase price of $1,500. The man made a $200 down payment and agreed to pay the balance in one year. The man also signed a security agreement that identified the bicycles as collateral for the unpaid purchase price and provided that the man "shall not sell or dispose of the collateral until the balance owed is paid in full." The retailer never filed a financing statement reflecting this security interest.

The man had bought the bicycles for him and his girlfriend to use on vacation. However, shortly after he bought the bicycles, the man and his girlfriend broke up. The man has never used the bicycles.

On August 1, the man sold one of the bicycles at a garage sale to a buyer who paid the man $400 for the bicycle. The buyer bought the bicycle to ride for weekend recreation.

On October 1, the man gave the other bicycle to his friend as a birthday present. The friend began using the bicycle for morning exercise.

Neither the buyer nor the friend had any knowledge of the man's dealings with the retailer.

1.   **Does the buyer own the bicycle free of the retailer's security interest? Explain.**

2.   **Does the friend own the bicycle free of the retailer's security interest? Explain.**

MEE RELEASED ESSAY QUESTIONS

SECURED TRANSACTIONS
February 2015

Acme Violins LLC (Acme) is in the business of buying, restoring, and selling rare violins. Acme frequently sells violins for prices well in excess of $100,000. In addition to restoring violins for resale, Acme also repairs and restores violins for their owners. In most repair transactions, Acme requires payment in cash when the violin is picked up by the customer. It does, however, allow some of its repeat customers to obtain repairs on credit, with full payment due 30 days after completion of the repair. In those cases, the payment obligation is not secured by any collateral and the payment terms are handwritten on the receipt.

Acme maintains a stock of rare and valuable wood that it uses in violin restoration. Acme also owns a variety of tools used in restoration work, including a machine called a "Gambretti plane," which is used to shape the body of a violin precisely.

Six months ago, Acme borrowed $1 million from Bank. The loan agreement, which was signed by Acme, grants Bank a security interest in all of Acme's "inventory and accounts, as those terms are defined in the Uniform Commercial Code." On the same day, Bank filed a properly completed financing statement in the appropriate state filing office. The financing statement indicated the collateral as "inventory" and "accounts."

Last week, Acme sold the most valuable violin in its inventory, the famed "Red Rosa," to a violinist for $200,000 (the appraised value of the instrument), which the violinist paid in cash. The sale was made by Acme in accordance with its usual practices. The violinist, who has done business with Acme for many years, was aware that Acme regularly borrows money from Bank and that Bank had a security interest in Acme's entire inventory. The violinist did not, however, know anything about the terms of Acme's agreement with Bank.

Acme is 15 days late in making the payment currently due on its loan from Bank. Bank's loan officer, who is worried about Bank's possible inability to collect the debt owed by Acme, has asked whether the following items of property are collateral that can be reached by Bank as possible sources of payment:

(1)   Acme's rights to payment from customers for repair services obtained on credit
(2)   Used violins for sale in Acme's store
(3)   Violins in Acme's possession that Acme is repairing for their owners
(4)   Wood in Acme's repair room that Acme uses in repairing violins
(5)   The Gambretti plane, used by Acme in violin restoration
(6)   The Red Rosa violin that was sold to the violinist

Yesterday, a creditor of Acme obtained a judicial lien on all of Acme's personal property.

1.   **In which, if any, of the items listed above does Bank have an enforceable security interest? Explain.**

2.   For the items in which Bank has an enforceable security interest, is Bank's claim superior to that of the judicial lien creditor? Explain.

MEE RELEASED ESSAY QUESTIONS

SECURED TRANSACTIONS
February 2016

Two years ago, a retailer of home electronic equipment borrowed $5 million from a finance company. The loan agreement, signed by both parties, provided that the retailer granted the finance company a security interest in all of the retailer's present and future inventory to secure the retailer's obligation to repay the loan. On the same day that it made the loan, the finance company filed in the appropriate state filing office a properly completed financing statement reflecting this transaction.

Six months ago, a buyer purchased a home entertainment system from the retailer for a total price of $7,000. The buyer paid $1,000 as a down payment on the system and agreed to make 12 additional monthly payments of $500 each. The buyer signed a "credit purchase agreement" memorializing the financial arrangement with the retailer and providing that the retailer would "retain title" to the entertainment system until the buyer's obligation to the retailer was paid in full. The buyer then returned home with her new home entertainment system. The buyer had no knowledge of the retailer's agreement with the finance company and acted in good faith in acquiring the home entertainment system. The retailer did not file a financing statement with respect to this transaction.

Two months ago, the buyer decided that she could no longer afford her monthly $500 payments for the home entertainment system. She contacted her friend, who had often expressed interest in acquiring a home entertainment system. After a brief discussion, the friend agreed to buy the home entertainment system from the buyer for $4,000 if the friend could pay the price 90 days later, when he anticipated receiving a bonus at work. The buyer accepted the friend's proposal, and the friend gave the buyer a check for $4,000. The buyer promised to hold the $4,000 check for 90 days before depositing it. The friend took the entertainment system and began using it at his own home. The friend had no knowledge of the buyer's agreement with the retailer or of the retailer's agreement with the finance company.

The retailer is in financial distress and has missed a payment owed to the finance company. Meanwhile, since the friend bought the home entertainment system from the buyer, the buyer has not made any of her monthly payments to the retailer.

1. **Does the finance company have an interest in the home entertainment system? Explain.**

2. **Does the retailer have an interest in the home entertainment system? Explain.**

3. **Does the retailer have an interest in the $4,000 check? Explain.**

MEE RELEASED ESSAY QUESTIONS

SECURED TRANSACTIONS
July 2016

Two years ago, PT Treatment Inc. (PTT), incorporated in State A, decided to build a new $90 million proton-therapy cancer treatment center in State A. The total cost to PTT for purchasing the land and constructing the building to house the treatment facility was $30 million. PTT financed the purchase and construction with $10 million of its own money and $20 million that it borrowed from Bank. To secure its obligation to Bank, PTT granted Bank a mortgage on the land and all structures erected on the land. The mortgage was properly recorded in the county real estate records office, but it was not identified as a construction mortgage.

Two months after the mortgage was recorded, PTT finalized an agreement for the purchase of proton-therapy equipment from Ion Medical Systems (Ion) for $60 million. PTT made a down payment of $14 million and signed a purchase agreement promising to pay the remaining $46 million in semi-annual payments over a 10-year period. The purchase agreement provided that Ion has a security interest in the proton-therapy equipment to secure PTT's obligation to pay the remaining purchase price. On the same day, Ion filed a properly completed financing statement with the office of the Secretary of State of State A (the central statewide filing office designated by statute), listing "PT Treatment Inc." as debtor and indicating the proton-therapy equipment as collateral.

Shortly thereafter, Ion delivered the equipment to PTT and PTT's employees installed it. The equipment was attached to the building in such a manner that, under State A law, it is considered a fixture and an interest in the equipment exists in favor of anyone with an interest in the building.

The new PTT Cancer Treatment Center opened for business last year. Unfortunately, it has not been an economic success. For a short period, PTT contracted with State A Oncology Associates (Oncology) for the latter's use of the proton-therapy equipment pursuant to a lease agreement, but Oncology failed to pay the agreed fee for the use of the equipment, so PTT terminated that arrangement. To date, PTT has been unsuccessful in its efforts to collect the amounts that Oncology still owes it. PTT's own doctors and technicians have not attracted enough business to fully utilize the cancer treatment center or generate sufficient billings to meet PTT's financial obligations. PTT currently owes Ion more than $30 million and is in default under the security agreement. Ion is concerned that PTT will soon declare bankruptcy.

In a few days, Ion will be sending a technician to the PTT facility to perform regular maintenance on the equipment. Ion is considering instructing the technician to complete the maintenance and then disable the equipment so that it cannot be used by PTT until PTT pays what it owes.

1.   **In view of PTT's default, if Ion disables the proton-therapy equipment, will it incur any liability to PTT? Explain.**

2.   If PTT does not pay its debts to either Bank or Ion, which of them has a superior claim to the proton-therapy equipment? Explain.

3.   Does Ion have an enforceable and perfected security interest in any of PTT's assets other than the proton-therapy equipment? Explain.

MBE SUBJECTS – RELEASED ESSAY QUESTIONS

TORTS
MEE Question – February 2009

Tenant lives in Landlord's apartment building. The furnace in the building was inoperable during three periods last winter, causing the loss of heat and hot water. On each of those occasions, Landlord made temporary repairs.

On March 25, the furnace again broke down. Landlord was promptly notified of the problem and he ordered the parts needed to fix the furnace on March 26, but they did not arrive until April 6, at which time Landlord fixed the furnace. Between March 25 and April 5, there was no heat or hot water in the building.

In order to bathe from March 25 through April 5, Tenant heated a large pot of water on the stove. After the water boiled, Tenant transferred the water to the bathtub, mixed in cold water, and then used the water to bathe.

On April 3, Nephew, Tenant's eight-year-old nephew, arrived for a visit. On April 4, Tenant was carrying a pot of boiling water down the hall to the bathroom when Nephew, who was chasing a ball out of a bedroom that opened into the hall, collided with Tenant. As a result of the collision, the hot water spilled on Nephew, seriously burning him. Nephew did not look or call out before running into the hall.

A state statute provides that "every apartment building . . . and every part thereof shall be kept in good repair. The owner shall be responsible for compliance . . . . A violation shall be punishable by a fine not exceeding $500."

Nephew, by his guardian, sued Tenant and Landlord for damages. At trial, both Tenant and Landlord argued that Nephew's negligence was the sole cause of the accident.

Based on these facts, may the jury properly award Nephew damages for his personal injury:

1. **From Tenant? Explain.**

2. **From Landlord? Explain.**

MBE SUBJECTS – RELEASED ESSAY QUESTIONS

TORTS
MEE Question – February 2010

Penny lives in an apartment on Oak Street across from the Fernbury Baseball Park ("the Park"). The Park is owned and maintained by the Fernbury Flies, a professional minor league baseball team. As she left her apartment building one day, Penny was struck in the head by a baseball that had been hit by Dennis, a Flies player, during a game.

The section of Oak Street that adjoins the Park was once lined with single-family homes. Over the past two decades, these homes have been replaced by stores and apartment buildings, causing an increase in both car and pedestrian traffic on Oak Street.

The ball that struck Penny was one of the longest that had been hit at the Park since its construction 40 years ago. During the last 40 years, Flies' records show that only 30 balls had previously been hit over the Park fence adjoining Oak Street. Fifteen of the balls hit out of the Park onto Oak Street were hit during the past decade.

The Park is surrounded by a 10-foot-high fence, which was built during the Park's construction. All other ballparks owned by clubs in the Flies' league are surrounded by fences of similar type and identical height. These fences are typical of those used by other minor league teams in the United States. However, in Japan, where ballparks are often located in congested urban neighborhoods, netting is typically attached to ballpark fences. This netting permits balls to go over a fence but captures balls before they can strike a bystander or car.

After being struck by the ball, Penny was taken by ambulance to a hospital emergency room. After tests, the treating physician told Penny that she had suffered a concussion. The physician prescribed pain medication for Penny. However, because of a preexisting condition, she had an adverse reaction to the medication and suffered neurological damage resulting in the loss of sensation in her extremities.

Penny has sued Dennis, the player who hit the baseball that struck her, for battery and negligence. Penny has also sued the Fernbury Flies. She seeks to recover damages for the concussion and the neurological damage resulting from the medication.

1.   **Does Penny have a viable tort claim against Dennis? Explain.**

2.   **Does Penny have a viable tort claim against the Fernbury Flies? Explain.**

MBE SUBJECTS – RELEASED ESSAY QUESTIONS

TORTS
MEE Question – February 2011

After recent terrorist threats, Metro Opera (Metro) decided to place metal detectors in its lobby. Metro also marked off an area just beyond the metal detectors in which to search patrons who failed the metal-detector test. Metro posted a sign near the entrance that read: "Warning! No metal objects allowed inside. All entrants are screened and may be searched."

Claimant and Friend saw the warning sign as they entered Metro. After entering, they observed several patrons being frisked. Claimant said to Friend, "I'm certainly not going to allow anyone to touch me!"

Claimant then walked through the metal detector, which buzzed. Without asking Claimant's permission, Inspector, a Metro employee, approached Claimant from behind and began to frisk Claimant. Claimant leaped away from Inspector and snarled, "Leave me alone!" Guard, another Metro employee, then used a stun device, which administers a painful electric shock, to subdue Claimant.

Unfortunately, the stun device, manufactured by Alertco, malfunctioned and produced a shock considerably more severe than that described in Alertco's product specifications. The shock caused minor physical injuries and triggered a severe depressive reaction that necessitated Claimant's hospitalization. Claimant had a history of depression but was in good mental health at the time of the shock. Claimant was the first person who had ever experienced a depressive reaction to the Alertco device.

The Alertco device malfunctioned because it was incorrectly assembled at the factory and therefore did not meet Alertco's specifications. Alertco's assembly-inspection system exceeds industry standards, and it is widely recognized as the best in the industry. Nonetheless, it did not detect the assembly mistake in the device that injured Claimant.

Claimant has filed two tort actions seeking damages for her physical and psychological injuries: (1) Claimant sued Metro, claiming that both the frisk and the use of the stun device were actionable batteries, and (2) Claimant brought a strict products liability action against Alertco.

Metro has conceded that the actions of Inspector and Guard were within the scope of their employment. Metro had instructed its employees to ask permission before frisking patrons, but on the day Claimant was frisked, a supervisor told employees to frisk without asking permission in order to speed up the entrance process.

1. **Can Claimant establish a prima facie case of battery against Metro for (a) the use of the stun device and (b) the frisk? Explain.**

2. **Does Metro have a viable defense to either battery claim? Explain.**

3.   Can Claimant establish the elements of a strict products liability claim against Alertco based on the malfunction of the device? Explain.

4.   Assuming that Claimant establishes either Metro's or Alertco's liability, can Claimant recover for her depressive reaction to the stun device? Explain.

MBE SUBJECTS – RELEASED ESSAY QUESTIONS

TORTS
MEE Question – February 2012

Paul, age eight, and Paul's mother, Mom, spent the morning at Funworld, an amusement park. Paul decided to ride the Ferris wheel. Mom, who was pregnant and tired, waited for him about 100 yards away.

After Paul entered a Ferris wheel car, the attendant, Employee, fastened the car's safety bar. As the Ferris wheel began to turn, Paul could hear loud screams from a car carrying two boys, both age six. The boys were rocking their car vigorously. Employee also heard the two boys screaming and saw them rocking their car, but Employee took no action to stop them.

As Paul's car began to descend from the top of the wheel, the two boys—whose car was right behind Paul's car—shook the safety bar on their car hard enough that it unlatched. Both boys fell to the ground. One of the boys struck Paul on his way down.

After the two boys fell, Employee stopped the Ferris wheel and sounded an emergency alarm to notify Funworld security guards of the incident.

Mom did not see the accident, but she heard the alarm and rushed to the Ferris wheel. A crowd had already gathered, and Mom was unable to see Paul. A bystander told Mom that "a little boy has been killed." Mom, panic-stricken, attempted to make her way through the crowd but could not.

Ten minutes later, the two boys who had fallen were taken to the hospital by an ambulance.

Paul and several of the other passengers begged to be taken off the Ferris wheel. Employee, however, refused without any explanation to restart the Ferris wheel. Thirty minutes later, a manager showed up and ordered Employee to restart the Ferris wheel and allow the passengers to exit.

Forty minutes after the accident, Mom was finally reunited with Paul. Both Paul and Mom went to the hospital, where Paul was treated for minor injuries caused by being hit when the two boys fell and where Mom suffered a miscarriage as a result of accident-related stress.

National accident records show that during the last 40 years, there has been only one other incident in which injuries have occurred as a result of passengers rocking a Ferris wheel car.

Paul and Mom have sued Funworld. Funworld has conceded that Employee was acting within the scope of his employment.

Based on the facts, could a jury properly find that

1.   **Funworld falsely imprisoned Paul? Explain.**

2.   Funworld was negligent because Employee failed to take action to stop the boys from rocking their car? Explain.

3.   Mom is entitled to damages for her emotional distress and resulting miscarriage? Explain.

MBE SUBJECTS – RELEASED ESSAY QUESTIONS

TORTS
MEE Question – July 2012

Susan, a student at University, lived in a University dormitory. Access to Susan's dormitory was restricted to dormitory residents and guests who entered the dormitory with a resident. Entry to the dormitory was controlled by key cards. Dormitory key cards opened all doors except for a rear entrance, used only for deliveries, that was secured with a deadbolt lock.

On November 30, at 2:00 a.m., Ann, a University graduate, entered the dormitory through the rear entrance. Ann was able to enter because the deadbolt lock had broken during a delivery four days before Ann's entry and had not been repaired. Ann attacked Susan, who was studying alone in the dormitory's library.

Jim, another resident of Susan's dormitory, passed the library shortly after Ann had attacked Susan. The door was open, and Jim saw Susan lying on the floor, groaning. Jim told Susan, "I'll go for help right now." Jim then closed the library door and went to the University security office. However, the security office was closed, and Jim took no other steps to help Susan. About half an hour after Jim closed the library door, Susan got up and walked to the University hospital, where she received immediate treatment for minor physical injuries.

One day after Ann's attack, Susan began to experience mental and physical symptoms (e.g., insomnia, anxiety, rapid breathing, nausea, muscle tension, and sweating). Susan's doctor has concluded that these symptoms are due to post-traumatic stress disorder (PTSD). According to the doctor, Susan's PTSD was caused by trauma she suffered one month before Ann's attack when Susan was robbed at gunpoint. In the doctor's opinion, although Susan had no symptoms of PTSD until after Ann's attack, Ann's attack triggered PTSD symptoms because Susan was suffering from PTSD caused by the earlier robbery. The symptoms became so severe that Susan had to withdraw from school. She now sees a psychologist weekly.

Since the attack, Susan has learned that Ann suffers from schizophrenia, a serious mental illness. From August through November, Ann had been receiving weekly outpatient psychiatric treatment from her Psychiatrist. Her Psychiatrist's records show that on November 20, Ann told her Psychiatrist that she "was going to make sure" that former University classmates who were "cheaters" got "what was coming to them for getting the good grades I should have received." Ann's Psychiatrist did not report these threats to anyone because Ann had no history of violent behavior. Ann's Psychiatrist also did not believe that Ann would take any action based on her statements.

At the time of the attack, Susan knew Ann only slightly because they had been in one class together the previous semester. Susan received an A in that class.

Susan is seeking damages for the injuries she suffered as a result of Ann's attack and has sued University, Jim, and Ann's Psychiatrist.

1.   **May Susan recover damages for physical injuries she suffered in Ann's attack from**

      (a)   University? Explain.

      (b)   Jim? Explain.

      (c)   Ann's Psychiatrist? Explain.

2.   Assuming that any party is found liable to Susan, may she also recover damages from that party for the PTSD symptoms she is experiencing? Explain.

MBE SUBJECTS – RELEASED ESSAY QUESTIONS

TORTS
MEE Question – February 2015

For many years, a furniture store employed drivers to deliver furniture to its customers in vans it owned.

Several months ago, however, the store decided to terminate the employment of all its drivers. At the same time, the store offered each driver the opportunity to enter into a contract to deliver furniture for the store as an independent contractor. The proposed contract, labeled "Independent-Contractor Agreement," provided that each driver would

    (1) provide a van for making deliveries;

    (2) use the van only to deliver furniture for the store during normal business hours and according to the store's delivery schedule; and

    (3) receive a flat hourly payment based upon 40 work hours per week, without employee benefits.

The proposed Independent-Contractor Agreement also specified that the store would not withhold income taxes or Social Security contributions from payments to the driver.

The store also offered each driver the opportunity to lease a delivery van from the store at a below-market rate. The proposed lease required the driver to procure vehicle liability insurance. It also specified that the store would reimburse the driver for fuel and liability insurance and that the lease would terminate immediately upon termination of the driver's contract to deliver furniture for the store.

All the drivers who had been employed by the store agreed to continue their relationships with the store and executed both an Independent-Contractor Agreement and a lease agreement for a van.

Three months ago, a driver delivered furniture to a longtime customer of the store during normal business hours. The customer asked the driver to take a television to her sister's home, located six blocks from the driver's next delivery, and offered him a $10 tip to do so. The driver agreed, anticipating that this delivery would add no more than half an hour to his workday.

In violation of a local traffic ordinance, the driver double-parked the delivery van in front of the sister's house to unload the television. A few minutes later, while the driver was in the sister's house, a car swerved to avoid the delivery van and skidded into oncoming traffic. The car was struck by a garbage truck, and a passenger in the car was seriously injured.

The passenger has brought a tort action against the store to recover damages for injuries resulting from the driver's conduct. Pretrial discovery has revealed that delivery vans routinely double-park; survey evidence suggests that, in urban areas like this one, 80% of deliveries are made while the delivery van is double-parked.

In this jurisdiction, there is no law that imposes liability on a vehicle owner for the tortious acts of a driver of that vehicle solely on the basis of vehicle ownership.

The store argues that it is not liable for the passenger's injuries because (a) the driver is an independent contractor; (b) even if the driver is not an independent contractor, the driver was not making a delivery for the store when the accident occurred; and (c) the driver himself could not be found liable for the passenger's injuries.

1. **Evaluate each of the store's three arguments against liability.**

2. **Assuming that the store is liable to the passenger for the passenger's injuries, what rights, if any, does the store have against the driver? Explain.**

MBE SUBJECTS – RELEASED ESSAY QUESTIONS

TORTS
MEE Question – July 2015

A boy lives in a northern state where three to four feet of snow typically blankets the ground throughout the winter, creating excellent conditions for snowmobiling. The boy is an experienced snowmobiler and a member of a club that maintains local snowmobile trails by clearing them of rocks, stumps, and fallen tree limbs that could cause an accident when buried under the snow. In January, the boy received a snowmobile as a present on his 12th birthday. The following Sunday, the boy took his friend, age 10, out on the boy's new snowmobile, which was capable of speeds up to 60 miles per hour. The friend had never been snowmobiling before.

The boy and his friend went snowmobiling on a designated and marked snowmobile trail that follows the perimeter of a rocky, forested state park near the friend's home. The trail adjoins forested property owned by a private landowner. Neither the boy nor his friend had previously used this trail.

The landowner's property is crossed by a private logging trail that intersects the snowmobile trail. The logging trail is not marked or maintained for snowmobiling, and access to it is blocked by a chain approximately 30 inches above ground level on which a "No Trespassing" sign is displayed. However, on the day in question, both the chain and the sign were covered by snow.

On impulse, the friend, who was driving the snowmobile, turned the snowmobile off the designated snowmobile trail and onto the logging trail. The snowmobile immediately struck the submerged chain and crashed. Both the boy and the friend were thrown from the snowmobile and injured. As a result of the accident, the snowmobile was inoperable.

About an hour after the accident, a woman saw the boy and his friend as she was snowmobiling on the snowmobile trail. After the woman returned to her car, she called 911, reported the accident and its location, and then went home. Emergency personnel did not reach the boy and his friend for two hours after the woman's departure. No one other than the woman passed the accident site before emergency personnel arrived.

As a result of the accident, the boy suffered several broken bones and also suffered injuries from frostbite. These frostbite injuries could have been avoided had the boy been rescued earlier.

The boy has brought a tort action against the friend, the landowner, and the woman.

1.   **Could a jury properly find the friend liable to the boy for his injuries? Explain.**

2.   **Could a jury properly find the landowner liable to the boy for his injuries? Explain.**

3.   **Could a jury properly find the woman liable to the boy for his injuries? Explain.**

MBE SUBJECTS – RELEASED ESSAY QUESTIONS

TORTS
MEE Question – July 2016

Six months ago, a man visited his family physician, a general practitioner, for a routine examination. Based on blood tests, the physician told the man that his cholesterol level was somewhat elevated. The physician offered to prescribe a drug that lowers cholesterol, but the man stated that he did not want to start taking drugs because he preferred to try dietary change and "natural remedies" first. The physician told the man that natural remedies are not as reliable as prescription drugs and urged the man to come back in three months for another blood test. The physician also told the man about a recent research report showing that an herbal tea made from a particular herb can reduce cholesterol levels.

The man purchased the herbal tea at a health-food store and began to drink it. The man also began a cholesterol-lowering diet.

Three months ago, the man returned to his physician and underwent another blood test; the test showed that the man's cholesterol level had declined considerably. However, the test also showed that the man had an elevated white blood cell count. The man's test results were consistent with several different infections and some types of cancer. Over the next two weeks, the physician had the man undergo more tests. These tests showed that the man's liver was inflamed but did not reveal the reason. The physician then referred the man to a medical specialist who had expertise in liver diseases. In the meantime, the man continued to drink the herbal tea.

Two weeks ago, just before the man's scheduled consultation with the specialist, the man heard a news bulletin announcing that government investigators had found that the type of herbal tea that the man had been drinking was contaminated with a highly toxic pesticide. The investigation took place after liver specialists at a major medical center realized that several patients with inflamed livers and elevated white blood cell counts, like the man, were all drinking the same type of herbal tea and the specialists reported this fact to the local health department.

All commercially grown herbs used for this tea come from Country X, and are tested for pesticide residues at harvest by exporters that sell the herb in bulk to the five U.S. companies that process, package, and sell the herbal tea to retailers. U.S. investigators believe that the pesticide contamination occurred in one or more export warehouses in Country X where bulk herbs are briefly stored before sale by exporters, but they cannot determine how the contamination occurred or what bulk shipments were sent to the five U.S. companies. The companies that purchase the bulk herbs do not have any control over these warehouses, and there have been no prior incidents of pesticide contamination. The investigators have concluded that the U.S. companies that process, package, and sell the herbal tea were not negligent in failing to discover the contamination.

Packages of tea sold by different companies varied substantially in pesticide concentration and toxicity, and some packages had no contaminants. Further investigation has established that the levels of contamination and toxicity in the herbal tea marketed by the five different U.S. companies were not consistent.

The man purchased all his herbal tea from the same health-food store. The man is sure that he purchased several different brands of the herbal tea at the store, but he cannot establish which brands. The store sells all five brands of the herbal tea currently marketed in the United States.

The man has suffered permanent liver damage and has sued to recover damages for his injuries.

It is undisputed that the man's liver damage was caused by his herbal tea consumption. The man's action is not preempted by any federal statute or regulation.

1.   **Is the physician liable to the man under tort law? Explain.**

2.   **Are any or all of the five U.S. companies that processed, packaged, and sold the herbal tea to the health-food store liable to the man under tort law? Explain.**

3.   **Is the health-food store liable to the man under tort law? Explain.**

MBE SUBJECTS - PRACTICE ESSAY QUESTIONS

TORTS
Question 1

Driver is a 16-year-old who recently obtained his learner driving permit. In Driver's state of residence the statute provides that a driver with a valid learner permit shall only operate a vehicle with a licensed adult driver seated in the front seat of the vehicle and shall only drive between the hours of 6 a.m. and 11 p.m. The purpose of the learner permit law is to allow new drivers an opportunity to learn to drive with the guidance of qualified drivers and to minimize risks to others who might be endangered by inexperienced drivers. The time restriction was intended to keep inexperienced drivers off the road during the hours when they are less likely to be fully alert. Driving without a valid driver permit or in violation of the learner permit law is a misdemeanor and subjects an offender to a fine.

Driver was driving a vehicle one night at midnight with a licensed adult driver seated in the front seat next to him. As Driver carefully drove through an intersection with a green light, his vehicle was struck by Thief, who inadvertently ran through a red light.

Thief was driving a car he had stolen 10 minutes earlier from Dealer using keys left in the unlocked car. Dealer is a car dealership which routinely leaves keys in cars on its lot for the convenience of its salespeople. Thief and others had stolen cars from Dealer's lot in the same manner on other occasions.

Passenger, an adult passenger in the backseat of Driver's car, was injured when the car Thief was driving struck Driver's vehicle. Part of Passenger's injuries were caused by her failure to wear a seat belt.

Passenger brings negligence claims against Driver, Thief and Dealer for her damages.

Analyze Passenger's claims against the defendants. Discuss the likelihood of Passenger prevailing on her claims in light of possible defenses.

MBE SUBJECTS - PRACTICE ESSAY QUESTIONS

TORTS
Question 2

More than one year ago, when Owner needed help with some work on his property, he hired Neighbor to do odd jobs. The tasks varied but there was always enough work to keep Neighbor busy. Owner expected Neighbor to work 10 hours a week and required Neighbor to work most Saturdays. Owner paid Neighbor a weekly fixed salary. Owner closely supervised Neighbor's work. Neighbor had a full-time job elsewhere but enjoyed the extra money he earned from doing work for Owner. Owner provided the tools and equipment necessary for the work Neighbor did.

One Saturday while working for Owner, Owner sent Neighbor to the hardware store to purchase supplies. Owner told Neighbor to drive Owner's truck to the store. On the way to the store, Neighbor noticed a post office and decided to stop and purchase some stamps for his own personal use. Unfortunately, while driving away from the post office, Neighbor nearly struck a car driven by Driver. When Neighbor swerved to avoid Driver he struck a utility pole. Neighbor was injured and sustained personal injury damages amounting to $20,000. Owner's truck sustained $10,000 damages.

Owner and Neighbor brought an action against Driver. The jury found that both Neighbor and Driver had negligently caused the accident. The jury also found Neighbor to be 50% at fault and Driver to be 50% at fault. The comparative fault statute in the jurisdiction states:

> Contributory fault does not bar recovery in an action by any person to recover damages for fault resulting in death or injury to person or property, if the contributory fault was not greater than the fault of the person against whom recovery is sought, but any damages allowed must be diminished in proportion to the amount of fault attributable to the person recovering.

What damages, if any, should each plaintiff recover? Fully explain your answer.

MBE SUBJECTS - PRACTICE ESSAY QUESTIONS

TORTS
Question 3

Attorney represents Hospital in a medical malpractice case. Plaintiff was admitted to Hospital for hip replacement surgery. Hospital records indicate that the surgery went well, without any apparent complications. Plaintiff, however, developed ongoing paralysis four days after surgery. Plaintiff has sued Hospital, Surgeon who performed the surgery, and one of the nurses (Nurse) responsible for Plaintiff's post-operative care. Plaintiff alleges that Surgeon committed unspecified acts of negligence, and invokes the doctrine of *res ipsa loquitor* in support of Plaintiff's claim. Plaintiff further alleges that Nurse committed negligence by allowing Plaintiff to get up from bed several days after the surgery.

Attorney has interviewed Surgeon and Nurse and found their stories entirely credible. Surgeon stated that nothing was wrong in the way the surgery was performed. Surgeon further stated that the risk of paralysis resulting from hip surgery is 1% (or 1 in 100 cases), and that Surgeon fully informed Plaintiff of this risk. Hospital has provided Attorney with a "Consent to Surgery" form signed by Plaintiff, which discloses this risk.

Nurse states that Nurse repeatedly instructed Plaintiff that Plaintiff could not get out of bed or put any weight on either leg for two weeks after surgery. Nurse also states that three days after surgery, Plaintiff disregarded these instructions and left the bed while Nurse was attending another patient. Nurse discovered Plaintiff and immediately put Plaintiff back in bed. Plaintiff's paralysis began to develop the next day.

Hospital has agreed to indemnify Surgeon and Nurse in any malpractice case brought against them based on allegations of simple negligence in the conduct of their professional duties at the hospital. Hospital is "self-insured" – i.e., no insurance company is involved in this case. Accordingly, Hospital has asked Attorney to defend Surgeon and Nurse, along with Hospital (together, "Defendants"), against Plaintiff's lawsuit.

Assuming there are no ethical impediments to Attorney's representation, draft a memorandum analyzing the potential merits of Plaintiff's claims and the likelihood of success.

MBE SUBJECTS - PRACTICE ESSAY QUESTIONS

TORTS
Question 4

Polly agreed to allow her next door neighbor Dunbar to graze his small herd of domestic sheep in her yard in order to keep the weeds down. Wanting to expand his stock by breeding, Dunbar purchased a ram (a male sheep), which he kept penned up on his own property. After he had the ram for a while, Dunbar noticed that many of his sheep were showing signs of injury. Apparently the ram had been butting them with its horns.

When Dunbar was out one day, Dunbar's nine-year-old daughter Claudia let the sheep out to graze in Polly's yard. This was one of the daily chores that her father expected her to perform. Despite the fact that her father always told her to completely secure the gate after letting the sheep out, Claudia did not do so, and the ram escaped. The ram followed the sheep into Polly's yard, where Polly was on her knees tending her garden. Although Polly heard the sheep, she did not turn around to see them. The ram then charged Polly and butted her with its horns, breaking her hip and sending her sprawling to the ground.

Claudia heard Polly's cries for help and ran to the house of another neighbor, Arthur. Arthur told Claudia to go home (which she did) and that he would "take care of the situation." Just then Arthur received a telephone call and, after speaking on the phone for 10 minutes, Arthur forgot what he had told Claudia.

In the meantime, the ram again attacked Polly, butting her repeatedly and causing her numerous other injuries. Eventually Polly was rescued. However, when an ambulance arrived on the scene, Polly declined medical treatment saying that her injuries would heal on their own without the need for expensive doctors.

The injuries eventually did heal for the most part, although Polly now walks with a permanent limp due to her fractured hip.

What claims does Polly have arising out of this incident, against whom, and what defenses might be reasonably asserted against her claims?

MBE SUBJECTS - PRACTICE ESSAY QUESTIONS

TORTS
Question 5

Art and Beatta are general partners in "AB Repo," a firm specializing in the repossession of motor vehicles in cases where buyers have become delinquent in making payments on financed cars and trucks. The office manager of AB Repo is Dan, the partnership's only employee. Art, Beatta and Dan each participate in the actual repossession activities from time to time.

Paul came to the AB Repo office and announced that AB Repo had mistakenly taken his truck from his home during the night. He calmly, but firmly, declared that he would sue AB Repo if they did not return the truck to him immediately. Without saying a word, Art and Dan took Paul by his arms, lifted him off the floor, carried him to the rear door, and threw him out of the office (which was down a flight of steps). Paul sustained a broken leg and a broken arm as a result. Beatta had not been present at the time.

Approximately 30 days later, Cal became a partner in AB Repo by making a $100,000 capital contribution to the firm. Thereafter, Art, Beatta and Cal acted as equal partners.

Paul wants to file a civil lawsuit and seeks your legal advice. Identify the potential defendants, then fully analyze and discuss Paul's potential claims against them, as well as the likelihood of his success.

MBE SUBJECTS - PRACTICE ESSAY QUESTIONS

TORTS
Question 6

Lu is the owner of an expensive house in a subdivision of 2-acre lots. Brad is Lu's neighbor. Lu's and Brad's yards are separated by a 6-foot tall privacy fence that prevents them from seeing into one another's yards.

Brad is an avid, though unskilled, golfer. He practices in his backyard daily during golf season. Almost daily, Brad manages to hit a golf ball into Lu's yard, which includes a swimming pool, flowerbeds, and a sculpture garden. But Brad's golf balls have never caused any physical damage to Lu's property. Brad's golf balls are specially made for him with his personal logo printed on them. Brad pays several dollars each for the golf balls.

Tension has mounted between Lu and Brad. Lu has asked Brad on many occasions to stop hitting golf balls into her yard, and he has asked her on just as many occasions to return the errant golf balls. Neither Lu nor Brad has complied.

The last straw occurred when Brad hit a ball that sailed past Lu's ear so closely that she heard it "zing" causing her to stumble while walking through the garden.

Lu filed a two-count suit against Brad for assault and trespass to land. Thereafter, Lu conducted a garage sale and sold a group of more than 100 golf balls bearing Brad's logo that she had collected from her yard. Brad answered the lawsuit, and counterclaimed against Lu for conversion.

Fully analyze and discuss the suit. Who should prevail on which claims and why? If you were representing Lu, what if any other legal action would you have recommended she take and why?

MBE SUBJECTS - PRACTICE ESSAY QUESTIONS

TORTS
Question 7

Able and Baker owned and operated "A-B Bar and Grill" as a general partnership.

They each alternated serving as the bouncer for their small tavern. One night a patron named Pat was talking too loudly to please Baker, who was acting as bouncer. It was about a half-hour before closing time, and all other customers had left.

Without any warning, Baker walked up behind Pat and struck Pat once in the back of the head with the baseball bat that was kept at the tavern's front door for security purposes. Pat was immediately knocked unconscious and injured.

Able saw what had occurred. Able and Baker allowed Pat to lay unconscious on the floor of the tavern for about 30 minutes, until closing time when they lifted the body onto the sidewalk in front of the tavern. A passing police officer discovered Pat and summoned medical care.

Pat was taken to the hospital where the injury was treated. The doctor concluded that the injury to Pat was somewhat aggravated by the delay in treatment. "Good thing that treatment was provided when it was," the doctor said after he treated Pat.

The next week, Carr joined as an equal partner with Able and Baker in return for a capital contribution from Carr of $300,000 to the partnership.

Pat seeks your advice about bringing a tort action. Analyze and discuss the tort theories upon which an action could be brought as well as the parties to be named. Discuss the likelihood of Pat's success against each of the parties on each theory.

MEE RELEASED ESSAY QUESTIONS

TRUSTS & FUTURE INTERESTS
July 2002

On February 5, 1999, Testator created a revocable inter vivos trust. This trust was validly executed. Bank was designated trustee of the revocable trust.

Under the terms of the trust, Testator retained all income for life. The trust then provided in Article II that "upon my death the principal shall be held in further trust with the income payable to my wife, Wanda, for life, remainder to my children."

Contemporaneous with the creation of the revocable trust, Testator validly executed a will devising Testator's entire probate estate to the trustee of the revocable trust to be disposed of as part of that trust. The will further provided that, if the trust was revoked prior to Testator's death, Testator's entire estate should pass to Wanda.

On March 1, 2000, Testator sent a validly executed trust amendment to Bank revoking Article II of the revocable trust and substituting for it a new Article II. This new article stated that "upon my death the principal shall be held in further trust with the income payable to my wife, Wanda, for the immediate two years after my death, and, at the end of the two-year period, the trust principal shall be distributed to my surviving children."

In March 2001, Testator and Wanda were divorced.

In March 2002, Testator died, leaving a probate estate of $100,000. The revocable trust had not been funded prior to Testator's death. Testator was survived by Wanda and by their three children, Adam, Ben, and Carrie.

Two months later, both Wanda and Adam died in an automobile accident. Under Wanda's probated will, her entire estate passed to a charitable institution, Hope, and under Adam's probated will, his entire estate passed to University. Ben and Carrie are alive. They each have one child who also survived Testator. Adam never had any children.

1. **Which instruments control the disposition of the property included in Testator's probate estate? Explain.**

2. **Upon Testator's death, what interest, if any, did Wanda have under the revocable trust? Explain.**

3. **Assuming that Wanda had an interest under the trust, what rights, if any, do Hope and University have under the revocable trust upon the deaths of Wanda and Adam? Explain.**

MEE RELEASED ESSAY QUESTIONS

TRUSTS & FUTURE INTERESTS
February 2003

Decedent died one year ago. Decedent's duly probated will created a $1 million trust. Trustee is the trustee of this trust. The trust provides that:

> Trust income shall be payable annually to my son Adam for 10 years. Adam's interest shall be free from control, debts, liabilities, and assignments by Adam and shall not be subject to execution or process for the enforcement of judgments or claims of any sort against Adam. After 10 years, I direct that the income be paid for 5 years to Charity, a charitable organization. After this 5-year period, the trust will terminate and the principal shall be paid to my daughter Beth.

Decedent was survived by Adam and Beth. Adam had a history of lavish spending, which Decedent deplored. Beth was very careful in her financial dealings.

Three months ago, Susan, Adam's former spouse, gave Trustee a copy of a judgment for alimony she had obtained against Adam and proof that Adam had failed to pay her the required $5,000. Susan demanded that Trustee pay her $5,000, which was less than the trust's annual income.

Two months ago, Beth gave Trustee a copy of a tort judgment that John had obtained against Beth. She then requested that Trustee pay John $10,000, the amount of that judgment, from the trust principal.

Last month, Adam, Beth, and Charity commenced an appropriate judicial action to terminate the trust and have the trust assets distributed to them. Trustee has filed appropriate objections in this action.

1.   **Is Susan entitled to be paid $5,000 from the trust income? Explain.**

2.   **Can Trustee properly pay John $10,000 from the trust principal? Explain.**

3.   **Should the court terminate the trust and distribute the trust assets to Adam, Beth, and Charity? Explain.**

MEE RELEASED ESSAY QUESTIONS

TRUSTS & FUTURE INTERESTS
February 2004

Testator, a widower, died one year ago at the age of 86 survived by his only two children, Angela and Brian (ages 40 and 45), twelve grandchildren (ranging in age from 17 to 27), and six great-grandchildren (ranging in age from 2 to 7). Testator's will bequeathed his entire estate to his "great-grandchildren living when my will is probated." Testator's will was probated two months after Testator died.

Before he died, Testator created a revocable trust with Friend as trustee. Friend was a longtime confidante of Testator and his family, with intimate knowledge of all of their financial and personal affairs. The trust provided that upon Testator's death the trust income could be paid to and among Testator's issue in such shares as Friend determined, with any unpaid income to be accumulated. It also provided that upon the death of Angela and Brian, the trust would terminate, and the corpus would be distributed to Testator's then living issue.

The trust contained no provisions relating to its administration. Because Friend was not very experienced in the administration of trusts and particularly in selecting appropriate trust investments, she interviewed a number of possible bank trust officers to assist her in administering the trust. Then she contracted with Bank, an institution wholly unfamiliar with Testator's family, to make all determinations regarding the distribution of trust income and how the trust's assets should be prudently invested.

Bank immediately sold all of the trust assets and reinvested all of the proceeds in XYZ Corporation, a telecommunications company whose shares are publicly traded. Bank paid $60 per share for this stock. Today, however, each share is worth only $21. The loss in value is due to the general decline in the telecommunications industry and not to any inherent weaknesses in XYZ. Twice, after contracting with Bank, Friend called Bank to see how things were going. On these two occasions Friend was advised that "all is well." Friend never made further inquiries.

The common-law Rule Against Perpetuities, as modified by the wait-and-see doctrine, applies in this jurisdiction.

1. **To whom should Testator's probate estate be distributed? Explain.**

2. **What fiduciary duties, if any, did Friend breach with respect to the trust? Explain.**

MEE RELEASED ESSAY QUESTIONS

TRUSTS & FUTURE INTERESTS
July 2004

Five years ago, Settlor created an irrevocable trust (the "Settlor Trust"). The trust provided that Trustee should pay annually "all of the trust income to my son Zack for life, with Zack to use such income to send Zack's children to college." The trust instrument further provided that, upon Zack's death, Trustee should "distribute the trust corpus in equal shares to Zack's children, issue of any deceased child to take his or her parent's share."

When Settlor Trust was created, Zack was married to Spouse. Zack and Spouse had three living children, Abel, age 23; Brian, age 19; and Carrie, age 15. Abel had one living child, Grandchild. Neither Brian, a college student, nor Carrie, a high-school student, was married or had children.

Two years later, Zack and Spouse had another child, Debbie. Following Debbie's birth, Zack stopped paying Brian's college expenses and told Carrie that he would not pay her future college expenses.

Trustee distributed last year's trust income to Zack. Shortly thereafter, Abel, Carrie, and Zack were all killed in an automobile accident. None of them had a will. Zack had not spent any of last year's income distribution. Zack was survived by Spouse, Brian, Debbie, and Grandchild.

Under state law, Abel and Carrie are deemed to have predeceased Zack. State law also provides that an intestate's estate passes to the intestate's spouse and children in equal shares or, if there is no surviving spouse or children, to the intestate's parents in equal shares or, if there is no surviving parent, to the intestate's siblings.

1.   **Can Brian impress a trust upon the income distributed to Zack from Settlor Trust to pay for Brian's college education? Explain.**

2.   **To whom, and in what shares, should the principal of Settlor Trust be distributed? Explain.**

MEE RELEASED ESSAY QUESTIONS

TRUSTS & FUTURE INTERESTS
July 2005

Two years ago, Testator died. By her duly probated will, Testator created two separate trusts naming First Bank as the trustee of each trust.

1. Testator left $100,000 to Friends' Trust and directed First Bank "to distribute the income annually among my friends in equal shares. At the end of ten years, this trust shall terminate and the trust corpus shall be added to the principal of Residuary Trust created under this will."

2. Testator left $500,000 to Residuary Trust and directed First Bank "to pay the income to Carrie for life and to distribute the principal, during Carrie's life or upon her death, to any or all of Carrie's issue as she appoints by deed or will and, in the absence of such appointment, to my alma mater, University, upon Carrie's death."

Last week, First Bank received two instruments in the mail. The first was a letter from George seeking a distribution of income from Friends' Trust and correctly claiming that he was a close friend of Testator.

The second was a deed labeled "Appointment" from Carrie directing First Bank to hold the $500,000 Residuary Trust in a new trust and to distribute income to Carrie's son, John, during his life. This deed further provided that upon John's death, First Bank should distribute the trust principal to Charity, a charitable organization, instead of to University as directed by Testator in her will.

1. **Can First Bank distribute income from Friends' Trust to George? Explain.**

2. **Did Carrie validly appoint an interest in Residuary Trust to her son John? Explain.**

3. **In light of Carrie's deed of appointment, what, if any, are the interests of Charity and University in the new trust? Explain.**

MEE RELEASED ESSAY QUESTIONS

TRUSTS & FUTURE INTERESTS
February 2006

Seven years ago, Settlor announced at a dinner party:

> "I am hereby creating the Settlor's Family Trust and naming myself as trustee. In about three years, I expect to sell some stock and to fund this trust with the sale proceeds. I reserve the power to pay to myself trust income and principal for my support at any time. When I die, all remaining trust assets are to be distributed to my daughter, Dawn. Neither my creditors nor Dawn's creditors can reach the trust assets to satisfy their claims, and neither of us is free to sell or otherwise transfer our respective trust interests. Please join me in a toast as I sign this cocktail napkin on which I have written the terms of the trust."

Five years ago, Settlor's sister-in-law, In-Law, executed a will leaving her entire $300,000 estate to the Settlor's Family Trust.

Four years ago, Settlor sold some stock and deposited the $100,000 sale proceeds into an account at First Bank in the name of "Settlor, as Trustee of the Settlor's Family Trust."

Two months ago, In-Law died. Had In-Law died intestate, her estate would have passed to her brother, Bill. Both Settlor, as trustee of the Settlor's Family Trust, and Bill claim In-Law's estate.

One month ago, Victim obtained a $75,000 tort judgment against Settlor because of injuries sustained as a result of Settlor's negligence. Victim immediately sought to collect that judgment from the First Bank account, notwithstanding Settlor's claims that this account was beyond the reach of his judgment creditors. Before this dispute could be resolved, Settlor died.

1.   **Was the Settlor's Family Trust validly created? Explain.**

2.   **Who is entitled to In-Law's estate? Explain.**

3.   **Can Victim reach the assets of the First Bank account to satisfy Victim's claim against Settlor? Explain.**

MEE RELEASED ESSAY QUESTIONS

TRUSTS & FUTURE INTERESTS
February 2007

Testator died three years ago. His duly probated will provided that:

1. I give $100,000 to Trustee to hold in trust and to distribute the trust income equally among those persons who are my friends at my death. After 10 years, the trust shall terminate and the trust property shall be distributed equally between my son, Sam, and the Fine Arts Program at State University. In no event shall this trust terminate earlier than 10 years after my death.

2. I give the rest of my estate to my daughter, Donna.

Both Sam and Donna survived Testator.

Walter and Janice, two neighbors of Testator, correctly claim they were good friends of Testator at the time of his death and demand that Trustee pay the income from the $100,000 trust to them. Claimant, who has a tort judgment against Sam, demands that Trustee immediately pay Claimant $25,000 from the trust to satisfy the judgment.

Two years after Testator died, State University closed as a result of a state budget crunch and the legislature's determination that the programs at State University, including its fine arts program, were largely duplicative of the programs at State Polytech, the other public university in the state.

1. **To whom should the income from the $100,000 trust be distributed? Explain.**

2. **Should Trustee immediately pay $25,000 from the trust to Claimant? Explain.**

3. **To whom should Trustee pay the trust principal at the end of the 10-year period? Explain.**

MEE RELEASED ESSAY QUESTIONS

TRUSTS & FUTURE INTERESTS
July 2007

Settlor, age 60, consulted an attorney, Attorney, about the creation of a trust. Settlor gave Attorney a memorandum containing the following information about his family:

Family Members	Relationship	Age
1. Wife	Spouse	48
2. Son	Child	21
3. Daughter 1	Child	16
4. Daughter 2	Child	10
5. Grandchild	Grandchild (Son's child)	1

Settlor also outlined his goals in creating the trust:

1. I want to fully control trust assets and enjoy all trust income until I die.
2. After I die, I want trust assets used to ensure that Wife is comfortably provided for. I also want Wife to be able to use trust assets to reward, in her will, whichever children have been most helpful to her. I don't want Wife to be a trustee; she doesn't have the financial background.
3. After Wife dies, I want my children to get the remaining trust assets. But, of course, if Son dies before Wife, I'd want his share to go to Grandchild.
4. I'm planning to fund the trust with cash and stocks. I may want to add some other assets later, but I'm not sure.

Based on the information provided by Settlor, Attorney drafted the following trust instrument:

SETTLOR TRUST AGREEMENT

1. I appoint Bank as trustee of the Settlor Trust.
2. I direct Bank to hold all assets listed on Schedule A in trust, and I direct Bank to dispose of these assets as follows:
   a. Bank shall pay all trust income to Settlor during Settlor's lifetime.
   b. After Settlor's death, Bank shall pay trust income and principal to Wife in such amounts as Bank, in its sole discretion, deems appropriate.
   c. After Wife's death, Bank shall distribute all remaining trust assets equally among Settlor's surviving children, share and share alike.
3. Bank accepts and agrees to faithfully carry out the terms of this trust.
   [Signatures, dates, and acknowledgments are omitted]

SCHEDULE A
12,000 Shares of XYZ Corporation, common stock
$150,000 (cash)

How would you revise the Settlor Trust Agreement to more fully meet Settlor's stated goals? Explain.

MEE RELEASED ESSAY QUESTIONS

TRUSTS & FUTURE INTERESTS
February 2008

Six years ago, Settlor created a valid inter vivos irrevocable trust. Settlor funded the trust with publicly traded securities, named Friend as sole trustee, and directed Friend, as trustee, to distribute all trust income to James, whom Settlor had been supporting for several years. Settlor also gave James the right to withdraw up to 5% of the trust's principal annually during the first 10 years of the trust's existence.

Four years ago, Friend sold all of the trust's publicly traded securities and reinvested 45% of the proceeds in the preferred stock of A Corp., 45% of the proceeds in the preferred stock of B Corp., and 10% of the proceeds in different publicly traded securities. Both A Corp. and B Corp. were closely held companies that were newly organized and cash poor. Their preferred stocks were not publicly traded and were subject to valid restraints on alienation that effectively made them nontransferable by the trustee for the next 10 years. Furthermore, although both preferred stocks guaranteed an annual 5% dividend, these dividends were not payable until after the 10-year restraint-on-alienation period had expired.

At the time Friend invested in the preferred stocks of A Corp. and B Corp., both companies were developing competing technologies to make ballpoint pens that also function as cell phones. Neither company had yet developed working prototypes of the proposed product. Friend honestly believed that the preferred stocks represented a safe investment that would produce returns in excess of those available from any other investment. Friend did not individually own any preferred stock of A Corp. or B Corp. However, Friend did individually own 70% of the common stock of A Corp., but had no interest in B Corp.

Despite Friend's confidence, the A Corp. and B Corp. investments have proven disastrous. Since the preferred stocks were purchased, neither company has succeeded in producing a marketable product or making a profit. Both are now near bankruptcy. Moreover, because the stocks have not paid dividends and cannot be sold, James's income from the trust has declined precipitously. Furthermore, because of the valid restraints on alienation, Friend has truthfully told James that any withdrawal requests cannot be honored.

Friend has consulted your law firm, concerned that he may have breached one or more of his fiduciary duties. Explain to Friend which duties, if any, he may have breached in carrying out his responsibilities.

MEE RELEASED ESSAY QUESTIONS

TRUSTS & FUTURE INTERESTS
July 2008

Ten years ago, Wife created a valid trust (Wife's Trust) and named Bank as trustee. The trust instrument directed Bank to: (1) pay all trust income to Wife during her lifetime; (2) upon Wife's death, pay all trust income to Niece during Niece's lifetime; and (3) upon Niece's death, distribute the trust principal to Niece's "then living issue."

Article Five of Wife's Trust provided as follows:

> Wife may revoke or amend this trust at any time prior to her death by a written instrument delivered to Bank.

Contemporaneously with the creation of Wife's Trust, Wife and her husband, Husband, executed separate wills. Each will devised the respective testator's entire probate estate to Bank "to hold as part of the principal of Wife's Trust, which was created simultaneously with the execution of my will."

Five years ago, Wife delivered to Bank a written instrument titled "Amendment to Wife's Trust." In this instrument, Wife directed Bank to distribute the trust principal to Niece's "children age 21 years or older who are living when Wife's Trust terminates."

Four months ago, Wife, Husband, and Niece were involved in an automobile accident. Wife was pronounced dead in the ambulance. Husband died three days later, and Niece died seven days later. Wife, who had previously transferred all of her assets to Wife's Trust, had no probate estate. Husband's probate estate was worth $300,000.

Niece had two children: Son, now age 20, and Daughter, who died one year ago at the age of 28. Daughter had one child (Grandchild), now age 4.

1. **Does the Amendment to Wife's Trust apply to the assets distributable to that trust from Husband's probate estate? Explain.**

2. **Is Son entitled to a share of the assets of Wife's Trust given the language of the Amendment to Wife's Trust? Explain.**

3. **Is Grandchild entitled to a share of the assets of Wife's Trust given the language of the Amendment to Wife's Trust? Explain.**

MEE RELEASED ESSAY QUESTIONS

TRUSTS & FUTURE INTERESTS
July 2009

Prior to his death, Settlor created a valid irrevocable trust and named Trustee as trustee. The trust instrument specified that:

1)   Trustee shall distribute trust income to Trustee's adult children, David and Edna, in such amounts as Trustee, in Trustee's absolute and uncontrolled discretion, shall determine.

2)   Trustee may distribute all trust income to either David or Edna.

3)   Trustee shall have the power to sell any trust property.

4)   This trust shall terminate in 10 years and, upon its termination, Trustee shall distribute 60% of trust property to David and Edna, in equal shares.

5)   In view of my long-standing interest in the area of education, Trustee shall distribute all remaining trust property to my alma mater, Business College.

During the last year of the trust, Trustee paid all trust income to David. Trustee's decision was motivated solely by her personal disagreement with Edna's political opinions.

During the same year, Trustee decided to sell certain trust assets. Solely to avoid paying a 6% sales commission that would have reduced the trust's sales proceeds, Trustee, in her personal capacity, purchased these assets for their undisputed fair market value. After the sale, the assets unexpectedly increased in value. Trustee recently sold these assets to a bona fide purchaser for a significant profit and retained the profit for herself.

The trust has terminated, and Trustee has discovered that Business College no longer exists. Trustee seeks judicial approval to distribute Business College's share of the trust to Settlor's estate.

1. **Did Trustee breach any fiduciary duty by paying all trust income to David during the last year of the trust? Explain.**

2. **Must Trustee return to the trust the profit she retained from assets she purchased from the trust? Explain.**

3. **Should a court authorize Trustee to distribute trust property that was payable to Business College to Settlor's estate? Explain.**

MEE RELEASED ESSAY QUESTIONS

TRUSTS & FUTURE INTERESTS
February 2010

Settlor created a revocable trust naming Bank as trustee. The trust instrument directed Bank, as trustee, to pay all trust income to Settlor and, upon Settlor's death, to distribute all trust assets to "Settlor's surviving children." When Settlor created the trust, he had three living children, Alan, Ben, and Claire.

Settlor died last year. Alan predeceased him. Settlor was survived by three children, Ben, Claire, and Doris (born after Settlor created the trust), and two grandchildren. One of the surviving grandchildren was Claire's child and one was Alan's child. Alan's child was his only heir.

When Settlor created the trust, he funded it with cash. Bank promptly invested the cash in a broad range of stocks and bonds and held this broadly diversified portfolio for just over twenty years. Although the portfolio had by then significantly increased in value, Settlor was dissatisfied with the rate of appreciation. Settlor therefore directed Bank to sell 90% of the trust portfolio and to reinvest the proceeds in the stock of XYZ, a closely held corporation that Settlor believed would substantially appreciate in value.

The investment in XYZ appreciated more than 50% during the first two years after Bank purchased the stock. However, during the five years preceding Settlor's death, the XYZ investment depreciated to about 70% of its initial value. This depreciation was largely due to mismanagement by XYZ's board of directors. Although Settlor was neither a director nor an officer of XYZ, he was fully aware of the management problems. He discussed these problems with Bank and told Bank, "I expect things will turn around soon."

Immediately upon Settlor's death, Bank liquidated the trust's interest in XYZ, thus avoiding further losses from this investment.

One month after Settlor died, Claire wrote to Bank disclaiming all of her interest in the trust.

1.   **To whom should the trust assets be distributed? Explain.**

2.   **Is Bank liable for losses on the investment in XYZ stock? Explain.**

MEE RELEASED ESSAY QUESTIONS

TRUSTS & FUTURE INTERESTS
February 2011

In 1994, Testator died, survived by her sons, Ron and Sam, and Ron's son, Peter. Under Testator's duly probated will, Testator created a trust and provided that

> Trustee shall distribute to Ron, for the duration of his life, as much of the income and principal from the trust as Trustee, in her uncontrolled discretion, deems advisable. At Ron's death, any remaining trust funds shall be distributed to my grandchildren, with the children of any deceased grandchild taking the deceased parent's share.

In another section of her will, Testator bequeathed property to her son Sam.

In 2006, Ron adopted Carol, who was then 14 years old.

On January 2, 2008, Ron borrowed $50,000 from a friend and gave the friend a note for that amount payable in five annual installments of $10,000 plus interest.

Between 1994 and 2009, Trustee distributed all the trust income (which averaged $15,000 per year) to Ron.

In 2009, Peter, Ron's son, died in an automobile accident survived by his wife, Ginny, but by no descendants. Under Peter's valid will, his entire estate passed to Ginny.

On January 2, 2010, Ron failed to make the required payment to his friend on the $50,000 note. Ron's friend then demanded that Trustee distribute that year's trust income to him instead of to Ron until the $10,000 plus interest due that year was fully paid. At that point, Trustee stopped paying trust income to Ron and refused to make payments to Ron's friend. Instead, Trustee began to accumulate trust income.

In late 2010, Ron died. He was survived by his adopted daughter, Carol; his daughter-in-law, Ginny; his brother, Sam; and Sam's wife. Sam has no children, but he and his wife plan to have a child in the near future.

1.   **Was Ron's friend entitled to any of the trust income earned during 2010? Explain.**

2.   **At Ron's death, to whom should the trust principal be distributed? Explain.**

MEE RELEASED ESSAY QUESTIONS

TRUSTS & FUTURE INTERESTS
July 2011

Forty years ago, Testator executed a valid will under which he devised his home to the trustee of a trust. Testator's will directed the trustee to

> retain the home to ensure that my Daughter has a comfortable residence throughout her life. The home shall not be sold until Daughter dies. After Daughter's death, I direct the trustee to sell the home and to distribute the sale proceeds to Charity, a charitable corporation organized to end homelessness in Capital City.

Thirty years ago, Testator died. At the time of his death, Testator still owned the home, which was located in Capital City in a quiet residential neighborhood of single-family homes near both a local college and the city's business district. The business district was commercially successful, but it had attracted a large number of homeless people.

During the last 30 years, the character of the neighborhood where the home is located has changed dramatically. Many apartment buildings have been built, greatly increasing population density and noise. Several bars and restaurants catering to college students have also opened in the formerly residential blocks near the home. Stores in the city's business district have moved to suburban shopping malls, and the vacated buildings have been converted to bars and dance clubs. This shift has increased public rowdiness, but it has also been associated with a marked decline in the number of homeless individuals in the business district.

Daughter recently decided that she wants to move from the home to a rental apartment in a quieter and less congested neighborhood. Daughter consulted a real estate agent, who correctly told her that the home is worth about $300,000 and will easily sell for that amount.

Daughter asked the trustee to sell the home, to hold the expected sale proceeds of $300,000 in trust, and to use the proceeds and the income to pay Daughter's rent, which will be about $2,000 per month. The monthly income from the $300,000 trust, however, is expected to be only $1,000.

When the trustee attempted to contact Charity to discuss Daughter's request, he discovered that Charity no longer exists.

The trustee has consulted the law firm where you work for advice on these questions:

1. **Can the terms of Testator's testamentary trust be reformed to permit the sale of the home? Explain.**

2. **Assuming that the trust can be reformed to permit the sale of the home, can the trustee also obtain authorization to use the sale proceeds and the earnings thereon to pay Daughter's rent? Explain.**

3. **After Daughter's death, will the trust assets pass to Testator's estate? Explain.**

MEE RELEASED ESSAY QUESTIONS

TRUSTS & FUTURE INTERESTS
July 2012

Thirty years ago, Settlor entered into an irrevocable trust agreement with Trustee. Pursuant to the terms of this trust, all trust income was payable to Settlor's Husband, and upon Husband's death, all trust assets were to be distributed to "Settlor's children." The trust also provided that Husband's income interest would terminate if Husband remarried after Settlor's death.

When the trust was created, Settlor and Husband had three children. Five years later, Settlor and Husband had a fourth child.

Ten years later, Settlor died.

This year, when the trust principal was worth $750,000, Husband wrote to his four children. Husband noted that he was about to retire and wanted cash to buy a retirement home. He asked the children to agree to terminate the trust and to direct Trustee to distribute $250,000 of trust principal to Husband and the remaining $500,000, in equal shares, to the four children. All four children agreed to Husband's proposal. Husband and the four children then wrote Trustee the following letter:

> We, the only beneficiaries of the trust, direct you to terminate the trust and distribute $250,000 of trust assets to Husband and the remainder, in equal shares, to Settlor's four children.

Trustee's response stated:

> I cannot make the requested distribution to you for the following reasons:

> (1) The trust is irrevocable and cannot be terminated.

> (2) Even if the trust were terminable, termination would require the consent of all beneficiaries. This is not obtainable because, if a child of Settlor predeceases Husband, one or more of Settlor's future grandchildren might be entitled to trust assets at Husband's death.

> (3) Even if the trust were terminable, only the three children living when the trust was created have a beneficial interest in the trust; therefore no distribution of trust principal can be made to Settlor's youngest child.

> (4) The actuarial value of Husband's interest is only $150,000. Therefore, even if the trust were terminable, any distribution of trust principal to Husband in excess of that amount would be a breach of trust.

Is Trustee correct? Explain.

MEE RELEASED ESSAY QUESTIONS

TRUSTS & FUTURE INTERESTS
February 2013

Ten years ago, Settlor validly created an inter vivos trust and named Bank as trustee. The trust instrument provided that Settlor would receive all of the trust income during her lifetime. The trust instrument further provided that

> Upon Settlor's death, the trust income shall be paid, in equal shares, to Settlor's surviving children for their lives. Upon the death of the last surviving child, the trust income shall be paid, in equal shares, to Settlor's then-living grandchildren for their lives. Upon the death of the survivor of Settlor's children and grandchildren, the trust corpus shall be distributed, in equal shares, to Settlor's then-living great-grandchildren.

The trust instrument expressly specified that the trust was revocable, but it was silent regarding whether Settlor could amend the trust instrument.

Immediately after creating the trust, Settlor validly executed a will leaving her entire estate to Bank, as trustee of her inter vivos trust, to "hold in accordance with the terms of the trust."

Five years ago, Settlor signed an amendment to the inter vivos trust. The amendment changed the disposition of the remainder interest, specifying that all trust assets "shall be paid upon Settlor's death to University." Settlor's signature on this amendment was not witnessed.

A state statute provides that any trust interest that violates the common law Rule Against Perpetuities "is nonetheless valid if the nonvested interest in the trust actually vests or fails to vest either (a) within 21 years of lives in being at the creation of the nonvested interest or (b) within 90 years of its creation."

Recently, Settlor died, leaving a probate estate of $200,000. She was survived by no children, one granddaughter (who would be Settlor's only heir), and no great-grandchildren. The granddaughter has consulted your law firm and has raised four questions regarding this trust:

1. **Was Settlor's amendment of the inter vivos trust valid? Explain.**

2. **Assuming that the trust amendment was valid, do its provisions apply to Settlor's probate assets? Explain.**

3. **Assuming that the trust amendment was valid, how should trust assets be distributed? Explain.**

4. **Assuming that the trust amendment was invalid, how should trust assets be distributed? Explain.**

MEE RELEASED ESSAY QUESTIONS

TRUSTS & FUTURE INTERESTS
February 2014

Ten years ago, a testator died, survived by his only children: a son, age 26, and a daughter, age 18.

A testamentary trust was created under the testator's duly probated will. The will specified that all trust income would be paid to the son during the son's lifetime and that upon the son's death, the trust would terminate and trust principal would be distributed to the testator's "grandchildren who shall survive" the son. The testator provided for his daughter in other sections of the will.

Five years ago, the trustee of the testamentary trust purchased an office building with $500,000 from the trust principal. Other than this building, the trust assets consist of publicly traded securities.

Last year, the trustee received $30,000 in rents from the office building. The trustee also received, with respect to the securities owned by the trust, cash dividends of $20,000 and a stock dividend of 400 shares of Acme Corp. common stock distributed to the trust by Acme Corp.

Eight months ago, the trustee sold the office building for $700,000.

Six months ago, the son delivered a letter to the trustee stating: "I hereby disclaim any interest I may have in the income interest of the trust." On the date the son delivered this letter to the trustee, the son had no living children; the daughter had one living minor child.

A statute in this jurisdiction provides that "a disclaimer of any interest created by will is valid only if made within nine months after the testator's death, and if an interest is validly disclaimed, the disclaiming party is deemed to have predeceased the testator."

1.   **How should the rents, sales proceeds, cash dividends, and stock dividends received prior to the trustee's receipt of the son's letter have been allocated between trust principal and income? Explain.**

2.   **How, if at all, does the son's letter to the trustee affect the future distribution of trust income and principal? Explain.**

MEE RELEASED ESSAY QUESTIONS

TRUSTS & FUTURE INTERESTS
July 2015

In 1995, a man and his friend created a corporation. The man owned 55% of the stock, and the friend owned 45% of the stock. When the man died in 2005, he left all of his stock in the corporation to his wife.

In 2009, the wife died. Under her duly probated will, the wife bequeathed the stock her husband had left her to a testamentary trust and named her husband's friend as trustee. Under the wife's will, the trustee was required to distribute all trust income to the wife's son "for so long as he shall live or until such time as he shall marry" and, upon the son's death or marriage, to distribute the trust principal to a designated charity. The stock, valued at $500,000 at the wife's death, comprised the only asset of this trust.

In 2013, after the stock's value had risen to $1.5 million, the trustee's lawyer properly advised the trustee to sell the stock in order to comply with the state's prudent investor act. Because of this advice, the trustee decided to sell the stock. However, instead of testing the market for potential buyers, the trustee purchased the stock himself for $1.2 million. Thereafter, on behalf of the trust, the trustee invested the $1.2 million sales proceeds in a balanced portfolio of five mutual funds (including both stocks and bonds) with strong growth and current income potential.

Recently, both the son and the charity discovered the trustee's sale of the stock to himself and his reinvestment of the proceeds from the stock's sale. They learned that, due to general economic conditions, the stock in the corporation that had been purchased by the trustee for $1.2 million had declined in value to $450,000 and the value of the trust's mutual-fund portfolio had declined from $1.2 million to $1 million. Both the son and the charity have threatened to sue the trustee.

The son has also decided that he wants to get married and has notified the trustee that he believes the trust provision terminating his income interest upon marriage is invalid.

1.   **Would the son's interest in the trust terminate upon the son's marriage? Explain.**

2.   **Did the trustee breach any duties by buying the trust's stock and, if yes, what remedies are available to the trust beneficiaries if they sue the trustee? Explain.**

3.   **Did the trustee breach any duties in acquiring and retaining the portfolio of mutual funds and, if yes, what remedies are available to the trust beneficiaries if they sue the trustee? Explain.**